THE ART OF FAIRNESS

Also by this author

The Secret House
Web of Words
E=mc²
Electric Universe
Passionate Minds
Einstein's Greatest Mistake

THE ART OF FAIRNESS

THE POWER OF
DECENCY IN A
WORLD TURNED MEAN

DAVID BODANIS

ABRAMS PRESS, NEW YORK

Originally published in the United Kingdom in 2020 by The Bridge Street Press, an imprint of Little, Brown Book Group, a Hachette UK Company

Library of Congress Control Number: 2021933482

ISBN: 978-1-4197-5635-1
eISBN: 978-1-64700-386-9

Printed and bound in the United States
10 9 8 7 6 5 4 3 2 1

Abrams books are available at special discounts when purchased in quantity for premiums and promotions as well as fundraising or educational use. Special editions can also be created to specification. For details, contact specialsales@abramsbooks.com or the address below.

Abrams Press® is a registered trademark of Harry N. Abrams, Inc.

ABRAMS The Art of Books
195 Broadway, New York, NY 10007
abramsbooks.com

In memoriam, Kathleen Griffin
(1954–2018)

"All good things . . . come by grace, and grace comes by art, and art does not come easy."

—Norman Maclean

CONTENTS

THE ART OF FAIRNESS

A QUIET TEA

JANUARY 2020, AND Özlem Türeci at home in Mainz, Germany, has a problem. She's just read an article on a new viral outbreak in Wuhan, China, realizes it's likely to develop into a pandemic that could threaten the planet—a world population of over seven billion is at risk—and believes the start-up she and her husband have created can play a central role in limiting that. Yet she also knows that a tremendous number of things will need to go right for that to happen: that there'll have to be accurate virus sequencing and lab research for initial tests, and big population studies for further tests—since putting powerful biological products into healthy people tends not to be a decision taken lightly—and then there will be production facilities to be built; huge series of them, $200 million each, with fermentation units and glistening steel holders and intricate airflow equipment to keep everything ultra-clean, and after that—for why not make it a bit harder?—the final product will need to be plugged in to distribution networks that can get it across the globe, ideally into every human being on the planet. To accomplish this in ten years would be impressive—the record for any major vaccine so far had been four—but she estimates they might have less than a year before economic and social collapse cuts in.

The technical details aren't what bother her. Türeci is an excellent organizer, and with her husband, Uğur Şahin, she'd made their medium-sized cancer research firm BioNTech into a masterpiece of organization on a tight budget. The problem is that as the vaccine gets closer to production, ever more players will start pulling and tugging at their work, including huge multinational companies—let alone the autocratic governments in Russia and China, not especially known for their adherence to gentlemanly, polite behavior. There will be crooks and cheats; cyberattacks and strong-arm tactics.

Türeci is known for being a decent, considerate woman. She and her husband—both in their 50s—live with their teenage daughter in a pleasant though not spectacular apartment; they bicycle everywhere; they used part of the funds that could have gone on an ostentatious house to help support scholarships instead. They like working at the breakfast table, sipping Turkish tea as they gossip. When they began their first company, Şahin bought a copy of *Business Plans for Dummies* and still keeps it up on a shelf.

Türeci's parents had emigrated from Turkey before she was born. Şahin had been born in Turkey near the Syrian border, then brought to Germany as a child, where his father worked on a Ford assembly line. They've taken to heart the belief of their parents' generation that one gets ahead by acting decently. They know a lot of fame and money is at stake, and wouldn't be entirely averse to having some of that. But it's a matter of pride for them not to be rude.

How could a couple like that have a chance of winning this world-shaking race?

I've always been fascinated by a simple question: "Can you succeed without being a terrible person?" At first it seems obvious that the answer must be "No." When a man like Donald Trump has been president, it's impossible to say that good guys always win.

Business seems to show us this all the time. Like a frog puffing up its vocal sac to look fearsome, a bullying tone in the office suggests the speaker has superior authority, or superior knowledge, or just a stunningly superior pedigree. If new hires gunning to rise in a consultancy or bank or in politics learn the further trick of bullying only those below them while smiling in a knowing yet ever-so-slightly-submissive way to those above them—a psychological two-step understood in seemingly every culture—their advancement is nearly guaranteed.

The logic appears impeccable. If someone's willing to take a shortcut to get what they want—if they're willing to shout and cheat and steal, if they don't care what it takes—it seems obvious they would triumph over someone who isn't going to act that way; proof, as the old saying has it, that "Nice Guys Finish Last."

But yet, does that mean you have to go to the other extreme and be a bully or Machiavellian to get anything done? What I've found, in my research, is that the answer is no. There really is a better path, leading neatly in between. When fairness is applied with the right skill, it can accomplish wonderful things. It led to the Empire State Building being constructed in barely a year, and to an English debutante becoming an acclaimed jungle guerrilla fighter. There's better information, better creativity, more honest alliances.

I've been looking into this path for years now into what that might be, starting in courses that I taught at Oxford, then moving on to observations in hi-tech firms, hospitals, banks, law firms, top military units, and other organizations. The same data kept coming up. Terrible people often succeed. That's a given. Yet when decent people get a certain sort of balance right, they also make it to the top, even in hard, competitive fields where they can help shift matters for the better. It's just often not noticed because more monstrous egos grab our attention.

The quest to advance this better way isn't new. The Bible asks, "What shall it profit a man, if he shall gain the world, and lose his soul?" It's especially pressing now, with society pushing selfishness to a stunning degree, and democracy under threat once again.

Success will often take longer. No one can teach you all the details in advance, for the needed skills are subtle ones, where advice is easy to state, hard to carry out. That's why it's an art rather than a science.

Biographies are a good way to help provide some of the needed experience, as authors since the Roman-era Plutarch have recognized. I've arranged this book as a series of profiles accordingly, concentrating mostly on ordinary, decent people who succeeded in life this fair way—albeit including enough about scoundrels to keep us on our toes.

The first half of the book goes through six detailed case studies, showing how to wield fairness skillfully in each of the basic domains of life: sensing what's around you, taking action, defending against danger. The Empire State Building and guerrilla fighter studies are there; so too are Texas pilots, English directors, the *Game of Thrones* producer—there's even a look at the man who coined the phrase "Nice Guys Finish Last" (yet who—his vindictive temperament putting him firmly on the scoundrel side—did himself end up finishing last). The positive stories are a proof that the decent approach can work, since here are numerous times when it did.

There are many ethical subtleties along the way, though in real life there's often a great deal on which everyone will agree. The producer Harvey Weinstein, for example, famously bullied and assaulted his way to the top in Hollywood, forcing individuals weaker than him to sign draconian nondisclosure agreements to keep what he was doing hidden. Yet Bernadette Caulfield, immensely effective as executive producer of *Game of Thrones*, was known for being the fairest of souls. There's no need for unarguable definitions of "good" or "fair"—there's no need even to insist that our preferred individuals are candidates for sainthood—to want to know, "How can I succeed in a way that's more like Caulfield or Türeci, and less like Harvey Weinstein?"

It also turns out that selfishness often sets up its own destruction through the resentment it creates, as well as by blinding those on top to things they really need to see. Sometimes—as with Weinstein—those consequences can take a long time to show their strength. Yet once dedicated reporters finally revealed what Weinstein was like, everyone who'd suffered from him watched in satisfaction as an awesome, Aeschylean collapse took place.

Having looked at individuals, the second half turns to what happens when you pull all the lessons together, and on the largest possible scale. Here I show how a master of human behavior—the president during World War II, Franklin D. Roosevelt—turned all the seeming constraints of fairness and decency into advantages, even in the harshest of settings, allowing him to help defeat one of the greatest evils the world has seen.

There's no guarantee, of course, that matters will always turn out this way; no magic that awaits. But often, surprisingly often, it works. The path to greatness doesn't require crushing displays of power or tyrannical ego. Simple fair decency can prevail.

You just have to handle it with skill.

That might seem hard to believe, so a brief taster of how successful it can be is in order. Türeci and Şahin's experiences in 2020 are ideal, displaying on a reduced scale everything we'll explore at greater length in the full studies to come. The entire book in miniature appears there.

Some successful science labs have been famous for their unfair culture. At the one run by the Nobel laureate Ernest Lawrence at Berkeley in the late 1930s, a young Italian physicist, Emilio Segrè, was on the staff. "You're a refugee, aren't you?" Lawrence asked him one day. Segrè explained that yes, he was: he and his wife were Jewish, and if they went back to Fascist Italy, they faced imprisonment, and possibly death. "And what am I paying you?" Lawrence asked. Segrè told him: it was $300 a month. "Let's drop it to 115," Lawrence said. "What choice do you have?" Segrè was furious, yet energized to work that ultimately brought a Nobel Prize for himself as well.

In the present day, one of the most prestigious labs in the Boston area is also known for the cutthroat competition its head encourages. Teams that are first in reporting successful results get rewarded; those who don't are dropped. Envy, theft—and yet a remarkable burst of energy among the young post-docs, desperate to get tenure, is the result.

In such labs, Türeci and Şahin's first step would be obvious. A race for a world-changing vaccine had immense rewards: in glory, and ultimately in raw cash. Since foreign spies or corporate intruders would give anything to disrupt the research, there would be no question that the harshest of possible nondisclosure agreements would be required. They'd have to confiscate all phones so no surreptitious photos could be taken; firm work schedules would need to be imposed as well.

For Türeci and Şahin, however, there was going to be no tightening of nondisclosure agreements, and no confiscation of phones, for they believed there was a better way to succeed. The exposure to their parents' generation had been fundamental; that period just a few decades before when so many immigrant Turks had been stuck in lowly jobs, yet wanted nothing more than the chance to be treated fairly and rise up.

Carl Jung once said that children try to fulfill not just the dreams their parents had, but the dreams their parents couldn't make come true. A woman wants a career, for example, yet circumstances don't allow it, and so her daughter becomes committed to having that career; similarly for a family's thwarted dreams of money or artistry—or for living in a realm where respect could become the norm.

The pressures, the reminders, had never entirely gone away. Germany was less prejudiced than when they'd been young, though even in 2010— two years *after* they'd founded BioNTech—a senior official at the respected German central bank had published a book explaining that with Turks in the country "the average intelligence of the population declines." It sold over a million copies.

What Türeci and Şahin were aiming to do at BioNTech, however, was create a world—or at least a 1,000-person community within the world—where the dream of their parents' generations could come true. No one at the company had to worry about being held back for coming from the wrong background. They knew about Şahin's own father labor- ing in a Ford assembly plant. Nor was there a smug old-boy network of those who'd gone to the very top universities—the MITs or Caltechs of the world—before being hired. Türeci had been a medical student at Saarland University Hospital in Homburg, a fine but definitely not world-renowned institution. Half the senior executives were women; over 40 nationalities were employed.

None of this would have worked if Türeci and Şahin had veered too far to the soft side. But one doesn't end up running even a medium-sized biotech company without a good amount of drive. A German journalist once asked how, as a couple, they resolved differences of opinion. Şahin's *Business Plans for Dummies* had explained it's wise to consult your spouse if you're planning a new venture. "We discuss it objectively," Şahin said. "And if I'm wrong, I admit it, even if I'm the boss in the office." Türeci smiled. "By the way, it's the other way around."

Now, late on the Saturday of the weekend when they'd read the Wuhan article, they faced one of the most important phone calls of the whole plan. It was with BioNTech's key financial backer, Helmut Jeggle, an experienced Stuttgart MBA who knew how cutthroat the business world could be. Jeggle wasn't convinced that dropping everything to focus on a virus that—this was still January 2020—had scarcely produced any reported cases in Europe or the US was a wise thing. But Türeci and Şahin didn't give an inch. It was a long phone call—two hours by Jeggle's recollection—and it's possible that "vigorous" language was used . . . yet at the end, it was Jeggle who'd changed, not BioNTech.

When Türeci and Şahin arrived at the office the next Monday—parking two mountain bikes neatly in front—they explained the importance of the new project, and how it was going to be run: without forbidding new security guards, and without the higher-ups imposing detailed work schedules—and, also, allowing any qualified scientists on staff to question Şahin's own first ideas about what vaccine design to focus on.

This was a delicate matter, for it turns out that with modern software, designing a potential mRNA vaccine is surprisingly easy (there's a link in the reading guide to an explanation). Şahin himself had outlined ten vaccines over the weekend, using his home computer at the breakfast table. The glory of having one of his designs becoming the vaccine that ended up produced would lead even a saint to keep competition away.

But although Şahin was far from a saint—he could get short-tempered, distracted, and sometimes short-tempered *and* distracted (an especially irritating combination)—he and his wife knew how often new hypotheses in science turn out to be wrong. If there was going to be any chance of success, they had to let any qualified scientist on the staff come up with alternate designs that might be better. If one of those bested the boss, that was what BioNTech would end up backing.

That's how decency in our first domain, of listening, can come out, and Türeci extended this in—quite optimistically—planning what to do if one of the vaccines really did work. BioNTech was big in Mainz, but Mainz is a small city. Locals weren't quite joking when they said the most exciting recent event had been Johannes Gutenberg's development of the printing press 500 years before. Once large international networks began to take shape, BioNTech could easily be sidelined; ignored, crushed.

To avoid that, Türeci would have to master even more on how to deal with specialist funding groups, and international patent committees, and above all, with the key regulatory agencies on the Continent, in Britain, and in the huge market of the United States.

Much of the expertise was concentrated in legal and compliance officers, those worthy beings, often sequestered many layers below the top, about whom books are never written, but who are exactly the individuals needed to understand the details that fast-track regulatory approval would require.

Türeci had to overcome her natural habits here. When she'd begun the switch from pure medicine to running a firm, "I dreaded the whole business of administration." Now she spent a lot of time with the legal and compliance teams, listening and taking notes about what had to be prepared.

Yet how to make sure the actual vaccine would be ready in time? Even with Türeci and Şahin putting their ego aside enough to listen, they still needed to get genuine creativity from their thousand-strong staff. BioNTech's focus was working with mRNA, and this is a very fragile molecule, dissolving with the slightest touch. They couldn't turn over all idea generation, of course, for then there would be chaos.

But what they could give—our second major pillar—was something else that labs like Lawrence's at Berkeley never provides: the respect and trust that everyone craves.

It helped that the employees could see their chiefs weren't above mundane tasks. Türeci often dressed in a nicely tailored jacket, but even so, "You need to take care of warehousing, refrigeration, transport chains," she said. "It sucks sometimes, but it's part of the job." It also helped that neither she nor her husband were guarded by ranks of secretaries and chiefs of staff, projecting power and status. They spent time in the labs, offering advice where they could, accepting the schedules that individual teams had decided on and put up in the hallways. Everyone also knew how Türeci and Şahin had stood up for them in the past against investors who'd tried to block their projects, or outside agencies trying to force development down paths that just wouldn't work. The department heads under them were doing the same.

As a result, a cascade of useful ideas poured out, and fast: better ways of purifying the mRNA strands; improved methods for helping those fragile genetic chains survive in the body; fresh machinery for measuring it all; managerial ideas on running hitherto separate tests in parallel as well. Technicians got to show what they were capable of, as well as top researchers, most spectacularly working out packaging to sustain the extreme cold the vaccine's fragile mRNA required. In that setting, no one was going to take a hefty sum from competitors to give away what was going on.

By the time February turned to March, the gamble seemed to be succeeding. BioNTech had become a superb vaccine-designing enterprise. Even the once-wary Helmut Jeggle was enthusiastically on board. One venture capitalist who'd been following the entire industry remarked, "None of the speed, none of the innovation, none of the quick decisions . . . would have been possible in any of the large pharma corporations."

But BioNTech still faced the problem of being too small.

The largest tests they'd achieved with the cancer therapies that had been their previous main products had taken place the year before. Those had been carried out on 250 people in Germany, and even so, all the supervision and testing had strained the firm's resources. To ensure their mRNA vaccine was safe, there would need to be observations on thousands, and then —for the all-crucial Phase III tests—on tens of thousands of human subjects. No start-up in tranquil Mainz was going to be able to achieve that on its own, but because of Türeci's advance preparations, it didn't have to.

Every organization needs a certain amount of self-defense. It's especially strong in biotech, where someone with ill intent could contaminate samples by casually not putting on their gloves properly. (How? Human skin has enzymes on it that degrade RNA, so putting on gloves while touching the glove's outside leaves skin flakes there. Anyone wearing the gloves will constantly be dropping those skin cells loose, destroying RNA it lands on.)

Türeci and Şahin had never been naive. They had lawyers keeping an eye on intellectual property, and employment contracts of course mentioned that privacy was expected; they also knew that friendly, easygoing colleagues at international conferences might well end up—in a friendly, easygoing way—stealing ideas that were too readily presented. There was a sensible arrangement of security passes and discreet guards. Because of the dangers of foreign spying, powerful cybersecurity systems were in place too.

Yet that was as far as it went—and this is the heart of how they handled the third main domain, of defense. If trust wasn't going to keep employees loyal, insisting on harsher nondisclosure threats wouldn't make it better. Beyond the sensible precautions, they'd never been the sort to encourage a vengeful air, and sensibly handled outside alliances were always encouraged.

When Türeci and Şahin got in touch with their contacts at Pfizer, accordingly—the huge American pharmaceutical that could bring them to the next step—the door was already open. Türeci had kept information flowing; the firms trusted each other, they'd worked together before. The head of Pfizer didn't have to bring in the lawyers at this stage, but rather said that he trusted BioNTech "100 percent." Plans for large-scale human trials, and for the complex $200 million production units, got started without delay. The details would be worked out later. Cooperation with regulators was the same.

Eight months after that first article about the outbreak in China, a Sunday night in November 2020 now, two calm researchers were back at home in their apartment, sipping Turkish tea, going over the latest tests. It was a pleasing moment. The numbers showed they had indeed created the world's first successful coronavirus vaccine, and it operated with 95 percent efficacy.

Once the news was released, Anthony Fauci, head of the National Institute of Allergy and Infectious Diseases, came as close to speechlessness as he gets. "We went from a virus whose sequence was only known in January, and now in the fall, we're finishing—*finishing*—a Phase III trial. Holy mackerel." Turks in Germany hadn't lowered "the average intelligence of the population" after all. Türeci and Şahin were lauded worldwide; soon on the cover of *Time* magazine, named Persons of the Year by the *Financial Times*; their company's value exceeding that of Deutsche Bank.

What they'd done had worked, and seemingly in the most natural way. Listening without ego had meant they received accurate information; being generous had brought in fresh ideas; being open to cooperation had let everything swiftly scale up.

But yet . . . a cynic might still insist that was a special case. Yes, it might be easy, in a white-coat lab setting, not to bully, to be considerate, to be open to sharing and collaboration. Other vaccine teams, finishing not far behind, had done much the same in Oxford and the US alike. The real world, however, is a harder place. Look at all the infighting and missed opportunities in so many countries' handling of the pandemic, from the first quarantines to the often bungled rollouts of the actual vaccines and everything that's happened since.

To see if matters really can be handled better in all our wider settings, we'll need to look more deeply into how the component parts of fairness are built up.

I

THE STORIES

WE SAW WITH Türeci and Şahin that at least sometimes you can succeed without being a jerk; that you need experience, and it helps if you can identify with adversity yourself. But with a skillful injection of fairness in the three domains everyone has to deal with—listening, giving, defending—it can be possible to carry it off. Those are the pillars that will stretch through the book, and they depend on having the right moral character—the "decency"—to keep them working well.

But how does "injecting fairness" work in the wider world? That's the key. Done with skill, it can achieve wonders; yet to understand how, we need stories that go into greater depth in one further domain after another. We'll start with fairness's role in the crucial first step of getting an accurate read of the outside world. No one can survive long if they get that wrong.

A close-up inside a jetliner high over the American Midwest shows what's at stake . . .

PART ONE

LISTENERS

CHAPTER 1

PILOTS

Al Haynes and Park Duk-kyu

("Listen, without ego")

"See what you can see back there, will ya?"

IT WAS 3:00 P.M. on July 19, 1989, and Al Haynes was the captain in the cockpit of a fully loaded United Airlines DC-10, traveling from Denver to Chicago. They'd been airborne for an hour now, everyone had finished their lunch, and Haynes, a seemingly easygoing 57-year-old from Lamar County, Texas, was leaning back, still nursing his coffee. His copilot, a younger man with less experience, Bill Records, was flying the plane.

It looked to be an easy journey, just a few tall, white cumulus clouds in the clear sky.

Aircraft had transformed since World War I, 70 years before. When pilots took off, they were lifted up in a biplane that might weigh 1,800 pounds. The larger biplanes could just about squeeze in a single passenger and had a main cruising speed no greater than a fast motorcyclist on the ground. The jet Haynes commanded carried nearly 300 people, weighed over 350,000 pounds, and flew at 560 mph: over 80 percent of the speed of sound.

Some of the cockpit controls would have looked familiar to earlier pilots, such as the modified levers that moved the rudder and other control surfaces. In World War I planes, pulling on those levers would tug a cable that stretched back to the rudder. In Haynes's jet, such a contraption would never have worked. The rudder at the back of the plane was bigger than a barn door. No human grip could pull a metal surface that size forward; not against air rushing at greater than hurricane speed.

Instead, tubes filled with compressed fluids stretched the length of the airplane. When the pilot moved their controls, he or she was adjusting systems that controlled those tubes, squeezing pressurized fluid to the desired spot. Without them working, the plane would skid randomly through the air, like a car on ice. Since they were so important, Haynes's DC-10 had three parallel sets of such tubes. Each had their own pumps, their own fluid reservoirs, and their own supply line. If one set failed, two would be left over to steer the plane. In an extreme emergency, the plane could be flown and landed with just one. To be extra sure, each system of hydraulic tubes was encased in tough steel. Only the throttles still worked in a way World War I pilots would have been familiar with. Push a throttle away from you, and more fuel was released into the engine it was connected to: the engine powered up. Pull it toward you, and less fuel went in: the engine slowed down.

Then, at 3:16 P.M., just as Records was beginning a gentle right turn, "there was this loud bang, like an explosion," Haynes remembered. "It was so loud, I thought it was a bomb."

The plane shook and started climbing. As Records struggled at the controls, the third crew member in the cockpit, flight engineer Dudley Dvorak, saw something horrible on his instrument panels. One by one, the dials showing fluid levels in the three hydraulic systems began to rotate backward. In just moments, all three were pointing straight down, to zero.

And with that, all the control surfaces—on the wings, and in the tail—were locked tight.

By this point the plane had stopped climbing, and all 350,000 pounds began rolling over to the right. The plane tilted five degrees, then ten degrees, then quickly passed 20 degrees and 30 degrees and more. Passengers on that side saw the ground begin to fill their view out the window; passengers on the left just saw the sky. At this rate the plane would roll on to its back, and from that there would be no recovery.

These are the times when our inner personality comes out. What happened next will show how one individual dealt with rushes of incoming information and the hierarchy available around him. Yet he believed that being fair was all-important.

How would that help him make everything work?

Hierarchy exists for a reason. Haynes was more capable than anyone else in the cockpit, and the most experienced. Records was still pulling on the central steering column, the yoke, trying to counter the right bank and fall, near-grunting with the effort, but Haynes could see it wasn't working. He took over, calling out "I've got it" to be clear, and—again an advantage of hierarchy—Records didn't fight back. He was trained to defer.

For a moment Haynes tugged at the controls too, for it's a reflex almost impossible to avoid, but then he stopped. If it hadn't worked for Records, it wasn't going to work for him. But . . . what if he reduced thrust on the wing that was rising and boosted it on the wing that was dipping? If ever there was a time to trust his own judgment, this was it. To Dvorak, what the captain did next was a blur: "[Haynes] took his hand off the yoke, swatted the [left] engine back, and on the way back up, pushed the [right] engine up, and was back on the yoke in just a matter of seconds."

Nothing happened at first, for a big plane has a lot of momentum, but slowly, painfully, the right wing came back up. Haynes evened out the two engines, yet since the explosion had happened in the middle of a turn, with the control surfaces locked, the plane kept on trying to roll to the right. There seemed no way to shift the controls now, so every pilot's nightmare began: the front started to lift up, even though Haynes had made no change. For half a minute it held at that angle, the plane losing speed as it pushed up against gravity and its wings provided less lift at that excessive angle. Then, with a shudder, the front tilted down and the plane began to speed up in a dive.

A roller-coastering path of this sort is called a phugoid cycle. In moderation it's not serious, but this was out of control. Worst of all, the downward segment was lasting longer than the upward one. To try to stop the oscillation, Haynes and Records both pulled back on the yoke, Records even wedging his knees under the handles to get additional leverage. It had no effect. The plane finished its downward dip 1,500 feet below where they had started, then it levelled out for a bit and began another uncommanded rise. But again, this was only a slight rise, while the down cycle was more extended. In another minute or two they would be a further 1,500 feet down.

Haynes knew that no plane this size had ever survived complete hydraulic failure. Just four years earlier, for example, a 747 in Japan without hydraulics had entered phugoid cycles, roller-coastering inexorably downward through the sky, the voice recorder showing the pilots increasingly frantic as their plane drifted out of their control. After a half hour, it crashed in mountains far off its intended flight path, killing over 500 people.

If there was going to be any chance of getting through this, Haynes would need to stop the plane's incessant banking to the right and, above all, understand what was causing the phugoid cycles. It had to be done quickly, before they lost so much altitude that they crashed. Maybe they had an hour, but most likely less.

Around this time, a flight attendant came into the cockpit. She had a message to deliver, yet at first was speechless at what she saw. "The pilots were struggling, it was just so frightening. It was like they were struggling to hang on to the controls." Finally she blurted out: there was another DC-10 captain in the cabin who was an instructor, a man named Denny Fitch. He was willing to come to the cockpit to help.

Haynes was at the most desperate moment of his life. When the flight attendant came in, he had to watch his instruments and grapple with the steering yoke, and work the throttle beside it, and keep in radio touch with local airports, and coordinate with his copilot, and identify changes in weather conditions ahead, and supervise the flight engineer. Earlier in the flight, before the explosion, a different United pilot, a trainee, had visited the cockpit to observe the flying. After he had returned to the main cabin, Haynes had seen no reason to call him back.

When the flight attendant blurted out this new offer, Haynes was too busy to turn around from his seat. When he answered, it wasn't in a raised voice, but just quick, nearly mumbled words.

. . .

Sociologists who want to understand attitudes to listening often use a measurement called the Power Distance (PD). It's a mark of how two individuals in an unequal power relationship are expected to act. A high PD score means both parties assume that juniors shouldn't question their superiors; there's a big power distance between them. A low PD score is the opposite: both parties feel that subordinates aren't as subordinate as all that and deserve to be listened to.

When aircrew from a number of nations were tested on this scale in the 1990s, those from Russia, China and India came out with the highest scores—there was a big power distance between superiors and juniors—and those from the UK, Germany and Sweden came out at the other extreme, being more egalitarian, with less of a presumed power distance between them.

But those figures are just averages, and although American pilots as a whole clustered near the egalitarian countries, there always were some convinced that hard hierarchy was right. One US flight engineer described to a government investigator what that meant working under his own pilot: "Whenever I speak up, he says, 'If I want your fucking advice, I'll ask for it.'"

The crash in 1999 of a Korean Airlines Cargo 747 outside London illustrates the dangers of this high-PD mindset. The pilot, Park Duk-kyu, was the same age as Haynes—57—and he too had been trained as a military pilot. His copilot, Yoon Ki-sik, was like Bill Records—younger, and less experienced.

Although Yoon was doing everything right in preparation to take off at night from London Stansted Airport, Park made clear to Yoon how inferior he was. In what language specialists later called a "derogatory" tone, he said, "Make sure you understand what ground control is saying before you speak!"

Then, before Yoon had the chance to respond, Park snapped at him again. "Answer them! They are asking how long the delay will be."

Despite that, the takeoff went ahead without problem. Moments later, Park was in control of the plane and began a planned banking turn to the left. What he didn't realize was that the instrument in front of him—the artificial horizon—that was supposed to show the turn, wasn't working.

When a plane is accelerating, it can be hard to feel how much it's banking, and so Park, thinking he hadn't gone far enough, increased the bank angle.

A warning buzzer went off, and Yoon's own artificial horizon—working properly—showed that they were indeed turning too hard. But after the chewing-out at takeoff, he wasn't going to say anything. The warning buzzer went off again. The tilt that Yoon saw on his artificial horizon was getting worse.

Their plane, with its hundreds of thousands of pounds of metal and full load of fuel, was speeding toward the ground. The warning buzzer kept on going off—a total of nine times—and the tilt Yoon saw on his artificial horizon kept on getting worse. Scarcely one minute into the flight, the 747 was flying with its left wing pointed nearly straight down, but Yoon still didn't dare to speak up to his captain. The flight engineer did shout out "Bank!" and then repeated it, but Park ignored him. The recovered flight recorder shows that Yoon stayed silent right until the point, moments later, that they hit the ground. All the crew died (as a cargo flight, there were no other passengers).

It's easy to criticize Park Duk-kyu, but until that point in his career, firmness had always worked. He'd been a skilled fighter pilot in the Korean Air Force, leading other flyers in one realistic training exercise after another. Hierarchies are effective at synthesizing information that pours in and ensuring that people you command will carry out your decisions. The problem is that this style of power is so attractive, it's easy to embrace it to excess. Letting go of your unquestioned place at the top of a hierarchy means you lose this automatic respect and have to respond to what someone else is initiating. For insecure people, that's too painful. You're vulnerable, dependent; for the duration of that interaction, "beneath" them. Staying planted Zeus-like atop a hierarchy avoids that.

Entire countries can match these different extremes. Russia and China (and North Korea) have legislatures laid out like a classroom: there's space for an instructor/dictator at the front, for obedient students in the seats. All those countries score low on indices of democracy, and their leaders assume it's natural to keep everyone who's lower down in their place. Whatever knowledge the participants might have is lost.

Western democracies are more on the semicircle model, where there's space for someone to keep order, but—at least in theory—the representatives are less passively obedient before that leader, and there's also space for them to speak to each other.

In ultrademocratic early Iceland, it's possible the informal legislature at times formed a circle; a model briefly copied by the then-West German parliament in Bonn.

What was Haynes going to do? He had been at United a long time; brought up there, as he liked to put it, "on the concept that the captain was THE authority on the aircraft. What he said goes." Although he lived in Seattle now, he was proud of being a Texan, and of his state's tradition of respect for men who could take care of themselves and be in control. (There's the story of a riot in a border town; the Texas Rangers are called in. The train arrives and a solitary man steps off. "But you're only one Ranger," the worried local sheriff says. "There's only one riot," the Ranger replies.)

On the other hand, Texas, like most regions, also has traditions of cooperation, where generosity gives you power. Once again, it's the choice we always have.

Haynes was the type of person who chose the more cooperative part of his background. He knew how hard it was to move up from copilot to captain. He'd been a Marine Corps pilot and instructor himself, going in straight after graduating from Texas A&M and building an excellent record. But even so, it had taken him nine years as copilot in DC-10s with United before being promoted. Bill Records was in the right-hand seat flying the plane because Haynes wanted to give him the experience; it was part of mentoring. If he could make the upward path easier for someone else, why not?

When he explained that at United, the captain traditionally was "THE authority on the aircraft," he would also say that he felt that was out of date. "Sometimes the captain isn't as smart as we thought he was." He hadn't called the trainee pilot back to the cockpit, but that was simply because a trainee doesn't have much to offer. A qualified flight instructor on board could be different. The flight attendant remembered walking back through the first-class cabin as quickly as she could without running, holding in her head what Haynes had told her. It was about ten minutes since the explosion, getting close to 3:30 P.M. She leaned forward to Denny Fitch. "They want you up there," she said.

The first thing Fitch noticed when he reached the cockpit was how hard Haynes and Records were working, the tendons in their forearms taut from their effort tugging on the yoke. Then he glanced at flight engineer Dvorak's control panel to the side and saw the awful, unimagined downturn on the hydraulic gauges, the three separate arrows all pointing straight to zero. In all the tests he'd given pilots at United's simulators in Denver, he'd never envisaged setting up one where all hydraulic systems were empty.

How could this happen? It must be linked with the second engine, the one in the tail, also being shut down. In a protective gesture, while mulling it over, he leaned forward and fastened Records's shoulder harness, which had been loose.

Haynes broke Fitch out of his reverie, introducing himself while still not looking away from the panel, just reaching one hand over his shoulder for a brief shake. They had a quick joke about getting a beer together when this was all over, and then they got down to business. Fitch crouched between Haynes and Records. From the black box cockpit recorder:

> FITCH: You lost the engine, huh?
> HAYNES: Yeah, well, yeah. It blew . . . Can't think of anything that we [haven't] done . . .

In the subtle etiquette of airline officers, this was a controlled way of asking for advice, the opposite of how Park Duk-kyu had handled his situation. But Haynes knew his crude engine-throttling could only stop the worst rolling, and that he was nowhere near getting the plane out of the phugoid cycle. The new arrival offered a suggestion:

> FITCH: The only thing I can think about that might help you at some point here [is to put] the [landing] gear down and that might hold the nose down a bit.

Almost simultaneously with Fitch's comments, however, other voices were calling for Haynes's attention. The main radio was on for contact with ground control from Sioux City, Iowa, and there also was another flight attendant who'd entered the cockpit.

> SIOUX CITY APPROACH: The [emergency fire] equipment is standing by.
> FITCH: Anything above about 210 [knots] is going to give you a nose-up moment.
> FLIGHT ATTENDANT: So we're gonna evacuate?

It would be hard for anyone to take in, plus Haynes had been hoping that as an instructor, Fitch might know of some special procedure that would get them out of this mess. But Fitch was giving no sign of that, and now it was embarrassing to have even imagined asking.

And this is the reality of listening in a difficult environment. There's too much information, we're distracted, we're emotional. Haynes let it pass. To the flight attendant he explained, as gently as he could, that although a few minutes before touchdown he would call out the brace position, her detailed questions about evacuation procedures afterward weren't realistic. (*"I really have my doubts you'll see us standing up."*) Fitch, however, was a source he could use for more information. It was hard to see from the cockpit whether there was any response on the wings' control surfaces, so he asked Fitch to walk back halfway through the cabin to the wings (*"See what you can see back there, will ya?"*).

It was a tense time. Fitch took about a minute, and when he knocked on the cockpit door to get back in, Haynes yelled at Dvorak, "Unlock that fuckin' door!" But when Fitch reported—nothing they'd been doing in the cockpit was making the wings' controls work—Haynes cooled down. Yelling wasn't going to make anything better, and he needed a clear head. If Fitch could take over the throttles, then he and Records would only have to concentrate on the yoke.

To Fitch, that was "an amazing thing, if you take into consideration that pilots don't give up control very easily." But to Haynes, it was obvious. If you're confident in your own self, you don't need to block others from helping you. One of the engine throttles was to Haynes's right, and another was to Records's left, so if Fitch stood between them, he could grab one throttle in each hand. With the distraction of handling the engines out of the way, Haynes could get back to work on trying to diagnose the problem, which was bringing them with sickening regularity in each cycle closer to the flat Iowa soil.

Fitch hadn't known about any secret reset buttons, but United had an engineering center in San Francisco with detailed information on every plane in the fleet. This was a storehouse of knowledge that even the simulator center in Denver lacked. Fitch himself hoped that "if there's a back doorway, some circuit breaker to pull, they'll know it." Dvorak had already started speaking to the San Francisco engineers, and Haynes pressed him to keep at it, even though the engineers couldn't seem to grasp that they really did lack all control of their flight surfaces.

Airline flight attendants know not to unnecessarily bother the cockpit in an emergency. Pilots of the "If I want your fucking advice" type would make them extra wary. But because Haynes had always been so polite, however busy he was, they were willing to come up when there was more information he might need to know. And around this time, one of them arrived to explain, after a bit of confusion, that she'd seen something wrong with "the rear wing."

This would have been easy to ignore, for there's no rear wing on the DC-10; she must have used the wrong term. But it was still possible she might have noticed something. If even the tiniest residual amount of hydraulic fluid had pooled up in back, pumping it forward could save their plane. Haynes sent flight engineer Dvorak to take a look. They were not going to give up, not on his flight.

Dvorak knew it was important to look calm as he walked through the long cabin, this time all the way back to the far end, but he couldn't help noticing how many children there were. United had been promoting discounts for parents with children and babies, and this was the result. The flight attendants had been telling everyone to get ready for a rough landing, to take off their glasses and remove any pens and combs from their pockets. To safeguard babies, they'd told parents to make piles of pillows and blankets on the floor, and when the adult was in the brace position just before impact, those would hold the baby still.

Dvorak was an experienced Air Force navigator and understood planes well, so this was testing. In the cockpit, he had a seat belt and full shoulder harness, yet even so knew it was unlikely he'd survive a landing. They couldn't aim the plane or properly control its descent. If they did manage to get down, landing in a cornfield would flip them over, while landing on a runway at this far-too-rapid descent would be like flying into a concrete wall. The pillows that the parents were earnestly pressing into position were useless.

Although some of the children were crying, Dvorak could see that others thought it was a game. At one point, near the third exit door, as a mother was bent down preparing pillows for her 2-year-old, her toddler climbed up on to the seat and giggled, giving a great merry wave to a passenger behind.

At the last door in the plane's tail, Dvorak grabbed hold of the seats to steady himself before looking out. The phugoid cycles were still repeating every minute, and it was hard to stay upright, especially this far from the plane's midpoint. A flight attendant called him to look at the other side. He took her arm, for a moment holding still, looking straight at her. It was startling. She felt, she later said, that he was saying his last goodbye. Then he studied what she pointed to out the window.

The DC-10 has three engines: one under each wing, and another in the tail. This tail engine was the one that had stopped working. In front of it is a big horizontal stabilizer, and Dvorak saw a chunk of that stabilizer had been torn away. Only an explosion from deep within the tail engine could do that.

As a flight engineer, Dvorak had the plane's schematics memorized. The three separate hydraulic networks were designed to survive almost anything, but they had one weak point. All three converged in the tail. When the engine there exploded, the metal pieces it threw out tore right through the stabilizer, shredding the hydraulic lines there. His gauge readings weren't faulty. There was not going to be any reservoir of useful hydraulic fluid left in the main lines of the system. All would have quickly been sucked out by the rushing air.

If there was ever a time when a captain was going to need more help in working out what to do, this was it.

Back in the cockpit Dvorak, reported what he had seen (*"All right . . . we got a lot of damage to the tail section"*). It was now about 3:45, a half hour since the explosion. Because the wing and tail controls were stuck, the plane had also been caught in a series of big looping right-hand turns, drifting it nearly aimlessly over the Iowa landscape; the phugoid ups and downs had been varying in intensity but left them at scarcely a mile and a half up, an enormous drop from the 7-mile height where they'd begun. They'd have to get control and orient to a runway, or field, or highway fast.

Their last hope was the San Francisco engineers, with their comprehensive library of every system the manufacturers had put in, and every contingency that successful flight emergencies had worked through. Under Haynes's eye, Dvorak radioed them again to give an update. It was a near repeat of what he'd told them before.

> DVORAK (TO SAN FRANCISCO MAINTENANCE): Roger, we need any help we can get . . . We don't have anything. We don't know what to do. We're having a hard time controlling it. We're descending . . .

But the conversation went nowhere. The San Francisco team was still asking if Dvorak was sure all three hydraulic systems were down. When he insisted, they went quiet for a while and then came on again: Was he really *absolutely* sure?

Haynes told Dvorak to drop it.

> HAYNES: . . . Forget them. Tell 'em you're leaving the air, and . . . and screw 'em.

There wasn't going to be any fix from the San Francisco team.

What does one do, feeling one's life is about to end? Fitch was struck with the ordinariness of the day. "Dear God, I'm going to die this afternoon. Here I am 46 years old and I'm going to die. My wife . . . loved her dearly . . . three beautiful children. The only question . . . how long is it going to take Iowa to hit me." What Dvorak felt he never said, but he was polite to San Francisco when he signed off; there was no need to make them feel any worse.

That was the attitude the whole cockpit had shared. They'd known from the start what was likely, and now, despite the ground getting closer and being scarcely able to steer (*"Sioux City . . . We're tryin' to go straight. We're not havin' much luck"*), they weren't going to change. Haynes joked to Records, his copilot aiming for promotion, *"I'll tell you what. I'll write off your damn PC [Pilot Certificate] if we make this."* Then he caught himself, and repeated it with a change: *"when we make this."*

There was more to this than just passing time. It was how they wanted to be remembered. Cockpits can be tight, exclusive communities, wary of newcomers, but Haynes had led from the top to make Fitch welcome—"He was now the fourth member of the crew," Haynes insisted—and in response, Fitch had given everything he could to find a way of adjusting their two remaining engines to regain some control.

Now, finally, it began to work.

Being a great pilot is like being a great horseman. Yelling and cursing at your horse for not doing what you want can have some effect, but not as much as being in tune with the animal. Haynes had given Fitch initial guidance on how to move the two throttles, and his tone hadn't been one where you swore at the dull metal and cables and fuel. You might do that for a moment—we're human—but if that's all you do, not much is going to happen.

Fitch had continued what Haynes showed him, making slight movements with each hand: one on the right engine's throttle, one on the left's. Each time he had then waited, listened, to how the plane responded. It was hard, for there would be a long—20- or even 40-second—lag between his moving a throttle and the resultant change in engine power shifting their phugoid path. Also, especially at first, each correction of the phugoid made the right-hand banking worse, while each correction of the banking made the phugoid cycles worse.

In the last few minutes, however—even while overhearing Dvorak's report on the San Francisco conversation, knowing the ground was going to be coming up soon—Fitch had a near-mystical feeling. "It became like the airplane was an extension of me . . . I could feel these stimuli coming at me before I actually felt them or saw them."

The phugoids had initially been big swirling things, tilting the plane way up for a climb, and then pitching it sharp down, for the even longer descent. What Fitch was beginning to sense now—edging the throttles just fractions of an inch forward or back—was a way to diminish that. He had been wrong to fight it. A skilled rider learns what his or her horse is scared of, and as much as possible tries to work with that. In a similar way, it almost felt as if the plane was trying to go back to the equilibrium speed it had been set for before the explosion. Pitching up and climbing was its attempt to slow down; pitching down and accelerating was its attempt to speed up.

Fitch began helping that along; making the plane finish each part of the phugoid more quickly (by performing the counterintuitive maneuver of accelerating into the descent, and decelerating into the rise). That meant there was less time rising and less time falling—and *that* meant the phugoid cycles were getting smaller. Under Haynes's encouragement now, giving feedback from Sioux City's radar and their own airspeed and compass indicators, Fitch managed for the first time since the explosion to bank the plane to the left.

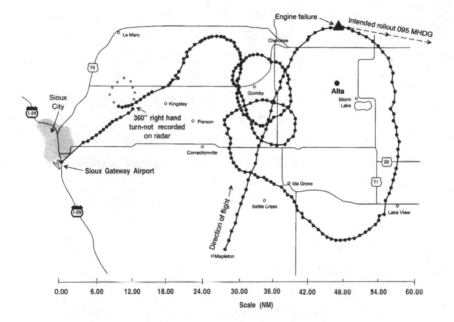

Radar track of United Airlines Flight 232. The explosion was at the top right. After that come the three unwanted looping right turns, before the all-important left where Fitch finally lined them up for Sioux City. *(NTSB)*

With that left turn, and the phugoids now at least slightly under control, everything changed. Sioux City's airport was straight ahead. They had a chance of making it. Suddenly there was a lot more to do: preparing the passengers, final arrangements for the location of the emergency equipment, locating highways that could be fallback landing sites. They also had to work out when best to bring the landing gear down; it might usefully slow them, but it might introduce more instabilities; it also would almost guarantee a flip if they missed the runway and had to try landing in a field.

Haynes elicited the opinion of everyone in the cockpit in a quick yet systematic way. He was in control, but everyone was cooperating. Scattered voices from the cockpit recorder as they approached:

> HAYNES: I want to get as close to the airport as we can . . . Get on the air and tell them we got about four minutes to go.
>
> SIOUX CITY APPROACH: United 232, can you hold that heading, sir?
>
> RECORDS: Yeah, we're on it now for a little while.
>
> FITCH: I got the runway . . . it's off to the right over there . . .
>
> HAYNES: We have the runway in sight. We have the runway in sight . . . We'll be with you shortly. Thank you for your help.
>
> SIOUX CITY APPROACH: United 232, you're cleared to land on any runway.
>
> HAYNES: (Laughter). You want to be particular and make it a runway now, huh?
>
> DVORAK (ON PA): Two minutes.
>
> (ATTENDANTS: shouting for passengers to get their heads down)
>
> · RECORDS: Okay. Here we go.
>
> DVORAK: Left turn just a hair.
>
> SIOUX CITY APPROACH: United 232 heavy, sir, you are well too far north . . .
>
> HAYNES (TO GROUND): We know. (TO COCKPIT): Pull it back . . .
>
> UNKNOWN: Left throttle, left, left . . .
>
> UNKNOWN: God!

. . .

Until the very last moment, it seemed they might have succeeded. They'd managed to line up with the runway and were close to putting down at its very start, thus giving them the maximum possible length to slow down. But they were coming in at over 270 mph, much faster than usual, and more dangerously, they were falling at over 30 feet per second, also much more than usual. (If a cement truck tumbles off a three-story building, that's how fast it will be going when it hits the ground.) Worst of all, although Fitch had managed to reduce the phugoid cycles, he hadn't been able to stop them. The plane was still inherently unbalanced.

A bare hundred feet up—seconds before they would have been on the ground—another phugoid began. The plane's nose tilted down, it started a steep right turn, and the right wing tip hit the runway. The landing gear gouged a trench 18 inches deep in the concrete before breaking off, and the plane fractured into four parts. Over 10,000 pounds of kerosene they hadn't been able to dump ignited. 111 people died, but because of the crew's work in getting there, 185 survived.

In the mayhem, the plane's cockpit was snapped off like a pencil tip and thrown into a soybean field beyond the runway. None of the medics and national guardsmen rushing to the jet bothered to look inside. As one physician remembered, "Here was this pile of aluminum and wires, and I couldn't figure out what it was."

It seemed impossible to imagine anyone was alive inside metal crumpled like that. But they were, all four of them, and after enough shouts alerting the rescuers, they were brought out with badly broken bones and deep cuts, but, wondrously, none so grave that their wounds couldn't be repaired. Within a year, each man was able to fly again.

When push came to shove, Haynes had succeeded, calmly, in finding out if any pressure was left in the hydraulic lines, as well as how to manage the plane's descent, despite lacking all usual controls. He had stopped panic, ignored extraneous news, told the airport what to prepare, kept updated on distance from Sioux City, sieved his resources skillfully (bringing in Fitch but not the other pilot on board; canceling the San Francisco conversations), and then worked the giant wobbling plane to approach a long runway at a nearly flat angle, having gained enough time for emergency services to get into position.

Despite the loss of life, this was, aeronautic historian Bryan R. Swope commented, "one of the finest displays of airmanship during an in-flight emergency since the beginning of aviation." The details were peculiar to this particular flight, to this particular hydraulic damage. As with Türeci and Şahin in their Mainz laboratory, no one could have told Haynes what to do in advance. But yet, permeating his actions was the same decent belief Türeci held: that everyone involved deserved to be treated fairly. In Mainz, that had led to initiative rising up, and a wide range of colleagues being listened to. Here over the Midwest, it led to useful ideas pouring in as well.

Both Türeci and Haynes understood that being fair wasn't the same as being soft. The baseball manager Leo Durocher—we'll see more about him later—was famous for saying nice guys finish last. In many respects, he was right. Someone who's "merely" nice will be walked over by everyone else. If Haynes hadn't been willing to keep the first trainee pilot out and ignore the ground teams when necessary—however much it hurt their feelings—he would never have succeeded. But on the other hand, if he'd gone to the other extreme and crushed anyone who might threaten his status, he wouldn't have succeeded either.

It's comforting to nestle within cocoons, sauntering along in the first person, in the most important person, where a great wave of tenderness for ourselves feels natural. It's especially strong today, where social media is fast and feedback loops can be slow. But the real world is remorseless. Back in 2020, when the first Americans were flown from Wuhan, China, to a military base in California, officials who met them were instructed not to wear protective gear because of the "bad optics." This did little to stop the virus's spread. Powerful individuals, who've accumulated multitudes of likes and yes-men, are always tempted by such defiance. But reality eventually impinges. Whenever there's enough time to see the consequence of those impulsive or narrow actions, it's the better person who has the greater chance to succeed.

Were Haynes's attitude captured in a koan—one of the brief, seemingly paradoxical statements in Zen Buddhism—it would be the one we saw with Türeci and Şahin too: "Listen, but without ego." Take advantage of hierarchy, but don't hide within it. That just blinds you.

Yet, although Haynes's considerate, fair listening was great, by itself it can easily lead into a trap. For there's a further precaution one has to take if one's consistently going to make intense listening work.

CHAPTER 2

DIRECTORS

Danny Boyle and Old-School Hollywood
("Listen, without fixation")

*"I really didn't know what I was doing . . . [but] I wanted the big-
ness, the power . . . and everybody saying 'Yes . . . yes . . . yes!'"*

EAST LONDON, 2010, and movie director Danny Boyle has been offered
one of the greatest opportunities of his life: the chance to organize the opening ceremonies for the forthcoming 2012 Olympics. When it goes live, he will
have a worldwide audience of over half a billion—an estimated 100 million
in the US alone—and he wants to use that for a very personal reason. He
loves how Britain had developed a comprehensive health service, along with
other reforms, and it would be a pinnacle of his career —greater even than
the Oscar he received for his acclaimed *Slumdog Millionaire*—to display that
in a thrilling way to the world.

From the outside, everything seems good. He's been given a great sum
of money to work with, and has the further advantage that London is, along
with New York, Los Angeles and just a few other cities, one of the great
centers of creative talent in the world. He also has an experienced team of
assistants from his movie days.

The problem is in the tremendous number of volunteers he'll need.
To tell the story as he wants, he'll need rehearsal after rehearsal; with aerial

choreographers and moving cameras; riggers on the new stadium's roof and stage operators far below; hundreds of dancers, singers, bicyclists (both flying and terrestrial); handlers of giant beds and a flaming cauldron; live sheep, inflatable chimneys, and a million-watt sound system; smoke generators, machine operators, animators, drummers, stagecoaches, video screens, the entire London Symphony Orchestra and, in an idea he and his team are especially proud of, great living Britons from Paul McCartney (of Beatles fame), to J. K. Rowling (of Harry Potter fame).

Just as with Türeci and Şahin at their biotech company, Boyle is not too worried about the technicalities of directing them all. He's had decades of experience getting large teams to work in complex shoots around the world. The worry he has is a different one. Boyle wants to keep everything a secret until opening night. Like a new product launch, it will have greater impact that way. Yet as the opening gets closer, ever more people need to be brought in. There'll be around 10,000 for the main year of rehearsal, and in the final run-throughs, just days before the official opening, the entire Olympic stadium will have to be filled.

Journalists from the popular papers, as well as bloggers, will do anything to get images of what's taking place. Making sure there's not a single leak seems insoluble.

But although Boyle doesn't realize this yet, listening—of the right sort—would crack it.

There were some people that he knew he could trust. He'd worked with his immediate team for years, treating them with respect, making sure they never had worse meals or hotels than he did, respecting their judgment where they had expertise too. They were rock-solid.

He also wasn't concerned about professionals like McCartney or the London Symphony performers. They too were used to keeping secrets. The difficulty would be with the thousands of new volunteers. Humans are malleable, vulnerable, fickle. A few of the volunteers might be trusted in all circumstances, and if asked once not to take pictures, would keep to that for all the months of rehearsal. Most, however, would respond to the dominant mood.

Boyle struggled through this with the section heads under him. He knew the focus would have to be getting everyone to keep the secret, and had them emphasize to the volunteers how important that would be. He also encouraged his section heads to work hands-on during rehearsals and construction so that ordinary volunteers would feel solidarity.

When deadlines were tight, accordingly, the head of construction was out there with everyone else, hammering away; the head of wardrobe was also amid the volunteers, often personally sewing costumes. And when it rained—and this being London, it rained a lot—Boyle too stood in the open with the volunteers at the disused car factory they'd taken over for rehearsals, helping the practice go ahead.

Boyle wasn't operating in isolation, however, and a range of outside authorities kept on getting in his way. The worst was the International Olympic Committee (IOC), based in Lausanne, Switzerland.

Even the most charitable observers would not present its members as brimming with the democratic, we're-all-in-it-together attitude that Boyle was so proud of and wanted for his opening ceremony. IOC chiefs lived in tax-free luxury in Switzerland, and when representatives flew in to London to observe progress, invariably in business or first class, they'd ask for chauffeured cars to meet them. Dinner at the finest restaurants—as well as accommodation in the finest hotels—were their due.

Some IOC officials had been known to insist upon 24-hour butler service; others had requested host countries to provide private helicopters or free plastic surgery—for their spouses. (One senior member would later ask the king of Norway to host a reception in the IOC's honor, and by the way, would the king mind paying for it himself? A separate entrance at Oslo Airport for IOC members would be appreciated too.) Seeing someone like Boyle—a man who was supposed to at their level—standing in the rain in support of lowly volunteers was incomprehensible.

Just below them was the London Committee for the Olympic Games

(LOCOG), and although not as supercilious as the IOC—who could be?—they also seemed different from Boyle and his team. The LOCOG offices were in an expensive tower in London's new business district of Canary Wharf. Boyle's headquarters were in London's grittier Soho neighborhood, in an office vacant because a new rental hadn't arrived yet, and where staff pinned sayings from William Blake and Jesse Owens on the wall.

Boyle's opposite number at LOCOG, its chairman, was the ex-Olympian Sebastian Coe, or rather, for his proper title, The Right Honourable The Lord Coe, KBE (Knight of the British Empire). Coe spoke with a neutral educated accent and liked expensively tailored suits, matching his perfectly knotted ties. He'd long been a member of the Conservative party, including when it had opposed sanctions on the apartheid government in South Africa. Boyle, by contrast, was a committed left-winger, and would later turn down a knighthood, explaining, "Not my cup of tea. I'm embarrassed even being called *Mr.* Boyle." He might wear a jacket over an open shirt, but ties were a rare occurrence.

Barriers had been rising from the beginning. Both the international committee and the London one had let it be known that in previous opening ceremonies, all camera phones were confiscated, and strict nondisclosure agreements had to be signed. Again, as with Türeci and Şahin, Boyle immediately told his staff that no phones were going to be confiscated, and nondisclosure agreements for everyone were out. That too wasn't his style. He also could see it would undermine the volunteers' enthusiasm.

The committees also expected all the participants to be paid. That way, the threat of not paying would keep them under control. But this wasn't Boyle's style either. He decided he would use unpaid volunteers almost entirely (except where special skills were needed, as with some of the camera operators, software engineers and the like).

Next, the Olympic committees pushed the importance of compartmentalization. If participants only knew one tiny part of the opening ceremony, then even if they wished to leak what they'd learned, the damage wouldn't be great. Boyle wasn't impressed. He'd seen enough big events where volunteers marched around confused. "They know they've got to raise their left arm at a certain point, but they don't know why." That wasn't the opening he wanted. He told the Olympic committee he would show the volunteers exactly how their actions fitted in the larger story starting from day one.

In all those matters, he'd been largely civil. But then the London committee, LOCOG, told him that the volunteers would have to pay for their costumes. Boyle said this had to be a joke. The volunteers were putting in hundreds of hours of work. For most of them, the costumes were the only tangible thing they were going to receive. Didn't LOCOG understand anything?

He *needed* the volunteers to want to keep the secret.

When others on the London committee insisted, the tolerant, we're-all-in-it-together Boyle let loose. Paying for the costumes was not going to happen. Did they want him to resign? Did they want anything other than some bland corporate crap? In the end, the volunteers got their costumes for free.

Yet Boyle was still stuck. Months of rehearsal stretched ahead. In the past, he'd always succeeded at getting out of tight spots. Although from his mother he believed that most people are good, he knew that not everyone was like that. He had grown up in a working-class Irish-Catholic family near Manchester, in the northwest of England. His father had left school at 14 and had needed to push vigorously to educate himself. "From him . . . I [also] inherited . . . aggression, stubbornness, doggedness." He'd had to hustle to get where he was. No one becomes a top director by being a pushover.

His personal motivation made it stronger. The spectacle he was rehearsing for the opening night would show Britain moving through the rough destruction of the industrial revolution into the more fairly arranged postwar society. That was the trajectory his own life had matched: his parents starting out poor, then being aided by the state—housing grants, free medical care, a scholarship for him—as they worked to move themselves up.

But what could he do for success here? He knew the volunteers needed a sense of ownership to do well, yet the calls for them to keep the secret just didn't feel effective enough. And more information was coming in, from his contacts in the journalistic world, that there definitely were infiltrators from

London's popular press among the volunteers, just waiting to break the secret. It was a sinking feeling.

He had to do better. But how?

It's hard to break out of assumptions that are leading you the wrong way. We've seen with the pilot Park Duk-kyu how easy it is to ignore those below you. But it can be just as hard when there's a group right at your own level which might have fresh suggestions you need. Hollywood's old-school directors, the Cecil B. DeMilles with their canvas director's chairs and riding crops, were masters of that approach: scorning any word from outside directors or producers, however experienced they might be. It's an excellent way to firm up your own superiority—albeit not especially useful for seeing when you're charging in the wrong direction.

Often the problem is simply ego. Something even the generally considerate Steven Spielberg once fell into. Early in his career, he'd made a point of listening to experienced outside directors, recognizing this was the ideal way to avoid getting stuck on ineffective approaches. Yet after his run of success with *Jaws* and *Close Encounters of the Third Kind*, he gave up on that. "I really didn't know what I was doing . . . [but] I wanted the bigness, the power, hundreds of people at my beck and call and everybody saying 'Yes . . . yes . . . yes!'"

The result was *1941*, and although that might not be the worst movie ever made—not when *Super Mario Bros.* is still available—it's definitely a contender. Spielberg himself later called it "a total conceptual disaster," and to his credit, later went back to eliciting high-level advice: *Raiders of the Lost Ark, E.T.* and *Schindler's List* were just some of the strong movies that resulted.

For Boyle, the temptation was a different one. When things are going wrong, when we're under a lot of stress—possibly even when preposterously arrogant officials are flying in from Lausanne to seemingly do nothing more than make one's job harder—it's tempting to switch off and turn inward, sticking to your own team to the exclusion of *any* high-level outsiders. Even those who, if you thought about it a bit more, might have something useful to offer.

Boyle had fallen into this a decade before with his big-budget movie *The Beach*, set in Thailand, with Leonardo DiCaprio. In previous movies, Boyle had always consulted with his main producer, Andrew Macdonald, as well as others with similar experience. But *The Beach* had a budget greater than anything in his career before. The need to take care of a huge crew, and deal with the most complex shoot he'd faced, and refocus a script that hadn't been designed for DiCaprio, who was then one of the world's greatest stars (for this was shortly after *Titanic*'s great success), all that made Boyle turn inward, fixating on the minutiae of day-to-day shooting.

Macdonald and others could see what was going wrong. Boyle was deciding whether the Khaosan Road in Bangkok should be duplicated else-where, and how well Moby's music would fit, and how to ensure stunt divers were safe. But what really counted—what sort of character DiCaprio was meant to be, and indeed whether the genre was action or social comment—he was missing entirely.

As Boyle became lost in the wrong problems, he became more and more oblivious to how he was treating others. "I don't think [I] behaved very well." He'd ignored his producer Macdonald, and by the time the filming was over, and despite weeks on one of the most beautiful beaches in the world, "I couldn't wait to leave." Boyle knew his whole approach to the movie had been wrong. But without outside advice from someone at his level, he'd been unable to see how to fix it.

In London now, for a weaker soul, that might have happened again. But to his credit, just like Spielberg, Boyle only acted so dismissively that once. How could he have let his family down by doing so again? His father had been dogged, but never bullying to outsiders; his mother really had insisted everyone deserved respect. It's easy to create an outside group to hate. But doing that—blanketly vilifying outsiders—would be the opposite of what they'd lived for.

That was crucial, for if Boyle had puffed himself up and kept mocking *all* Olympic committee member as interfering "suits," he would have missed the key insight he needed for the opening ceremonies—which came from the most unexpected source.

It came from The Right Honourable The Lord Coe, KBE.

All Boyle needed to do, whatever his irritation at other committee members might have been, was see Coe as a real person, and listen to what he had to say. This was wise, for the ex-athlete Sebastian Coe had superb experience with international crowds.

Boyle's first plane flight from Britain had come in his mid 20s. Coe, by that age, had competed in Spain, Belgium, Norway, Switzerland, Italy and Moscow (where he'd won the first of his two Olympic gold medals). With his father—a working-class boy who'd bettered himself through education—he'd long worked with sports physiologists in America, getting a start in understanding different individuals there long before Boyle had ever visited.

Preconceptions block us from everything. Boyle was from the north of England and tended to let everyone know. Coe had moved around when he was young but was also mostly from the north, having grown up in the city of Sheffield. While the 11-year-old Boyle had passed a national test, sending him tuition-free to a relatively elite middle school, Coe had failed that test and ended up in a more mediocre ordinary school. There, "If you've got a name like Sebastian, you either learn to fight or to run."

Coe had certainly risen high in Britain's baroque class system, but that had come from effort, not inheritance. His grandfather was Indian, from Punjab—little advantage in the relatively racist 1970s, when he was first coming to public attention—and he'd been elevated to the House of Lords for his service as chief of staff to a Conservative politician. When he'd spoken out against the apartheid regime in South Africa, the constituency that he represented in Parliament had tried to stop him from running. "I'm not a classic Tory," he'd softly explain to anyone interested in asking.

And both men shared something deeper. Boyle admired his father and was shattered that he'd died a year before the Olympic opening, never getting to see his son's achievement. But his father could have a temper, and had pushed a poisonous academic competition between Boyle and his twin sister, and "when I was growing up, I hated my dad like you do."

Coe had a similarly complicated relation with his own father. Peter Coe had been a gifted mathematician who ended up in engineering. Although setting up the network of physiologists and sports scientists that had been indispensable to his son's career ("there was simply nobody better to have in my corner"), there's also an interview where Seb Coe says, sadly, that his father was the sort of man who'd never use one word when none would do. In important years, communication was tough.

Both Boyle and Coe, accordingly, understood what it was like to wield power . . . and why those who used it had an obligation not to close off. As they got to know each other—not as categories, but as people deserving of respect—they each learned from the other. Coe would sometimes wander the rehearsal spaces before the Olympics; quiet, just watching, admiring how Boyle demonstrated to his volunteers what to do. And Boyle got to learn what Coe had gained from his own wide international experience.

The word "secret," Coe explained, could feel malign, dangerous, with overtones of something pressing to get out. Abusers, for example, terrify their victims into believing they must keep a secret.

Why didn't Boyle break with the idea that there was a great "secret" to keep, he proposed, and instead call it a surprise? A surprise is something you can feel ownership of, something that you get the pleasure of revealing later. It was only because Boyle had fought the reflex to denigrate all "suits" that Coe was able to bring this up.

Boyle accepted Coe's idea immediately. This was what he'd been missing. As tens of thousands of more volunteers were brought in for the technical run-throughs, it would be crucial. "Kids love surprises, and there's nothing sinister," he said. From the next set of rehearsals, at a disused car factory in East London, then on to the final full practices at the new Olympic stadium, the bold hashtag "SaveTheSurprise" was displayed on screens everywhere. The fixation on "secrets" was over.

There was still a lot to do. One of Boyle's assistants was from California, and helped make sure the British story was clear for the American audience; there were technical difficulties galore (including an emergency use of hair dryers when enormous glowing Olympic rings suspended over the stadium got soaked in the rain); problems with various committee members less helpful than Coe as well.

But yet, with no phones confiscated and nary a nondisclosure agreement in sight, when Boyle saw no leaks at all were appearing, he realized he had, indeed, brought even the infiltrated, never-quite-identified journalists on board. By not singling them out, he'd made clear that he believed in them—and that was one of the finest results of all. They'd come to believe it was their role to #SaveTheSurprise along with everyone else.

"You may not have exactly the same values," he remembered, "but you can still be on the same side . . . They didn't write a word."

Coe's suggestion had triggered exactly the transformation Boyle needed. On the planned opening night, everything came off: magnificently, wonderfully, Olympically. It was the largest global audience British television had ever had, reaching record numbers in America as well, and not a single participant had leaked. When the ceremony finally went live—with Mary Poppins and J. K. Rowling and enormous trampoline beds all telling the story of innovation and British social reform ("They're pretty sound values," he liked to say)— the surprise, as Boyle had so wished, was complete. At one point, enormous screens in the Olympic stadium, transmitting worldwide, displayed a video clip of Queen Elizabeth II. She was being collected by the James Bond star Daniel Craig at Buckingham Palace and led into a helicopter. That turned into the real event of her—or a stuntman dressed like her—parachuting into the stadium, then walking up to the VIP section. When her own grandsons Princes William and Harry turned around and saw their real grandmother appear behind them, they were overwhelmed—even they'd had no idea how Boyle had saved this surprise.

Just as Al Haynes had a head start because he could put his ego to the side, here too being considerate can give a great advantage. When you're not disparaging all those around you—when you're not terrifying your co-equals and are modest enough to know you're fallible—you can set up the channels that will help you avoid fixation.

That brings us from one koan now to two: "Listen, without ego," and "Listen, without fixation." They're linked. Putting ego to the side—listening to those below you, as well as to "outsiders" at whatever level—magnifies what you can learn, neatly allowing you to avoid fixation along the way.

Bullies miss this, but so do the merely clueless. In one large Johns Hopkins University study, 64 percent of the surgical specialists interviewed felt their operations had high levels of teamwork. Only 28 percent of their nurses agreed.

As always, it's important not to go too far in the modest direction, for you still need to be able to take command. But when it's handled properly, being considerate is not a constraint. It's a strength. Otherwise, your ego in desperate control, you'll miss what's going on around you and be on track for failure.

Next? Fairness has something more to reveal: not just benefits for the individual enacting the fairness, but for those receiving it too. When that's skillfully handled, it can go even further: to create mighty buildings, and motivate fighters for the most deadly of missions.

PART TWO

GIVERS

CHAPTER 3

BUILDERS

Paul Starrett and Frank Lorenzo
("Give, but audit")

"Gentlemen, when the enemy is committed to
a mistake we must not interrupt him too soon."

JUNE 1928, AND the solid Midwesterner Paul Starrett—born in Lawrence, Kansas—has wangled an appointment in New York with the elegantly dressed financier John Jakob Raskob. Mr. Raskob, bored, has just asked Starrett how he could possibly do better as a contractor than all the others who have presented their pitch for the new skyscraper planned for 34th and Fifth.

That was a hard question to answer. Starrett and his four brothers had managed projects before, but they owned none of the equipment that would be needed for a building this size. Starrett's father had been a farmer and carpenter, his mother a schoolteacher. He'd worked as a stock boy in a hardware store, and earlier on a ranch in New Mexico. He'd always been blunt, veering on abrasive, and now in his 60s he suffers from depression in a way he's embarrassed to admit. Why bother with social niceties? He does something very odd in contracting circles.

He tells the truth.

Raskob is incredulous. He's enough of a New Yorker to know the word "chutzpah." How can a hick who doesn't have any equipment—and the construction of a building designed to compete with the fast-rising Chrysler Tower would require dozens, hundreds, of unique pieces of heavy machinery—imagine he could get the job?

He repeats what he has just asked: "*How* much equipment have you got on hand?"

"Not a damn thing," Starrett says. There's nothing to lose now. "Not even a pick and shovel."

But before Raskob can shoo his visitor out—at least in Paul Starrett's later account—the hick from the Midwest explains why there's merit in what he said. He, a balding man with wire-rim glasses and emphatic in what he says. No one, he says, has the equipment such a vast job would entail. But the Starrett men will design and then purchase every piece that will be needed, from steam shovels to on-site kilns. When the project is done, they'll sell their equipment and give Raskob and the project's other financial backers the difference.

"Will that make a profit?" Raskob asked.

Starrett said that sure it would. The other contractors were trying to pull a fast one over the financiers, he explained, for they would have to rent secondhand equipment that didn't work very well. The Starretts' way would guarantee there'd be good equipment left at the end. He was giving an honest offer. And—with a deep breath—Raskob accepted.

It was one of the best decisions he ever made. With the difficult-but-honest Starrett committed to telling the truth, a space was being created in which impressive things could happen.

The entire Empire State Building was constructed on that site in just thirteen months.

This was before computers or AI, when draftsmen used T-squares and compasses to sketch blueprints by hand; when stenographers had clanking machines and carbon paper to get instructions multiplied and out. Nor was thirteen months simply the amount of time to get the main steel frame built. It was almost everything, from disassembling the massive Waldorf-Astoria hotel that was standing there already—and taking away the thousands of truckloads of rubble that would produce—to designing, constructing, then topping out the new building, its windows and flooring all complete, to its full soaring height above New York City.

The approach Starrett used can be introduced by an anecdote from the life of the British prime minister Benjamin Disraeli, a man with a kind but notably plain-looking wife who had stood by him in the darkest moments of his parliamentary career.

"I saw you walking in the park with Mrs. Disraeli, Ben," the sarcastic Tory Member of Parliament Bernal Osborne said, "and I can't for the life of me understand what sentiment she can possibly inspire you with."

"A sentiment quite foreign to your nature, Bernal," Disraeli replied. "Gratitude."

By cold logic, Mrs. Disraeli's kindness toward her husband in the early years made no sense. If you're giving something away, you possess less of it than someone who hasn't given anything away. But that misses human nature. If I throw away something which I own, it's true that subtracts from me. But if I give it to someone else, as with Mrs. Disraeli's kindness to her husband, it needn't be a loss—as long as I can trust my gift will someday be reciprocated. That return journey is what Benjamin Disraeli summarized with the word "gratitude." What happened in the New York building industry was similar.

Workers in the years leading up to the Empire State Building's construction had generally been treated awfully, with wages kept low, at best $7 a day for laborers. If they wanted a hot meal during the day, they lost pay for the time it took to get down to the ground, find a food wagon or diner, and then climb back up. Safety laws scarcely existed, and there were numerous deaths as the perilous cranes went up.

Paul Starrett's doctors couldn't help his depression, a feeling he described of being "lost and unhappy—detached from the activities that satisfy me." He was never going to be the sort to enthusiastically stand around with his workers like a Danny Boyle. But it meant a great deal to him that those who were powerless were treated fairly. However gruff he appeared on the outside, it was the one thing he could hold on to. Sometimes he would be slightly stooped, with the burdens of life, but for the duration of the project, it helped keep the worst of his inner darkness from getting worse.

Raskob knew that Starrett had completed several buildings before, but only now did he learn more of how he'd gone about it. In one of the earlier projects, terse as always, Starrett had lobbied against a star architect's design that would have left ordinary clerks far from any natural light. In another— just as grumpy, yet again just as considerate—he'd had his company's office boys and janitors look through an architect's plans to make sure the final layout would be convenient for all the junior staff in that finished product.

Now, with the Empire State Building, Starrett and his brothers were going to continue that decency. For safety, they'd assign dedicated squads to make sure all sudden gaps in floor cover—for elevators or hoists—were well marked and protected. They would provide full pay on days when the wind was too high to go up safely.

Oh, and Starrett was going to more than double basic wages for all workers on the site, making the rate $15 a day—and there would be good-quality, subsidized restaurants on floor after floor of the building as it rose up.

Raskob wasn't a cruel man, but he was puzzled. He had prospered in America's 1920s. Businesses didn't usually pay more than they had to. Could Starrett's plan—the offering of generosity, and the assumption that gratitude would result—actually work here?

What Starrett and his brothers were planning to do was what economists call providing efficiency wages. Pay more, treat workers better, and you get better, more motivated staff. Progressive business schools are full of examples. But one can be reminded of the physicist Enrico Fermi's remark when presented with explanations of why there was likely to be a multitude of advanced civilizations among the stars. "Then where is everybody?" he gently asked. If what progressive firms do is so effective, why doesn't every organization run this way?

The answer is that generating gratitude is far from being the only way to succeed.

Around the time the Empire State Building was getting under way, Raskob had become involved with funding a small regional airline named Eastern Air Travel. Its first CEO, the famous World War I aviator Eddie Rickenbacker, was like Starrett in that on the outside he was grumpy and swore a lot. But also like Starrett, that masked the fact he was exceptionally considerate. He'd guaranteed mechanics a 40-hour week (an industry first), linked pay with the company's profits (also a first), and brought in a company-wide pension. By the time of his death as a revered industry elder in 1973, that consideration had built Eastern into the third largest airline in America.

Then, in 1986, Frank Lorenzo assumed control, and what he did next shows all the obstacles people like Starrett are liable to face in their efforts to make fairness work. (Again, I chose this case out of many more recent ones because the details are so clear at this distance in time.)

Lorenzo had grown up in middling circumstances, his father running a bar—their home actually under the approach path to New York's La Guardia Airport, where Eastern Airlines flew daily. But while Rickenbacker had been drawn to aviation—"When I look up and see the sun shining on the patch of white clouds," he'd written, "I think how it would feel to be up above it watching the earth below"—Lorenzo was immune to such vistas. What he was drawn to was money, the more of it the better, and although that is an attitude many of us wholeheartedly share, he had a distinctive way of acquiring it.

It didn't harm Lorenzo that he was a handsome, seemingly easygoing man—the opposite of the blunt, irritable Starrett or Rickenbacker—and on the surface, he could make himself appear concerned, earnest, polite. Yet his reflex wasn't to build but to take. The first thing Lorenzo started taking from Eastern employees was their salaries. He cut wages, starting with Eastern's mechanics and ramp-service personnel. Then he began breaking off assets, first selling landing slots, and then jets, and finally an industry-leading reservations system his immediate predecessor had developed.

This wouldn't have been too bad if he'd used the profits for new aircraft or purchasing new routes Eastern needed. Aviation is a tough business. "If the Wright brothers were alive today, Wilbur would have to fire Orville to reduce costs," Herb Kelleher, founder of Southwest Airlines, once said. But Lorenzo wasn't building anything. Rather, he set up holding companies where he funnelled much of the savings from these sales. The reservations system he sold at a low price to a group largely under his control. He then charged Eastern for using it, racking up gains of nearly half a billion dollars. Lorenzo knew how he'd be judged if his acts were uncovered—as Machiavelli put it, "Those best at playing the fox . . . have to know how to disguise their slyness; how to pretend one thing and cover up another." Service quality and the amount of time allowed for repair went down, while a Federal Aviation Authority study showed Eastern's maintenance rates falling to last among major airlines in America. To cover over that, Lorenzo simply continued to show earnest concern in any public interview.

What he was actually plotting to do was make Eastern's workers so resentful that they would go on strike. With new laws the conservative president Ronald Reagan had recently promoted in the 1980s, once Eastern went bankrupt, he'd be able to fire everyone, skip severance pay, then start again with new hires on lower wages. He'd even get to break the "previous" company's agreement to pay his employees the pension savings they'd built up.

Unfortunately for Lorenzo, he'd surrounded himself with yes-men, none of whom were aware enough, or brave enough, to warn him how much federal laws and the mood among his employees had been changing.

To make his strategy work, Lorenzo had to trigger the ground crew, mechanics and others in what was known as the machinists union to go on strike, while ensuring the pilots stayed at work. Then the airline would keep earning money in the brief period until full bankruptcy protection came into effect.

To keep the pilots on his side, Lorenzo decided to send a video—this was before streaming—to each one of them. It showed him avuncular, trustworthy, sitting on his couch at home in Houston. He held up an agreement which, he said, guaranteed that if for any reason there was a strike with the machinists union and the company entered bankruptcy, Eastern would *not* go to a judge and attempt to cut the pilots' pay. He then solemnly signed the agreement before the camera.

As word of the video spread, the machinists union lawyers gasped in wonderment at their luck. Lorenzo was misleading the pilots. By the law of the time, a declaration of bankruptcy invalidated all previous guarantees. The machinists' lawyers spread the word. Lorenzo wasn't the friendly, trustworthy guy he pretended to be. He wanted the pilots to go along with an agreement that he knew wouldn't be worth anything.

A few days after the video, when the machinists went on strike, Eastern's pilots—conservative Republicans almost to a man—joined them. For good measure, the flight attendants joined in too.

This was in 1989. With his workers united against him, staying out as March turned into April and April turned into May, and then, as the once most-profitable-of-all flying months of the summer began, Lorenzo became frantic. At this rate, his income would crash during the strike.

What he had missed is how much people hate being cheated. That's why cheats have to be so ingenious in hiding what they do. This resentment is the flipside of gratitude, and a powerful force indeed. There's been the worldwide resentment at bankers who escaped the 2008 crash with no penalties, while China's indignation at Western bullying under the Qing dynasty shows little sign of going away after more than a century.

In Reagan's time, just a few years before the Eastern strike, the resentment of the pilots, machinists and flight attendants wouldn't have mattered. The law would still have protected Lorenzo, allowing his subterfuge to work. But Reagan's successor, George H. W. Bush, had brought in fresh laws that helped employees on strike. When Lorenzo finally managed to get the airline into bankruptcy, almost a half year after the strike began, there was no money left for him to take.

All this time, an entirely different approach had been possible. While Lorenzo was destroying Eastern, other airlines were achieving record profits, not through warring with employees, but, as Lorenzo's immediate predecessor (the distinguished astronaut Frank Borman) had already begun, through innovation in reservations systems, better route planning, and better customer service. Smug amid his yes-men, Lorenzo entirely missed that.

At the end, in the grand tradition of kicking a man when he's down, Michael Milken, the junk bond king later jailed for fraud, came out against Lorenzo; the not-usually-Marxist *Wall Street Journal* declared that he had gone too far in milking the airline; even—and for this you almost begin to feel sympathy for the poor man—Newt Gingrich piled in against him. After a final effort by Lorenzo to stiff his main investors, Eastern was broken apart. The Scandinavian firm that bought the largest fragments specified that Lorenzo could not be involved with their work in any way. He ended up at a loose end in corporate America, widely shunned, and calling out forlornly for a job.

Now back to New York, 1930. If the Empire State Building builder Paul Starrett had gone to the opposite extreme from Lorenzo—if he had been naively generous to everyone—he too would have failed. But Starrett had survived years in New York construction, a life experience which disabuses anyone of belief in the inherent benevolence of humankind. If the principles he applied as work on the project began were to be summarized in a koan, it would be a blunt "Give, but audit."

Building sites are magnificent locales for scams. A foreman, for example, might invoice for 100 workers but only supply 94. Workers would nonchalantly borrow tools which they were never going to bring back. And suppliers across New York had become expert in skimping on the quality of bricks, of bolts, of glass and of virtually every other component known to man, as the original procurement documents for the Empire State Building's construction reveal.

It hadn't been chance that Starrett was the last person interviewed by Raskob. Starrett had known the tendering contractors would plot against each other. When a friend on the planning committee, Robert C. Brown, let him know the others were going to play up his lack of equipment, he'd pulled in favors to be sure he was called in last, the ideal position in which to present his rebuttal.

Since he'd need extra help to block all the tricks once construction began, Starrett brought in a Canadian engineer named John Bowser. In his heart, Bowser was a romantic who appreciated the grandeur in architecture. He even dreamed of having a miniature Empire State Building in limestone for his tombstone one distant day. But Bowser also had left home at 11, worked construction around the world, and knew every possible subterfuge. Notes from the time describe him as having "the qualities of tact and infinite patience," combined with, as archivists delicately put it, "a forceful personality."

That's the mix you need to make generosity work in a complex new project. To ensure that unions stayed honest about how many men were there, Bowser hired staff to physically visit each man on the construction site: this happened twice in the morning, and twice in the afternoon. Many of the workers spent their day on beams dangling up to 1,000 feet above the ground, so that was not an easy job. But as Bowser's records coolly note, "This method takes away from the foreman . . . the temptation of favoring [non-existent] accounts."

To keep inventory from walking away, Bowser created a department of accountants who'd also clamber through the building to check that equipment was remaining where it was supposed to be. (It's much the way a huge bureaucratic process operates behind the scenes at Wikipedia and eBay to keep cheats from taking advantage there too.)

All this was a Borgesian task in his era, given that there were no computers, and all directives had to be dictated or handwritten, then typed, filed and cross-filed; also given that the inventory being sought was constantly scooting around on monorails, trolley cars and steam engines. Detail was crucial. The hard to categorize chrome-nickel for the window trim needed to be distinguished from the chrome-nickel for the vertical dividers; the 15,000—not 14,990—bags of marble chips needed to be counted and then marked as counted (so they wouldn't be double-counted); and on and on.

Starrett's lack of naivety was crucial. He knew that he could only continue being fair to the workers if by auditing thoroughly enough he made sure they were just as fair in return; giving the work that was their side of the bargain. Yet he also was decent about it, having Bowser block potential cons without humiliating the workers.

All his initial promises were followed through. The subsidized restaurants duly appeared, scattered among the building's floors as the construction rose. The crews used them to take away hot sauerkraut, stews, soft drinks and "near beer" (Prohibition making alcohol illegal) for lunches on their work sites, which sometimes—as a great photograph showed—took place on exposed beams far above the Manhattan streets.

Creativity poured out, just as with BioNTech's vaccine researchers generations later. Workers suggested building a miniature railway line to transport bricks into the site, instead of, as was usual before, stacking them on wheelbarrows to be more laboriously pushed along wobbling wooden gangplanks. With a peak of 100,000 bricks arriving in every eight-hour shift, that sped up construction a lot. Electricians spontaneously came up with wired signaling systems to replace the usual bell ropes for announcing when a shipment was coming up.

Other ideas had consequences still visible on the Empire State Building today. Expert craftsmen were traditionally called in to smooth the edges of the large stones that served as such a large structure's facing material. But others quickly pointed out that it would save time to take stones still rough from the quarries and simply cover their joins with thin metal panels bolted deep into the stone. Junior architects perfected that, and the famous art deco front for the building was the result, with its shining stainless steel strips leaping out from their gray limestone surround.

Starrett and Bowser were getting back a lot more than they gave out, but that's the magic of gratitude. Since the project's multitude of subcontractors found that they too could depend on what each other said, a powerful form of fast-tracking started up; one of the first for a construction project of this size. Foundries knew they'd been given the honest date by which they'd need to have the first steel beams ready. Likewise, suppliers of elevator cables and producers of the cement needed for floor pouring and structural engineers and mechanical engineers and hundreds of other participants could trust what they were being asked to do.

Starrett was also spared the usual high turnover on such construction sites, with all the retraining costs that would have entailed. Workers didn't want to quit their jobs, not with these wages and attitudes.

Starrett still rarely smiled, and grumpily snapped out his decisions. But that didn't matter. You don't have to love someone to respect them. You don't even have to like them. If they're fair and you see their competence, that's enough. Unpack the word "fair" and everyone can understand the ideas inside: that there's a justifiable amount to push people, and anything else would be excessive. Not only was Starrett aware of this as a noble goal—many people are—but he also was decent enough to *choose* to act that way. The handsome, easygoing Lorenzo was friendlier on the surface, but he was hated once people realized he was violating that. It was the irritable, grouchy Starrett who was loved.

When ironworkers on comparable buildings to the Empire State Building across the river in New Jersey, earning far less, went on strike, Starrett's workers felt no reason to join them. Rather than being shunned in corporate America, searching forlornly for work, he and his brothers ended up among the leading contractors in the country.

There's an insight to all this from the ancient sage Hillel, writing two thousand years ago. What he asked, in essence, were two linked questions: "If I am not for myself, who is for me? But if I am only for myself, what am I?"

The idea is that neither extreme will do. You need to stand up for yourself; otherwise, in a rough world, you will be destroyed. But if that's all you do—if you're only for yourself—what kind of person are you? The Starretts were opting for a middle path, and since they had the savvy to guard against cheats—what came out as "Give, but audit" in a brief koan summary—the gratitude they unleashed was the reward.

This applies more widely than just to skyscrapers of the last century. When the Soviets left Eastern Europe at the end of the 1980s, a near half-century of seeming loyalty vanished in a blink. The Russian state had given nothing, and nothing was all they were going to get back.

Style is never the issue. At the rehearsals for the 2012 Olympic ceremonies, Danny Boyle was more like the easygoing Lorenzo than the grumpy Paul Starrett. But no one had to worry he was merely Machiavellian: agreeable on the outside, conniving on the inside. He too constantly demonstrated to his thousands of volunteers that he really was out to help them . . . and from gratitude, confidence, they too offered up a tremendous range of new ideas about set design and social media and modern dance, all so important to his opening ceremony's great success. And, of course, if he'd been scornful toward Sebastian Coe, it's likely he would have never received the crucial idea to #SaveTheSurprise that made it all possible.

How much further can audited generosity go? The business world is important, but there are domains where even deeper commitment—where matters of life and death—are at stake. A series of events in the jungles of northeastern India during World War II is revealing.

CHAPTER 4

FIGHTERS

Ursula Graham Bower and Old-School Colonialists
("Give, by letting others give")

*"New Delhi, Dec 8, 1945. The dramatic story of a female
'Lawrence of Arabia' emerged from the wild jungles of Burma
today—the story of a beautiful British woman who has been leading
fierce head-hunting tribesmen against the Japanese . . ."*

IN THE SUMMER of 1942, British general William Slim was at the lowest point in his life. Japanese troops had stormed through Burma, where Slim had been based, killing thousands of British and Indian forces, and sending the rest into humiliating retreat. Only an all-out sprint to the Burmese border allowed Slim to get his army across the Chindwin River. He'd had to protect them from strafing by Japanese fighters, as well as try to help at least some of the refugees hurrying to keep up; knowing that if they didn't make it by the time the monsoon started, they would be hunted to their death.

When he staggered into the Indian hill town of Imphal, he had only bare fragments of the divisions he had started out with months before. "Tactically, we had been completely outclassed," he admitted. His army had rarely had good intelligence from behind Japanese lines and been continually surprised by where the attacks came from. Much as with commanders at Dunkirk, he'd also had to leave almost all his heavy equipment behind.

Most of his men had some mix of malaria and jungle sores and longed for dry lodgings. Yet many of the British officers in Imphal looked down on them as cowards and failures. They were forced to live huddled in tents as the rain poured down and mud pooled around them.

Over the next two years, Slim transformed his army, building it up for an intended assault back into Burma. But Japan struck first, early in 1944, again disconcerting him, its troops crossing the Chindwin to advance into the main pass from Burma into India.

Soon the vast British military supply depot near Kohima was under threat, as well as the crucial junction at Imphal. If they were lost, it was not only all of India that would be vulnerable: America needed Slim's region for the supply flights into China that supported anti-Japanese forces there. Without Chinese resistance, Japan would have more troops free for the campaigns against America in the Pacific.

Amidst that confusion, however, a message soon came to Slim's headquarters:

GOING FORWARD TO LOOK FOR THE
ENEMY STOP
KINDLY SEND RIFLES AND AMMUNITION
SOONEST

One officer, hearing that equipment was being assigned to a "Miss Bower," thought it all a joke: "Ha ha—very funny. Who made this up?" Hadn't there been some sort of London debutante with the double-barreled last name "Graham Bower" traveling through the region in the past?

Slim's more experienced officers told him to shut up. Miss Bower was one of their most successful agents, now operating behind enemy lines. Her message came from within the Naga Hills: dense jungle where headhunters had until recently roamed, and which looked to be part of the Japanese invasion routes.

How could a young woman, on her own—who had, indeed, been a London debutante not long before—survive in a setting like that and help

them? Her story shows how much the deepest manner of giving can yield—
and what inner transformation we need go through to be able to offer that
at all.

Ursula Violet Graham Bower had been born in 1914 to wealthy parents in
the English coastal town of Harwich, where her father was a Royal Navy
commander. He loved taking his daughter hiking and teaching her to shoot:
rifles, shotguns, automatic pistols and whatever else he could get his hands on.

Her mother had different views about how a girl was to be raised. "What
she wanted," Graham Bower remembered, "was a really attractive debutante
daughter, which was a desirable thing for her generation; [one] who could
dance and play tennis and well—what she got was me."

Since a daughter who didn't fit in was embarrassing, not only did Mrs.
Graham Bower leave most of the childrearing to nannies—usual enough
in her class—but she also took to parking her daughter with a conveniently
generous grandmother who lived far away. That made her own socializing
in London much easier, and if months at a time went by without her seeing
her child, that was just something young Ursula would have to accept.

Boarding school was supposed to help, giving freedom for the parents
and a social life for the students. But even there Ursula offended her mother.
She was at Roedean, one of the best boarding schools for girls in Britain,
and she'd come to relish her studies, at age 16 being top of her class in Latin,
and scoring near top in English, French and history. She was eager for university, and her school thought even Oxford might be possible. But to her
mother, that was ridiculous. "I heard it said," Ursula remembered, "that it
was no good spending money on me because I wouldn't want a career, but
of course, that wasn't so." It was only her brother, she was told, who would
be going on to university, not her. "I didn't kick much, [but] just folded like
a wet umbrella. It all seemed pretty hopeless."

Being back at home didn't make things better, for she hated the rounds
of London debutante balls her mother forced her to attend. Society girls were
supposed to be fragile and willowy, but although Graham Bower was fit—
still delighting in long hikes with her father whenever he was on leave—she

was never going to be that fashionably slim. She tried to make up for it with careful dressing, but that was an impossible task, since her fashion-conscious mother wouldn't go shopping with her to help. The disapproval only got stronger. Coming down the stairs once, dressed in what she thought were clothes that would finally make her look acceptable, her mother called out, "What *are* you wearing?!"

Decades later, Ursula's own daughter explained how "completely devastated" she'd been by that remark; by the never-ending pressure to be perfect in this world where she could never fit.

What was she to do? Although the family wouldn't give her money for school, there was plenty if she wanted to spend it on a car. She bought an Aston Martin ("the joy of my life") and surprised everyone by entering amateur rallies, taking a course in mechanics to fix it as needed.

Her father thought that was excellent, but Ursula knew it wasn't going to be meaningful enough for long. When her mother decided to send her to India in the hope she'd find a wealthy white husband there, Graham Bower for once didn't argue against what was expected, and with resignation just agreed.

She ended up at the hill station of Imphal in August 1937. The Englishwomen there were eager to have this fresh, well-off arrival join them, but she found their life intensely boring. The women spent their time idling, or meeting at the golf course, or twice a week watching polo. A few of the men engaged in more adventurous duck-hunting, but though they gossiped about who might try to catch her in marriage, the fact that Graham Bower was a good shot meant nothing. She wasn't going to be asked along for manly pursuits.

This was no better than back in London. If she'd come all this way here, there had to be more interesting ways to engage herself.

Stretching beyond Imphal were the Naga Hills, their ranges "running down from Tibet," then turning into thick jungle at this lower altitude. Graham Bower made an awkward first expedition in. And there, even with other Europeans clattering along, something unexpected happened. "As we topped the ridge and met the view, I stopped short." Mist was boiling in the hollows, rising raggedly as the sun struck it. "Beyond the first, forested hills below us lay range on range and ridge on ridge . . . they rolled on until they melted into the lowering sky.

"That landscape drew me as I had never known anything do before, with a power transcending the body, a force not of this world at all." The Naga tribesmen* they saw were too wary of her and the other visitors to communicate much. Britain had conquered their lands just two generations before. Colonial officials had more than once offered the inhabitants "free" sacks of grain, which they then later insisted, at gunpoint, had to be paid back with exorbitant interest, for a period running into years, impoverishing entire villages.

Back in Imphal, Graham Bower was "dazed, tired, bewildered and not sure what had happened." The Europeans expected her to simply pick up with the usual social rounds, but she couldn't. Graham Bower was 23 years old. As the weeks stretched along, she felt "not yet of the hills, but already divorced a fraction from my own race."

What does one do to create a meaningful life?

It's the question at the heart of Graham Bower's transformation to being an important intelligence agent, and a topic that had fascinated the Franco-Dutch anthropologist Arnold van Gennep, who coined the phrase "Rites of Passage." He found people generally went through three distinct phases if they were going to change.

First they separated from the world they'd been in before. Then they entered into a free-floating alternate world: a limbo that existed seemingly out of time. Only then—the third stage—could they leave that timeless zone and reconnect with the world. When they did, they'd be transformed.

Ursula Graham Bower had completed the first stage when she left Britain. Life on the distant Indian/Burmese border was her second, transitional stage. The third, stable stage, everyone had told her, was to be marriage and children. But that didn't feel like enough; not yet, at least.

---

* The Naga were a loose confederation of different peoples; their home terrain spread over several adjacent regions, only one of which was officially termed "Nagaland." For simplicity I'll refer to "Nagaland" and "the" Naga throughout; see the reading guide for details.

How was she going to live instead?

After her expedition, she barely had time to reflect before she was forced by her family to return to England. She tried her previous life—the motorcar races; the cafes and social gatherings—but that was impossible. "I had to go back." She arranged with professors at Cambridge and her still-desired Oxford to study the peoples living in those hills, and then she sailed to India again.

Her renewed expeditions into the Naga Hills were hard, as the Europeans in Imphal now mocked her. "There was a great deal of tut-tutting and firm belief that at the end of three days I should be borne home in a fainting condition." Yet as the weeks and then months went on, in this setting she described of "green jungle, of bamboos and elephant-grass and trees," Graham Bower began to shift. At first she had experienced a distance from the Naga, for she represented the authorities, and "there stood between the [Naga] and the Government a wall of misunderstanding, fear, suspicion and mistrust." Finally, in the hilltop village of Laisong, she decided to give her word—written down by visiting government officials—that she would cut herself off from protection by any British colonial law. Although she couldn't "become" a Naga herself, she was henceforth going to put herself entirely under their law.

This changed everything. She was far from medical help or newspapers—or even banal yet comforting English-language conversations while watching a polo match. There were storms with hailstones that shattered walls, once even blowing her roof away. In daytime, the humidity was brutal; she had to defend herself from young men who at the start tried to peer at her undressing. It didn't matter. She was going to stay—this final stage in her rite of passage—and with that, at last, she was accepted. "When I first reached Laisong, I was outside it. As their reserve melted, the wall dissolved, and [finally] I found myself on the far side looking back."

She began to work harder at learning the Naga's Tibeto-Burman language. Reciprocity grew, for seeing her commitment they began to teach her too: practice on how to handle the slippery stepping-stones necessary to cross the fastest rivers that shot through their valleys; knowledge of traditional medicines; help in locating elders who could best pass on poetic tribal lore.

It was genuine respect. When clouds of locusts damaged crops so much that famine seemed possible, Graham Bower didn't just help in getting quantities of food in (though of course she did that where she could). She now understood the Naga's superior knowledge of their land, and the subtle supply connections between the different villages. She helped protect them from administrators who might impose solutions as disastrously as had happened before, when entire regions ended up in debt.

In 1942, when the Japanese stopped short of the Naga Hills, Graham Bower had set up a small reconnaissance force to search for downed airmen, or help in other ways. That's how Slim's officers first heard of her. Now, amid the fresh dangers of 1944—the Japanese no longer just threatening India, but actually pouring in— Slim needed groups like hers, but properly armed, and on a far larger scale. Finding the leaders to do that was hard. Many British civilians and officers in the region had let the previous decades of military superiority go to their heads. Once Japanese battle victories cut that superiority away, although there were notable exceptions, many showed little concern for anyone but themselves.

Bower's* initial work with these reconnaissance teams back in 1942 had shown she wasn't like that. The fact that she was willing to take the initiative now in 1944, when the Japanese were actually present in India—her "going forward to look for the enemy" message—was even better.

From the outside, her prospects might not have seemed good, for, as she put it, "the Japanese advance [had come] on like a tidal wave, and we suddenly found ourselves some 200 miles in advance of everyone else." But Slim needed any information she could provide. He gave instructions that she was to be supported with all possible urgency. Her group, along with other reconnaissance and ambush teams, became part of what was labeled V Force.

---

* As she began to use just the single last name "Bower" for communications efficiency at this point, that's a shift I'll now make too.

Up in Laisong, Bower was just glad she hadn't been fired after her initial telegram ("I was always afraid they'd find an excuse"). But she also knew that if she was going to do a good job, she'd need to transform her operation. There were at least 800 square miles of jungle to monitor, with numerous tracks the Japanese could be advancing along. It wasn't going to be enough to have a few friends from Naga families she knew well in Laisong helping. She'd need a force of over a hundred to help Slim properly.

That wasn't going to be easy. In the two years Slim had spent building up his army, his officers had devised numerous ways to get their vast, multi-ethnic force to cohere. There were lectures and shared promotion schedules, and training camps where recruits of every ethnicity and religion got the delights of crawling through mud while sergeants yelled equally at them all, and—usually pretty safely—machine guns went off overhead. Bower, by contrast, had no training camps, no sergeants, and no heavy machine guns; no MPs or threats of court-martial either.

What she did have, though, was trust, at a level which sometimes even she didn't grasp. At one point in her recruiting for this new, more dangerous operation, a group of the fittest Naga who'd said they'd join suddenly asked for "24-hour leave." She thought that was it. "We've got this very small chance of getting out of it alive, and I simply cannot ask them to go with me on a suicide mission. So I said, 'All right—you go' never thinking I would see them again." She knew they had every reason to believe they'd be safe from Japanese attack if they simply sat out the war in their villages.

In fact, they did return, and within the promised time. Most had young children, and they'd simply been arranging for guardianship of their families in the event of their deaths. "This had taken me so much by surprise that Namkia [one of the group] said, 'What did you expect? How could we have abandoned you?'" Because Bower had doubted their sincerity, "I felt about six inches high."

Once again her "giving" hadn't meant imposing on the Naga. It had meant *enabling* them—as a Zen-style koan might have it, "Give, by letting others give"—and now for the most significant of acts. This went beyond generosity and gratitude on a construction site. She was asking them to put their lives on the line.

By then a small British party of young troops, exhausted, had managed to climb up from the lowlands to drop off what she'd requested. "I never thought a box of grenades would look beautiful," she recalled, "one of the nicest gifts I've ever received." There also were rifles and ammunition.

Once she had the guns, Bower's Naga friends helped work out the likeliest tracks the Japanese could be taking. This soon resulted in Bower leading an expedition to a hill above the position where three important routes converged. Getting to the top was exhausting—"Frightful sweat, higher and higher . . . burning heat"—but she wasn't going to let any of her men see her give up. Once in position "we . . . had to do the best we could for about a week. There were all sorts of refugees and enemy agents, and Lord knows what coming through all this time, and we had to deal with them."

When it was possible, she and her men simply arrested looters or AWOL conscripts and took away their weapons. Sometimes, though, the looters operated in large armed gangs, and there was no alternative but to shoot. Even with the smaller submachine gun known as the Sten gun, the results could be messy.

"I had to collect the bits [of body parts] and bury them. [At first] I thought I was never going to manage it, but when it came to the point I was so wild about having had the villages looted that I didn't care a hoot . . . Word went round that we meant business, and the looting was under control from then on."

If Bower hadn't been willing to take lives, she would have failed. But if she'd merely exulted in her power—if she'd threatened and tried to dominate the Naga in every way—the group that left for that 24-hour leave would never have come back.

Slim understood that kind of relationship; it was one of his great strengths. He repeatedly told the story of how, during the worst moments of the 1942 retreat, he'd come across a group of officers who'd made themselves a comfortable bivouac, while leaving their men without food or shelter. He laid into them: "You will neither eat, nor drink, nor sleep, nor smoke, nor even sit down until you have personally seen that your men have done those things. If you do not, I will break you." A pause, then the essence of the contract that fair treatment could create: "[But] if you will do this for them, they will follow you to the end of the world."

His 14th Army headquarters occasionally sent additional liaison officers on missions to try to reach Bower, but this wasn't always as helpful as expected. Even men who had been around since 1942 often associated the extreme jungle where Bower operated with ambush, dank smells, terror. She reassured them. The Japanese weren't natural masters of the jungle, she explained, for there were no jungles in Japan. If they had any skills, it was because they had learned them, just as she had learned from the Naga. For example, if the enemy appeared behind you, that didn't mean you were surrounded. Act quickly to attack from the side, and *they* would be the ones who were surrounded.

As to the liaison officers' greatest worry—the fact that these villagers still had a reputation as headhunters, and macabre "head trees" still sometimes existed in their palisades, where trophies until recently had dangled—she explained that this hardly occurred anymore. Anyway, it did have an internal logic. "If you come home with a head, the rest of the person is not looking for you."

When she was with the Naga themselves, she wasn't going to give them any instruction on survival—no one on the planet was more skilled in this terrain than they were—but she did encourage her men to spread out more than they were used to, with a scout at least fifty yards ahead, and formations ending with "an officer, which in this case was generally me." Some of the men carried spears, but most had tommy guns. It was because its ammunition was heavy for Bower to carry that along with her kukri—the Gurkha-style knife she'd lived with for years now—she carried the smaller Sten gun.

The patrols were tiring. On a previous outing, "The path fell suddenly, through grass and woods," she remembered, "down by zigzags, by steps, by twists, by long slants—down, down, down, turning and dropping."

The terrain changed quickly at different altitudes. "A warm, wet, muggy quiet enveloped us; tiger-mosquitoes swamped. Giant bamboos replaced the lighter types."

The formation discipline she taught proved useful when on one patrol the leading Naga, turning a corner, ran into a large force of Japanese directly in front of him. He might have had a chance of escaping had he run back, but that would lead the heavily armed Japanese to his own men before they were prepared. Instead, making a quick calculation, he fired at the first enemy soldier he saw.

The other Japanese instantly shot back and killed him, as he'd known they would, but the noise of their weapons alerted the others still out of sight around the corner behind him. That spacing Bower had insisted on gave them time to shift a few yards away from the path. Since the jungle was exceptionally lush, they were now invisible. When the Japanese finally came—thinking the sole Naga they'd met had been on his own—they were ambushed in turn.

For basic reconnaissance strategy, Bower also now understood to work with the Naga rather than presuming she'd know best, as she might have earlier. The result was a geometrically ingenious system of scouts and runners—some stationary, others roaming—which gave her information on enemy sightings with optimal speed.

Agreeable, thoughtful Bower had been generous to her Naga friends, offering up her entire life. All the lessons we've seen so far applied. She'd listened without ego, and thus learned from them. Their advice had helped her keep the right focus in her original anthropological studies (in times of peace), as well as now in these choices about where and how to scout (in these times of war). She'd given generously but hadn't let herself be taken advantage of, be that by the occasional peering village male or the gangs of armed looters whose body parts, after battle, had been so messy to dispose of.

All of that was triggered by her commitment, and letting them take the initiative. That was how—"Give, by letting others give"—the gratitude and initiative she helped channel arose: the effective patrols, the detailed scouting information, the help for escaped prisoners and bailed-out airmen. Before that she'd been like many of the Europeans, engaging in little more than a monologue. Now, like all real connection—like all real giving—she'd entered a dialogue.

Bower's success led to the Japanese setting a bounty of one hundred rupees on her, literally for her head. She tried to laugh it off, saying that since it hadn't been cut off yet, *she* was the one the Japanese owed the hundred rupees to. But she also knew that a number of V Force camps in adjacent regions had been located; some of the officers escaping, others most terribly not. She could no longer stay in Laisong, for with its single entrance up a sharp hill, it was a perfect trap. Bower and selected bodyguards took to sleeping in shelters cut tunnel-like into the scrub, moving regularly.

It was exhausting, and one particularly unpleasant week, when torrential rains came, "Our nerves were in rags . . . and we snapped and squabbled like bad-tempered children." Later, she came down with malaria. She also knew her efforts were only a small part of the army's intelligence and scouting work.

But yet, the sightings that came in through Bower's network—both the information about where the Japanese were and, just as importantly, where they were not—were recognized as distinctly trustworthy, helping Slim and his officers safely reassign forces. In time, the sieges of Kohima and Imphal were lifted, and within a year, Slim's army had crossed the Chindwin and was on its way to pushing the Japanese entirely out of Burma. Bower was awarded the distinguished MBE honor from the King George VI, and taught jungle survival techniques to RAF crews and others. When peace came, she went back to her anthropological studies, while continuing to help with health and other matters among the Naga. She married a fellow V Force officer.

Before all that, in the latter months of 1945, she was briefly famous, with wildly exaggerated stories of her derring-do spreading across the world's press (including a luridly colored comic book titled *Jungle Queen*). *Time* magazine, then with an audience of millions, tracked her mother down in Wiltshire for a comment on her extraordinary daughter. Mrs. Graham Bower pondered. Life had never been easy with Ursula, but it wouldn't do to say anything that might sound untoward. Then she had it. The important thing to understand about my daughter, Mrs. Graham Bower said, was that "she never would sit still."

Years before, when still living in London, Ursula had been nearly broken by her mother's disparagement. But that was long past. In the new world she'd created, forgiveness could lift its consoling head. Her mother hadn't meant any harm. She'd merely acted as she'd been taught.

So did it matter that her mother still didn't grasp what drove her and could only remember, for an audience of millions, that she hadn't sat still? Not really, not anymore. She easily wrote back, unbothered: "Did you, Mother darling? The things you say!!!!"

For now, in the Naga Hills where she had been granted welcome, Ursula Violet Graham Bower was, finally, at ease.

This is what fairness, decency, can lead to. The actions we need to take will differ according to the setting—be that cockpit or Olympic stadium, construction site or isolated hilltop village—but the ideals of fairness mean we don't have to start from scratch each time. These ideals really can guide us to impressive results. Any listener who develops skill at putting their ego aside gets a boost in understanding what's coming up. Any skilled "giver" has the chance to open up the gratitude that sped the Empire State Building upward, and helped Bower's V Force to success in her dangerous setting.

None of that's automatic, which is why we're in the realm of art, and detailed knowledge of our particular fields is always going to be needed. Listeners must navigate the line between being too open and being too closed, "givers" the line between too much selfishness and too little auditing.

One might wonder how much Bower's style of deep, connected giving is needed in ordinary life. She was, after all, on her own in the Naga lands, with no authority or military strength at hand to force the tribes to work with her. Back in our large cities, however, where companies and other organizations have clear lines of authority, it can seem odd to waste your time with such time-consuming, indirect approaches. Why not just insist on what you want?

This is where a closer look at our third pillar of action, the realm of defense, is needed.

A visit to a baseball stadium in the middle of the last century—where a famously cynical expert is about to create an immortal phrase—shows how to make this work.

PART THREE

DEFENDERS

CHAPTER 5

COACHES

Leo Durocher and Gil Hodges
("Defend, by not overdefending")

"What are you doing, Leo? What are you doing?"

IN JULY 1946, Leo Durocher, the combative Brooklyn Dodgers manager, is sitting with a group of newspapermen in the Dodgers' old brick-walled Ebbets Field. They're watching the opposing team, the New York Giants, jog up from their dugout to take their turn at batting practice.

Durocher likes to talk. He gestures at the Giants players. "All nice guys. They lose a ball game, they go home, they have a nice dinner." The reporter beside him—Frank Graham of the *Journal-American*—lets Durocher continue. "All nice guys. They'll finish last." Graham is good at shorthand, and knows he's on to a winner. Above his article in the next day's paper, the *Journal-American*'s headline writers boil down Durocher's words, and the famous saying "Nice Guys Finish Last" is born.

The idea is compelling. Being polite and fair and gentle is all very good, but it seems like a description of the dull manner of partner your parents might like you to marry. In a crisis or creating a business, it's natural to want a more hard-driving person working on your side.

By now we can recognize this is a false opposition. Although being gentle in all circumstances will indeed mean you get walked over, fairness doesn't need to mean being meek. On the contrary, when applied well, it can crush most bullying types—as an account of Durocher's battle with his greatest opponent, Gil Hodges, reveals.

Durocher needed to act the way he did, or at least he thought he needed to, for he was a small, wiry man, the sort easily picked on in a clubhouse. It didn't help that he came with a strange French-Canadian name, and that in his playing days he had been far from a gifted batter. Babe Ruth famously once said that Durocher couldn't hit the floor even if he was dropping a cigarette.

All he had were good reflexes—he became a quick infielder—and above all, the ability to hustle. As a player he cheated a lot, with a propensity to spike opposing players. "I'd knock over my grandmother if she was blocking second base," he liked to say.

Later, as a manager himself, Durocher intimidated umpires, threatened journalists, encouraged his pitchers to hit opponents in the head with their fast balls (a potentially fatal act in this era before helmets) and installed a hidden telescope to steal opposing teams' signs.

The year of his remark to Frank Graham, everything worked, and Durocher's Brooklyn Dodgers won the National League East by eight games. The blue-collar Brooklyn fans loved his style. They resented wealthy Manhattanites who could hide their inherited privilege behind a mask of genteel good manners, and anyone who cut through the rules had their vote.

But the next year, Durocher was fired for going too far—rigging card games against his own players hadn't helped—and ended up moving through the league, sometimes with great success, sometimes not, until finally, pulling strings, in the mid-1960s he was able to get himself a job managing the Chicago Cubs.

The new job should have been a chance to bring his career to a triumphal end. Chicago had done poorly recently, but had strong players and doggedly loyal fans. Competition in the NL included such jokes as the newly formed New York Mets team, which had lost a record 120 games when it was founded in 1962, and finished last or next to last every year after that, and in 1969, the Montreal Expos.

Durocher pushed and bossed and harangued his players, and by the 1969 season, the Cubs took an early lead in the standings that they kept for months. Clearly it seemed his approach worked. By mid-August, they were far in front. The Mets were 9 games back, a seemingly insuperable gap so late in the season.

It was Durocher's inability to avoid over-attacking, however, that brought Chicago's success to an end.

Publicity agents tried to present him as a lovable curmudgeon, but the reality was different. Earlier in his career, outraged by a fan who he felt had insulted him, Durocher got an off-duty policeman to hustle the poor man out of sight of anyone else. Being proportionate in defense was not going to be enough. After the policeman winded the fan with a lead-filled club, Durocher started punching the man in the face so hard and so repeatedly—breaking his jaw, then keeping on hitting—that the policeman ended up scrambling to pull Durocher off. "What are you doing, Leo?" he said according to his testimony later in court. "What are you doing? Let him go."

Here too the spillovers from his temperament spread far beyond his day job. Durocher found it hard to keep friends, for he kept stealing from them at cards, just as he also found it hard to keep girlfriends and wives. (One did turn the tables on him, though, neglecting to inform him when they got married that she was, in fact, currently also married to someone else.) The single indisputably good thing he did in his life—screaming in his typically charming manner at his Brooklyn players who petitioned against the Black athlete Jackie Robinson joining the team that they could go fuck themselves, as well as their petition—was marred by his complete inability to keep from needling and goading Robinson, once hired, to the degree that soon Robinson hated him as much as everyone else did.

Back in Chicago in 1969, the summer that was supposed to complete his career, Durocher pushed his players for week after week without the rest they begged for in the hot, humid Midwestern summer, so much that they turned against him. He ragged his third baseman, Ron Santo, as a cowardly Wop, weak from diabetes, until, Santo remembered later, "I grabbed Leo and had him around the neck. I could have killed him." Durocher also encouraged fans to throw batteries and metal spikes at opposing teams so frequently that they played harder than ever against him.

Finally, in a move to match Lorenzo's abusing of Eastern airline employees, Durocher berated and humiliated umpires to such an extent that "whether or not Leo ever united the Cubs against the umpires," one sportswriter wrote, "he certainly united the umpires against the Cubs." As an earlier general manager Durocher had worked under put it, Leo "possessed the fertile ability to turn a bad situation into something infinitely worse." His Cubs fell into a record-setting losing streak.

And the Mets won the pennant.*

To Durocher this was incomprehensible, the way democracies being stronger than dictatorships is incomprehensible to strongmen around the globe. The phrase "Nice guys finish last" had stuck with him ever since Frank Graham's old headline, and he'd liked it. "I don't think," he said, "it would have been picked up if it hadn't struck a chord. Because as a general proposition, it's true." Durocher had known the Mets manager, Gil Hodges, years before; Hodges had played on one of his teams. Everyone knew him as one of the most decent men in baseball. Yet here *he* was the one finishing first!

What Durocher missed was the space available between being too aggressive and being too soft. Clearly you need to defend yourself. As we saw in aviation with Haynes, being "merely" nice would put you too far at the pushover extreme. But going as far in the other direction as Durocher—being so disproportionate—is also a mistake. The Starretts' site director, the Canadian John Bowser, had understood this perfectly. It's a cliché to talk about sowing the seeds of your own destruction, but that summer in Chicago, this is what Durocher had done.

The conclusion is not that unfair or constantly furious coaches never succeed. Vince Lombardi managed to be an exceptionally effective football coach, yet with an erratic brutality toward his players that made almost all of them detest him. When the quarterback Bart Starr heard Lombardi was

---

* I was there. It was agony.

coming to take over the Green Bay team, "I could hardly wait to meet a man that went to church every day. I worked for him for two weeks, and then I realized that this man *needs* to go to church every day."

Possibly, as Lombardi's biographer suggests, this stemmed from the fact that he had used a family exemption to evade service in World War II even though he was a fit, strong man, and on the practice field he could allay that by making even stronger men cower before him. But such insecurity never ends, for the underlying wound is never dealt with. He seemed just as tense and prone to yelling at home as on the field.

Whatever the cause might be, the significant point is that Lombardi's is just one way forward.

A single episode from the summer of Hodges's great competition with Durocher shows how a fairer leader can get the balance right. It came near the end of a long doubleheader, and Hodges's star player, Cleon Jones, had started to give up.

Jones was playing in left field, and it was hot, and he was tired, and the Mets were down by nine runs already in the second game, so when yet another ball came near him he didn't sprint forward to nab it, but instead, letting everyone know how he felt, just trotted lackadaisically toward the ball. He was a star, and his team was probably going to lose anyway, so why should he bother?

Hodges knew why he should bother. The team looked up to Jones. If one of their best players started taking it easy, who would be next? It was usual in Hodges's time that, when a manager wanted to pull an outfielder from the game, he signaled to the player or had one of his coaches do that. Hodges didn't do this, nor did he yell. This wasn't out of weakness. Durocher had spent his life around grown men who wore children's woollen outfits and played a game with a ball and stick, running around bases to score a run. Hodges was a coal miner's son who'd been a Marine in the World War II battle for Okinawa and won a bronze star for heroism in combat. He was making a choice.

In the Pacific, appropriate defense was violent, and deadly. On a base-ball field, however, aiming it differently was right.

What Hodges did was call out to the umpire to pause the game, then stand up from his seat in the dugout and—the entire stadium puzzled—start walking across the infield. Only his wife, watching from home, realized what was going to happen. "Oh my God," she remembered thinking, "he's not going to . . ."

Hodges passed the pitcher's mound slowly, and then passed the shortstop's position, still slowly, and kept on walking—strolling actually, just as lackadaisically, it might seem, as Jones himself had strolled toward the line drive—until finally, quite at ease, not breathless at all, he reached his player. It had rained earlier, and the turf here in the deep outfield was soaking. Jones remembered, "I looked down and he looked down and both our feet were in water up to our ankles."

Hodges was relaxed; perhaps the two men would chat for a while, but well, everyone was waiting, that wouldn't be fair, so he turned back, on the wet turf, gesturing for Jones to walk beside him, and the two men—everyone in the stands, and also the players from both teams, and the umpires, still staring—walked together, squelching slightly with each step, all the way back to the dugout, where players who weren't in the game waited. Hodges was just as casual as before. By the time they'd reached the dugout—and under Hodges's instruction, one of the coaches had sent out a replacement player far below Jones's caliber—he had made his point. "If you're hurt, tell me," Hodges would say. Otherwise, he expected commitment. Jones had the highest batting average in the league, but Hodges was letting everyone know, as one player remembered, "that you play this game one hundred percent all the time or you're not playing."

Keeping a firm defense and sustaining order are central, but the art came in the way that everything Hodges had "injected" was fair. "Cleon [Jones] didn't resent this thing," another player recalled of the forced walk back from the outfield. He realized that what had happened was no more than he deserved. He had no need to feel resentful.

The next day, with no hard feelings, Hodges let Jones play again. Jones was transformed, as was the team. It was exactly the balance that we've repeatedly seen. Hodges had been fair to his own goal of firmly shaping a team that was going to win, yet remaining considerate enough to preserve Jones's dignity. Soon the Mets tore past Durocher's Cubs, won their division and the pennant, and were in the World Series.

There they faced the heavily favored Baltimore team. In the fifth game, Jones batting, the Baltimore pitcher threw the ball inside. Jones said it hit him, the umpire said it didn't—and Hodges immediately, absolutely, backed his player, not giving in until the umpire relented. That put Jones on base. When a home run after him gave the Mets two runs, they turned the game around and soon won the World Series—with a spectacular running catch by the now far-from-lackadaisical Jones securing the final out.

The koan that Hodges was implicitly following could be phrased as "Defend, by not over-defending." All the successful decent sorts we've seen were following it. In line with Hillel's outlining of a middle path, they couldn't be too soft, but nor could they be unnecessarily brutal, Durocher style. Even aside from the ethics, it would be counterproductive.

Danny Boyle was excellent at getting the balance right, for from the movie world, he already knew the sort of dangers that could arise. His main Indian colleague on *Slumdog Millionaire*, for example, Loveleen Tandan, had been warm and kind, and indispensable in educating him about India. But when *Slumdog*'s filming was at its peak and he needed her the most, she'd announced that she had to stop and work on another film. Boyle's project would be ruined if she left.

Boyle understood her motive. "Everyone in India does it; it's a bargaining tool to get more money." He'd acted much the same himself at other times. To progress in a competitive field, anyone needs a healthy desire for money or success. The trick was to stand up to Tandan without unnecessarily offending her. She didn't get a raise in salary, but Boyle promoted her to co-director, which she deserved, and both were happy.

It had been similar with ensuring his volunteers got their costumes for free. He'd exploded at the Olympic committees that had tried to stop that. "You've got to be willing to push people around sometimes to get things done." But he'd been like Hodges, not Durocher; these blow-ups were rare, and he apologized immediately after. That's what kept the channels open with Coe and the other experienced outsiders who could help.

We've already met Bernadette Caulfield, executive producer of that 2010s hit *Game of Thrones*. Her problem on that show's huge shoots—with Hollywood-level budgets and more crypts, castles and armies of the undead than even Mr. Boyle had to synchronize—was not just to fix conflicts herself, but to encourage the production's many warring factions that doing so with the minimum escalation possible was wise.

The specials effects teams (SFX), for example, were often in battle with the visual effects teams (VFX). SFX did traditional stunt work: blowing things up, having battered gates burst open, creating snow and rain. They knew those were tough, active actions, yet often felt looked down on. VFX, did the complex, computer-based CGI work the show also depended on. Each field attracted different sorts. As the stereotype had it, you could identify the VFX group by their wearing chinos and sipping espressos; the SFX crew after hours by their wearing jeans and drinking beer.

It was easy for the two sides to feel defensive. How should a stabbing take place? It could be with SFX putting a miniaturized blood reservoir in place to be triggered by radio signals or compressed air tubing. Or it could be done by VFX using computers in postproduction. Neither side would enjoy giving in. SFX blood was more realistic and felt natural, so SFX supervisors felt that was the approach that should be taken. But VFX effects could guarantee perfectly illuminating spurting arcs—and so, *their* supervisors felt, that was obviously how the effect should be done.

Caulfield, in her response, however, was invariably like Hodges and Boyle. New hires noticed that she was firm when needed—firing those who couldn't shape up—but because she was secure in herself, she didn't overdo that. She also had enough practical experience to be certain she wasn't going to be manipulated. "I know how heavy cable is," she explained, "I know what the crew has to go through—I'm actually married to a dolly grip."

When the two effects teams were at an impasse, she'd sit down with them together, sometimes saying she had a suggestion: Maybe the two sides yelling at each other some more would solve the problem? When they accepted, reluctantly, that no, this probably wouldn't help, she'd get into better solutions. Often a compromise was possible. SFX, for example, might rig up a real spurt for the first take, while VFX handled later takes in postproduction. That way the actors and director would have one experience with a "real" stabbing, yet could try further variations without delaying the shoot.

Even when a compromise couldn't be worked out, she showed the teams that instantly counterattacking didn't help. It just got the other side angry.

Caulfield encouraged this moderate approach across the show. This didn't make everything perfect. There was one shot, famously, where a modern take-out coffee cup was left in a scene. But that was rare. Caulfield won multiple Emmys, was lauded by everyone she worked with, and was, as the *Game of Thrones* writers put it, "the single best thing that ever happened to the show."

Much of that approach—of Caulfield, of Boyle, of Hodges—can be scaled up even more to some of the largest businesses on the planet. But when we do that, yet further skills have to be brought in.

CHAPTER 6

TECH EXECUTIVES

Satya Nadella and Steve Ballmer

("*Defend, by opening gateways*")

"*Fucking Eric Schmidt is a fucking pussy!*"

IF LEO DUROCHER had been taller and heftier, he would have been an excellent prototype for Steve Ballmer, the man who took over Microsoft after Bill Gates's retirement. Their ways of defending their organizations had much in common.

Some big men are careful not to abuse their size. The one-time NFL linebacker and consistently good-natured actor Terry Crews is a case in point; the man-mountain Dwayne Johnson is also known for his gentle manner. But early on, Ballmer—a giant of a man, six-foot-five and with the shoulders to match—discovered that intimidation worked, that screaming at subordinates, lunging forward until you're almost in their face, veins popping out on your neck, was an effective way to get them to do your bidding.

Under his mentor, Bill Gates, he learned business techniques of a similar nature. Memos from the time show senior staff at Microsoft talking about competition as a jihad; of planning not just to defeat rivals, but to "smother" and "extinguish" them. When a new-style browser from Netscape threatened Microsoft's position, executives decided to "cut off Netscape's air supply";

they would destroy it entirely by giving away its product for free. When called to court, they doctored videos to mislead opponents.

None of this would have surprised the great theorist of capitalism, Adam Smith. Merchants always tried to connive against their competitors, and even more so against the public, he observed. It was the government's job to adjust rules, and where possible, societal mores to make that manner of action harder and fair competition easier.

Because Microsoft in its early years had an effective monopoly in desktop software, profits poured in. Back in 2000, when Ballmer became CEO, the company was dominant; a tank, unstoppable. University students discussed how to answer likely interview questions if they were lucky enough to be considered for a job there.

But tech rarely stays still, and soon new competitors such as Google and once-mighty Nokia were threatening Microsoft's dominance. In theory, this could have been Ballmer's chance to understand what had succeeded in the past and work out what to do next. He wasn't a man who operated like that, however. If there were threats coming from outside, he felt, his job wasn't merely to block them. His job was to obliterate them.

At one point, for example, the software engineer Mark Lucovsky told Ballmer, as a matter of courtesy, that he was leaving to work at Google, where Eric Schmidt was then executive chairman.

Ballmer channelled his inner Durocher.

First there was the verbal expressionism. "Fucking Eric Schmidt is a fucking pussy!" he shouted. Then, according to court documents that the startled Lucovsky later submitted, there was the hunt for an appropriate weapon: in this case, a chair in Ballmer's office. Ballmer lifted it up, screaming, then heaved it. Lucovsky ducked.

Ballmer wasn't done. "I'm going to fucking bury that guy!" he added. The chair had missed Lucovsky but bounced off a table. The court documents Lucovsky filed are unclear on what additional objects were propelled his way, but he does remember Ballmer going on. "I have done it before and I will do it again! I'm going to fucking kill Google." Finally, Lucovsky escaped.

Everything that threatened from the outside had to be crushed. The Linux operating system was directly targeted, since Ballmer saw its free (or relatively free) model as a direct threat to Microsoft's cash fountains in Windows and Office. Ballmer, accordingly, tried to deter Linux's customers by warning that it was a "cancer," and as bad as "communism." When Steve Jobs announced the first iPhone in 2007, that also needed not just to be criticized, but undermined in its entirety. Ballmer discouraged the many business customers who looked to him for advice from buying one. "It doesn't have a keyboard," he explained, his tone heavy with mockery. "Which makes it not a very good email machine." The iPhone would also be foolish to buy since it was "by far the most expensive phone in the marketplace." To further harm Apple, he kept Microsoft's developers from working with the new ecosystem of apps that the smartphone was opening up—an ideal way, from Ballmer's past experience, to starve Apple of funds.

Outside developers were scorned as well, especially if they'd ever worked with the enemy. When Microsoft did have to associate with them in joint ventures, they weren't made welcome, let alone brought along to the most important Microsoft retreats.

Executives within Microsoft who threatened the Windows cash fountain by suggesting new business models were abused with special belligerence. They weren't merely wrong to suggest that the separation of chips, systems, and software that Microsoft had profited by so far could be changed. They were attacking the company, and no retaliation could be too hard.

Videos can still be found floating around online of Ballmer in a sweat-stained shirt, rampaging in front of his employees, bellowing to the point of hoarseness what he wanted, and what he didn't. As that was how he acted in public, insiders have suggested—as Lucovsky's court deposition indicates—that he was even less moderate in private, storming as his company kept falling behind.

People convinced this style is the only possibility often take heart from the sixteenth-century political writer Niccolò Machiavelli, and primarily his work *On Principalities*, translated as *The Prince*.

Being good is foolish, Machiavelli wrote, for "a man who strives for goodness is sure to come to ruin." Being truthful is also unwise. "A lie, convincingly told, is among the most powerful weapons in the ruler's arsenal." And, most memorably, why constrain yourself by being kind? "Since love and fear can hardly exist together," he wrote, "if we must choose between them, it is far safer to be feared than loved."

But although cynics through the ages have relished these principles, inked at Machiavelli's isolated farmhouse in the Tuscan hills, as you can by now imagine, they're not quite as wise as he thought.

They weren't even wise for Machiavelli himself.

The reason he was stuck in an isolated farmhouse was that he'd completely failed in his own career. He had been a senior official in the Florentine Republic, but apparently so imperious that organizing the citizens into a militia to defend the city from invaders, they faded away at the enemy's approach. He'd ended up taken prisoner by the subsequent rulers, tortured (in a cell where lice were "as big as butterflies"), and then expelled to that farm.

Life didn't get better after he finished his manuscript. Although it was the Medici family who'd tortured him, he very much wanted a job, and dedicated his new book to Giuliano de' Medici. But Giuliano died before Machiavelli was done, and when Machiavelli rededicated it to Giuliano's thuggish nephew, Lorenzo, the result was no better. In one story, when Machiavelli tried to present his master the manuscript, Lorenzo ignored him for a visitor who was offering a pair of hunting dogs. The Medici had been living these cynical approaches for generations and didn't need a failed minister to restate them.

Generations of leaders and citizens in Italy took equally cynical, duplicitous paths, with few constraints on authority or mechanisms to tell leaders when they were traveling blind. The outcome (helped along by other factors) was centuries of chaos, weakness, loss. Where nobody trusts anyone else, it's impossible to work together. The few scattered individuals who tried to act in a better fashion were crushed.

.   .   .

In fairness to Ballmer, most of what he did as CEO had once worked well for him: using his physical presence to intimidate others, playing hardball to make the young Microsoft grow. But even in the early days, it probably hadn't been necessary, and when his tenure finally ended, after over a decade of fury at enemies, his achievement was one for the history books.

Not only did *Forbes* magazine describe Ballmer as "the worst CEO of a large publicly traded American company," his furious, border-closing defenses had ensured his company missed out on smartphones, social media, key aspects of the cloud and pretty much every other major development in tech during his tenure. Although incumbents often have a hard time in quick-changing fields such as tech, this took some doing. An investor who put $100 into the company when Ballmer first took charge would have ended up, fourteen years later at the end of his bellowing tenure, with just $80 in hand.

The issue wasn't just one of being closed to fresh ideas. Ballmer was an intelligent man—he'd done well in math at Harvard, along with Gates—and he read omnivorously. In calmer moments he could be almost sheepish about raging so often, even if he might defend that as merely the outpouring of powerful feelings. But whatever chagrin he later felt, the results were the same.

On the day he announced his departure, Microsoft's stock jumped 7 percent.

Ballmer's successor, Satya Nadella, was the opposite in almost every way that counted. From the time he took over in 2014, he showed that in this domain it was also possible, Gil Hodges or Bernadette Caulfield-style, to resist attacks—to fight entropy and build up complex structures and make a company profitable indeed—without intimidating, yelling or bullying.

It's easy to say this was because Nadella was a better person. But who's born better or worse? It's illuminating to see, as much as anyone can, what made him choose the different approach, where he resolved to be as open as possible to what the outside world has to offer.

Nadella had grown up in India, the only child of a senior civil servant father who moved regularly. As a teenager, he tried for the holy grail of middle-class Indian families, the prestigious Indian Institutes of Technology, but flunked the entrance test. His father—a man, Nadella remembered, who had never met an exam he didn't ace—was bemused that a child of his could be so incompetent. On his 21st birthday, Satya Nadella was flying to America to try graduate school after those failures, his destination not the prestigious MIT or Caltech that so many Indian students got to, merely the electrical engineering department of the University of Wisconsin in Milwaukee.

In fact, Milwaukee was strong in electrical engineering then, and his training was good enough that he ended up at Microsoft. Once he got there, he slowly moved up the ladder (keeping a soft spot for students who'd made it from lesser-known universities). The company was moderately racist against Indians at the time—"we could get to a certain level but not beyond," Nadella remembered—and a number of executives looked down on him because of his Hindi accent. But his home country had been even more strongly divided by its multitudes of castes and races and religions, so he could live with this. He wasn't a standout executive, nor was he a terrible one; he was seen to have a good strategic sense, but otherwise was just one of the very many slightly awkward, slightly wary, skilled engineers the company was so good at utilizing.

Soon he married an architectural student, Anu, whom he'd known from India. Although his colleagues thought it charming that he would uncon- sciously rotate a cricket ball in one hand when he was on the phone—he'd been mad about cricket as a student in India—yet otherwise the country he'd left was far away.

But then, when Satya was 29 and Anu, 24, was pregnant with their first child, just weeks before full term, they noticed that their baby seemed to have stopped moving. There was a rush to the hospital and an emergency cesarean, and when their son Zain was born, everyone in the room realized something was seriously wrong. "He did not cry." There was another hurried journey, an ambulance with siren wailing to transport Zain—"all of three pounds"— across Lake Washington to the Seattle Children's Hospital. Gradually the diagnosis became clear. Their baby had suffered oxygen deprivation that would severely limit his physical and cognitive ability.

A single day before, Satya had been about to finish their nursery, and wondering when Anu would go back to her architectural practice. "All these plans I'd had were thrown up in the air." Zain would never be independent. "I was sad for how things turned out for me and Anu." They'd had a care-free lifestyle, and now this. He had been tumbled into van Gennep's rite of passage, but what would he be like when he emerged?

He was dutiful to his child as the diagnosis of severe cerebral palsy was confirmed, and one operation after another took place. But why had this happened to him? That was his overwhelming question. "I distinctly remember who I was [then] . . . I won't say I was narrow or selfish or anything, but there was something that was missing." Today, it's common to feel that we exist in a void; that it's up to us, bravely, to create our personalities alone. But that's not how it works.

Satya couldn't break from his self-focus on his own—he had no extra generosity to give at his company—and it was only through longer experience with his wife Anu that he began to change. They had settled in America in a striking way. Satya already had a green card when they married in India; the precious document which granted permanent residency in the US. But holders of green cards couldn't bring their wives over. In a story he often repeated, he'd flown from Seattle to Delhi, went straight to the US embassy, marching past the lines waiting to get in, and declared that he wanted to give back his green card.

The clerk he spoke to was startled—no one gave up a green card—but Satya Nadella insisted. He would apply for a temporary H1B visa instead. That would allow Anu to live with him in Seattle, at least for a while. If he couldn't later convert that to permanent status for both of them, then he'd move back to India. It was a grand gesture, yet in a sense a selfish one. He was helping Anu, but he remained the center of the drama: a romantic hero, assembling the life he wanted. (And in fact, they did both soon achieve permanent status.)

By the time his son was 2, Nadella was beginning to understand what more there was. Anu had dropped her job to care for Zain; driving him to the successive operations, sitting with him in intensive care. There were hard moments for them all. "Did I do something to cause this?" she remembered thinking.

When Zain had a fit in a grocery store, she could see people's scorn; she judged herself harshly. But then she made a point of breaking from that. "I forced myself to respond to the man offering to unload my cart rather than the cashier rolling her eyes." By feeling for the cart-helper's generosity— giving that appreciation—she could be free. The new life with Zain had a richness she hadn't expected.

These were the experiences that gradually transformed Satya too. He watched Anu and slowly, eventually, "without [her] schooling me, I got schooled. Nothing had happened to me; what happened was to my son. It was time for me to see life through his eyes." He'd hated how permanent his son's condition was, but although Zain was quadriplegic and legally blind, he also was clearly delighted by music, by human contact.

Why shouldn't that be what counted?

Finally Satya stopped blaming himself, and his fate, and the universe. "Anu deeply taught me how to forgive myself." He recognized the Buddhist roots. Understand the limits of what you can control, and "only then," he wrote, "would you be ready to develop . . . empathy and compassion for everything around you." That, if we were to summarize it, could be seen as another wise, seemingly paradoxical guide: "Defend, by opening gateways."

That was how to become more humane, and that was what the trans- formed Nadella could bring back to Microsoft. He didn't have to close off from the outside world. Instead, he could understand it, and connect to it. Gil Hodges succeeded with a baseball team by being firm yet not overly aggressive in defence. Nadella, running a huge corporation, had to go further. He defended by opening gateways—carefully accepting more of what the outside world presented—in a way that would let in benefits, not dangers.

Even as Nadella was still working in Microsoft's server division, far from senior staff with their reflex to "smother" all rivals, his colleagues saw something was changing about him. There was a confidence where his awkwardness had been. It wasn't arrogance, but rather he'd ask: What if a rival is merely someone who's on a different path? Of course you'll have to be ready to defend yourself in case they hurt you. But if you insist that's the *only* possibility, who knows what you might lose. Combined with his already good strategic sense, that was a powerful mix.

He was given more responsibility, and then more—his measured, decent approach leading him to hit one financial target after another—until finally, when Ballmer left in 2014, he was appointed head. His first task was to stop his firm's steady, stately decline from its eminence under Gates. For that, he realized, he would need to change Microsoft's notion of what an enemy was. Ballmer had grown up in Detroit, the son of a Ford executive, where it was obvious that competitors were there to harm you. If General Motors' market share went up, Ford's went down. It had been natural to encourage the same attitude at Microsoft. Nadella could understand this. Immediately after Zain's birth, a similar trade-off had seemed obvious to him too: a child was impaired, and so the parents suffered. His wife Anu, however, had shown him how limited that was. Empathy and respect could be an active tool. "The computer scientist in me loved this compact instruction set for life."

That was the attitude he was going to spread.

He wasn't a saint. As the worldly philosopher Mick Herron once noted, "With power comes responsibility, along with the opportunity to stick it to those who've annoyed you on your way up." Quite possibly he went too far in removing high-level executives he didn't trust. But that was rare, and pretty quickly he succeeded in shifting the focus toward careful openness.

Ballmer had called Linux a "cancer" and as bad as "communism," so at an early presentation, Nadella stood smiling on stage as he nodded for a large "Microsoft ♥ Linux" slide to be projected above him—what one analyst called a "hell freezing over" moment. Microsoft was going to be in partnership with the open-source movement now.

Ballmer had hated Apple, and particularly the iPhone. In an incident hallowed in company lore, he'd once grabbed an iPhone that an unwitting Microsoft junior had brought to a public event, then proceeded to "jokingly" stomp on it, smile-glaring at the humiliated employee all the while.

Nadella—again to set out his different view—made a point of holding up an iPhone at another early presentation, as he explained the work Microsoft would be doing in the Apple ecosystem too. He also set up close relations with Google (to get Office to work on their Android platform), with Facebook, and many others. "Partnering," Nadella observed, "is too often seen as a zero-sum game—whatever is gained by one participant is lost by another."

To make the new attitude catch hold, there was one more in-house change he had to undertake. Employees can't take an open stance toward the outside world if they're constantly used to the opposite at work. Ballmer had encouraged a promotion system at Microsoft called stack ranking, where members of a team were always rated against each other. If ten engineers and marketers worked on a project, two would have to be ranked as superior, seven as mediocre, and one as inadequate.

The idea makes sense, sort of, for we can often tell who the stars of a project are. But it was handled so mechanically that it created a true zero-sum world. Everyone realized that if one of their colleagues smarmed his or her way up to be labeled superior, they themselves would be cast down to the category of mediocre—or even the Dantean pits of "inadequate," from which few mortals escaped. And since projects took months or years to come to fruition, yet these rankings were instant, the company's focus shifted from how good products turned out to be when they were finally released to what you could make others, in-house, think of you right now. Stealing credit from others and pretending that all good ideas were your own became indispensable.

A famous cartoon from the Ballmer era captured the results. Dully efficient Amazon was a simple hierarchy; internally warring Microsoft had everyone pointing pistols at one another.

Stack ranking had been an excellent way to create cascades of miniature Ballmers: reflexively harsh to each other and focused almost solely on the world inside Microsoft. To Ballmer's credit, he had started to dismantle much of this when he finally recognized its effects. Nadella, however, made sure that the remaining vestiges of that system came to an end. There still were assessments, but they were more rounded.

Warily, tentatively, Microsoft employees began to peek over the internal parapets they'd created and see what might happen if they trusted each other more and accepted that a range of views might be valid. It was the attitude Bernadette Caulfield independently established among her different effects teams on *Game of Thrones*. There it had been enough to open up from one specialist team to another. Here at Microsoft, there was a whole world outside. Özlem Türeci being willing to link her BioNTtech firm with trustworthy outside groups was more of the same.

It's important not to go too far in lauding one executive. Microsoft works in a complex, constantly changing environment. Nadella had to make a number of trade-offs—on user interfaces, on privacy—that are far from ideal. There's another, more general proviso. Personal virtue only travels so far. Mark Zuckerberg, the Facebook founder, for example, was known for being generous in philanthropy, and thought it a matter of honor to be considerate to his staff. But no one would say that the firm he created—so easily used to enable political extremism—has been an unambiguous good for humankind. It's the same reason there's no admiration for tobacco executives, however kind they might be to their assistants, or however fairly they rose to the top.

But although the jury's still out, his efforts in his first years as CEO paid off. In the Ballmer era, Microsoft had disparaged the wider world and looked within. In the Nadella era, bringing in partners was going to make his company stronger, not weaker. This is what allowed the revitalized firm to pick up on the trends toward mobile and cloud computing; that's what put sales teams at ease with subscription-style services, where constant monitoring of what buyers felt was central.

Whereas Ballmer had been *Forbes*'s "worst CEO," Nadella, five years after taking over, was named the *Financial Times* Person of the Year. And while Ballmer, over 14 years, had miraculously shrunk each $100 invested into barely $80, Nadella, over just seven years, turned each $100 invested in the firm into more than $700. Opening to the outside world had let it escape entirely from the world of legacy, slowly growing firms where it had been stuck before. At the end of Ballmer's tenure, Microsoft had a similar market capitalization to IBM. In 2021, its market cap was worth that of IBM plus Oracle plus Cisco—three times over.

Hearing the various plaudits, Nadella always says, with honesty, that he helped, but it's his employees who did the work. Where the attitude that reenergized his company came from, however—that he does know. His son Zain is in his twenties, confined to a wheelchair. He can't communicate with his father in words, but, as Nadella says, "The one thing that he can communicate is, when I get close to him, he'll smile. And that makes my day, and makes my life."

Nearly halfway through the book now, and we've seen how, with skill, our fairer sorts have repeatedly been able to make difficult situations better: from operating theatres to construction sites, jungle pathways to world-spanning companies.

Their decency can succeed in all three domains—all three pillars of action—we've considered. Those are natural categories: organisms have to assess their environment and initiate actions, and defend against others' actions. The advantages of the decent approach are manifold. With ego-free listening, you're not advancing blindly—and if you're modest enough to prearrange matters to avoid fixation, you'll do even better. With the offer of generous giving, creativity and gratitude land on your side. And properly aimed defense can turn enemies into colleagues, as with Özlem Türeci at BioNTtech being far from naive and carefully auditing potential collaborators.

To see how effective this is, simply flip it around. Wouldn't you like working with someone who was willing to listen to you, helped bring out what you were best at, and protected you during it all?

Although little of that can be formalized, there are some useful guides, in particular when it comes to steering the line between Hillel's being too selfish and being too easily pushed around. It is good to offer generosity, so long as you're sensible enough to audit; it's wise to keep a powerful deterrent like a personalized Spitfire squadron in reserve as well.

A handy aide-mémoire comes in the Buddhist-style koans from each chapter:

— *Listen, without ego*
— *Listen, without fixation*
— *Give, by letting others give*
— *Give, but audit*
— *Defend, by not overdefending*
— *Defend, by opening gateways*

None by themselves can do the necessary work for you. Success in business, as in life, is never a matter of following one single rule. Instead, one needs to work through thousands of small decisions. The koans are just good checklists to hold in mind along the way.

Personal style was never the issue, for as seen, you don't have to love someone to respect them. Nadella was genteel, Starrett and his Empire State Building foreman Bowser very much were not, but that didn't matter. It's fairness and competence that leap out. These take time to perfect, and if handled naively—forgetting to audit, listening to everyone and never taking a decision—they won't succeed at all.

Türeci and Şahin managed to put all these parts together in their successful race to create a vaccine: levelheaded and assured as they engaged in listening, giving, and defending their 1,000-plus employees. The better figures in all our paired biographies did the same.

Many people want to be like that but fail. To understand more about what's needed, a look now at one man who spent years on the agonizing cusp: who wanted to stay good.

But found it very, very hard.

REFLECTION

WHO ARE WE?

CHAPTER 7

VOYAGERS

On the Loving Kindness of Captain William Bligh

("Include, including yourself")

*"Until this Afternoon, I had hopes I could have
performed the Voyage without punishment . . ."*

BRITAIN'S ROYAL NAVY in the late 1700s was not known for the restraint with which its officers addressed their men. But even in that era, William Bligh stood out, so much so that at one point the Admiralty officially reprimanded him for immoderate use of language. Given the anatomical and genealogical impossibilities of the language that was considered acceptable, this staggers the imagination.

His name has become a byword for foul behavior, and he's famous for the mutiny on the *Bounty*, deep in the South Pacific in 1789. On the way out, he'd whipped one member of his crew simply from a secondhand report that he had been insolent. Anchored in Tahiti, where he was supposed to collect breadfruit trees for Jamaica, he whipped his crew much, much more; excruciating, formal sessions with men half-stripped and tied to the ship's mast or a metal grating, there to be slashed a dozen times or more by a whip with nine knotted cords, the dreaded "cat-o'-nine-tails."

To our sensibilities, that makes him a monster, and in one sense he was even worse than is popularly imagined. British sailors in his era knew that the Royal Navy would track mutineers to the ends of the earth, so the act was never undertaken lightly. Yet the mutiny on the *Bounty* wasn't the only time Bligh was forced from his command.

In official accounts, it happened four times.

The *Bounty* mutiny took place in the South Pacific in 1789. Eight years later, Bligh's men expelled him from the 64-gun *Director* that he was commanding in the English Channel and North Sea. Seven years after *that*, officers on the HMS *Warrior* put their freedom in jeopardy by bringing him before a court-martial for behaving "in a tyrannical and oppressive . . . manner."

That's when the Admiralty ruled against Bligh and he was told to watch his tongue. The final mutiny was still to come. In 1806, the original backer of Bligh's breadfruit expedition thought it would be best for Bligh to be sent far from England. The post of governor-general in Australia's New South Wales was vacant, and surely he would be out of trouble there. But although Bligh was older and notably weaker, little in his manner seemed to have changed.

On the way out to Australia, on one of several ships traveling together, he argued with his convoy's commander so persistently and so irritatingly— about the right compass bearing and where to stop for provisions, and who deserved to be in charge—that the commander ended up ordering cannon to be shot at Bligh's ship to shut him up. Once on land, matters got worse. Within a year, the army unit under his command marched with fixed bayonets and loaded muskets to arrest him, the local citizens by one account "enthusiastically encouraging them on." He was confined offshore for two years before finally being allowed to sail home.

Despite two sea mutinies, however, one failed Admiralty court-martial, and—in a land/sea combined-op rare in history—a further mutiny by imprisonment from his own ground troops, memory has been unfair to Captain William Bligh. Most of the time on his voyages, astonishingly, he was the opposite of how this appears. He was a little shorter than average for the time, yet sturdily built, and cheerfully helped everyone along in the roughest of weather, and made a point of ensuring his sailors had dry, warm feet. He vacated his bed for men whose hammocks had become soaked by the cold seas; he deplored the backwardness of commanders who took to the lash.

While most of us have the capacity to act quite differently under different conditions, few life stories illustrate these shifts possible in our personality quite as starkly as the career of William Bligh. It shows the range of possibilities we all have within.

The story starts over a decade before his *Bounty* voyage, when he was a mere 21-year-old midshipman, serving on a Royal Navy vessel cruising in the Irish Sea just to the west of England, on the lookout for smugglers, notably ones from the Isle of Man.

He didn't fit on the ship. The young Bligh had attractive, pale skin—of an "ivory whiteness"—and was an artist with an attractive freehand line. He loved reading and mathematics, and was good at spherical trigonometry. His ideal was the sophisticated men of the Royal Society, heirs to Newton and the other great rationalists who were transforming the world. His family, however, hadn't been rich enough to get him into the Navy through the usual channels, so at 16 he had begun on the lower decks.

There he was very much among the rough men of the oceangoing fleet. He'd had to rise on his own. On shore leave on the Isle of Man, he finally met a young woman who loved books as much as he did. Her father, pleasingly, had been friends with the philosophers David Hume and Adam Smith; her grandfather principal of Glasgow University.

Before long they "came to an understanding" that they would get married, but that was going to be delayed for two years and possibly more, for something more wonderful had happened in Bligh's professional life. His drawing skills and navigation talents had been recognized by none less than Captain James Cook. Would young Midshipman Bligh be willing to serve as navigator on his next voyage?

Midshipman Bligh said yes, definitely yes, overwhelmingly yes. James Cook was the greatest explorer of the age. Even more, he represented everything that Bligh dreamed of for himself. Many sea voyages were run by captains who treated their men little better than slaves. It had been known for junior officers to beat the sailors with cudgels every morning, herding them from their hammocks like cattle. On another British ship, the captain had a rule that the last man down from a mast was automatically whipped, however quickly the descent took place.

Sailors died constantly, from falls, infection, scurvy and these beatings. The rats that swarmed through almost all ships invariably outnumbered the men, being capable of eating thousands of pounds of food in a single month. The remaining food the sailors depended on often included weevil-laden biscuit, rotten meat, rancid butter. Sewage and grotesquely filthy water pervaded the decks, the bilges and almost all open space. Pigs, goats, ducks and dogs wandered amid it all.

Cook was one of the first to change that. His ships would not be festering slave-holds. Isaac Newton, the Royal Society's most respected president, had perceived a universe of crisp, crystalline-clear laws. James Cook's ships would match that. Men from the lower orders of society were not inherently impulsive or violent, Cook believed. They could be improved with fair treatment. Cook ruled accordingly that no man on his ships should be flogged unless it was absolutely necessary.

Disease also did not have to be accepted. It was not an act of God. It was a failure of science. He had his men wash down the decks with vinegar almost every day. The latest scientific literature was studied to see what mix of fruits, malt and brine-soaked cabbage—the newfangled *Sour Krout*—would keep deadly scurvy away.

It worked. Captain Cook's first great ship, the *Endeavour*, was one of the models for *Star Trek*'s *Enterprise*, and for good reason. Not only was it a machine with technology seemingly landed from the future, the spirit of adventure was the same. Cook boldly wrote that he planned to go not only "farther than any man has been before, but as far as I think it possible for man to go."

The *Endeavour* left England in 1768 when Bligh was just 13, and when it reappeared three years later, it had covered 70,000 miles, exploring unimagined cultures, discovering new species of plants and animals, carrying ornaments and clothing and weapons never seen in Europe before. Just as notably, following Cook's new methods, only one member of the crew had died. That was unprecedented—and this was the magnificent, advanced machine young William Bligh was getting to join fresh from the Isle of Man in 1776.

Then, at 22, he served as Cook's sailing master on the *Resolution*, the successor vessel to Cook's beloved *Endeavour*. Navigation was complex, and Bligh had to use sextants, charts and the newly invented accurate marine clock; he used his spherical trigonometry and worked through calculations to correct for magnetic variation that had been developed by Newton's contemporary Edmund Halley. Cook deferred to him, and Bligh navigated the ship with accuracy. They went from England to Tahiti and Hawaii in the Pacific, then up through the Bering Straits to the ice-rich bays of what the Russians had reported as a huge frozen island they called "Alaschka." Bligh led exploration parties that ventured from the main ship in small boats. Only when finding walls of ice 12 feet high in mid-August did they turn back.

Back home in England, Bligh married his Isle of Man young lady, Elizabeth Betham, and they started a family; he continued on other voyages, becoming one of the most experienced officers in the Royal Navy, known for his navigation and precise, beautiful sketches. When, in 1787, now in his 30s, he was given command of HMS *Bounty*, it was the revered Cook's model he would follow. The mission was simple. Tahiti had breadfruit trees, which produced nutritious large fruit (starch-dense, they indeed tasted somewhat like bread). If living trees could be brought to the Caribbean, that would be another useful crop for the British Empire there.

The breadfruit trees Bligh had to collect were big, so he designed ingenious modifications for his ship, which he ensured were properly carried out before departure. At its heart was a huge nursery, with skylights and air vents, with a stove to keep the plants warm, with wooden frames set out to hold over 600 plant pots, and a clever recycling system to reuse fresh water that drained out.

The *Bounty* was a cutter, a fast vessel of a size just one down from Cook's ships. By regulations of the time, Bligh couldn't be named a captain—the commanding officer could only be a lieutenant—but he knew how important it was to keep the men on his side. Why not educate them and treat them well? When they were well out into the Atlantic, near the volcanic island of Tenerife, he unfurled the official orders and read the chief point aloud. "We are proceeding to Otaheite [Tahiti] without stopping," he announced. They might not be able to get around South America, he explained, since they'd left several weeks later in the year than he would have liked, and the southern hemisphere's winter would be upon them when they reached Cape Horn. If that were to happen, they'd need to switch east and go the other way, around Africa.

Since that would mean a longer journey, he went on, as a precaution the biscuit ration now would be reduced. But—a move he knew would sustain morale—he was now proclaiming a great innovation. It was usual to have the watches arranged so that each portion of the ship's company had four hours on and four hours off. On the *Bounty*, that would now be adjusted so that each group could have eight hours of uninterrupted sleep.

Bligh wrote in his log, "I have ever considered [extra sleep] among Seamen as Conducive to health . . . it adds much to their Content and Cheerfulness." Nor was he deluding himself about his popularity. One of the crew who later became a mutineer wrote that Bligh's words were "cheerfully received."

And so it went on for the months until they reached Tahiti. Bligh kept the decks scrubbed regularly with vinegar, so disease stayed low (which was useful, for the surgeon turned out to be a drunk, staggering aimlessly from his bed for a few hours each day as he looked for his liquor stashes, before falling back into a stupor). Porpoises swam alongside the ship in numbers so dense they became a living wall. One afternoon, a cloud of butterflies blew past, to everyone's wonderment. Bligh instituted free time for music and dancing every day the weather allowed. "What has given me much pleasure," he wrote, "is that I have not yet been obliged to punish any one."

Because Bligh was known for being so genial, men who'd sailed with him before had volunteered to be on this journey, even more than had volunteered to repeat with Cook. One of them, a tall, dark-haired younger man named Fletcher Christian, was pleased to be making his third voyage with Bligh. Before departure, he spent time with Bligh's family and played with his children. Once on the *Bounty*, Bligh promoted him so they could eat together more often. Since Christian's family was as educated as the family Bligh had married into—Christian's older brother was a fellow at Cambridge—the conversation they shared had a special satisfaction. "I saw your partiality for the young man," a chief mate from one of those previous voyages wrote to Bligh, remembering how "[you] had him to dine and sup every other day in the cabin." Soon Bligh announced to the crew that he was promoting Christian to acting lieutenant.

When the *Bounty* passed the latitude of the Falkland Islands, their late start began showing its dangers. The sweet ease of the tropics had ended; winter, and greater waves, were upon the ship. As they pushed to get around the tip of South America, rain became sleet, and sleet became snow; the sails began to crack with ice—the men who came down from the masts could scarcely move their hands, and "sometimes for a While lost their Speech."

Bligh was in his element. There was a solution for every problem! To make stable sightings in the jostling waves, he lashed himself to the mast. Since his men needed to stay warm when a catastrophic wave one midnight poured tons of ocean water through the tightly sealed hatches—as if the Cliffs of Dover had come alive and were tumbling down on them—Bligh vacated his cabin, turning it over "to the Use of those poor fellows who had Wet Berths."

Bligh was particularly concerned to make sure his sailors had dry feet. Two men were assigned to work the stove, spreading everyone's clothes to keep them dry. He upped everyone's rations so that along with hot porridge and sugar for breakfast, there would be hot soup however late the work ran. On one of the very worst days at the Cape ("the Snow fell so heavy that it was scarce possible to haul the sails from the Weight and Stiffness") he ordered one of the ship's last hogs killed for morale, and the extra nutrition they needed.

As storms slamming in from Antarctica kept getting worse, Bligh realized his men's safety was in danger. "I cannot expect my men and officers to bear it much longer," he wrote in his journal, then told his men they would stop this useless effort to get around South America. The ship was going to turn around and head east. Traveling around Africa would make the journey months longer, but "I [need] to Nurse my people with care and attention."

There were cheers, and other crew members continued jotting down how wonderful he was. "It was a fine boat," another future mutineer wrote, while the surgeon's assistant noted how the captain was taking "extreme care of the Ship's company." There was nothing miserable, hate-filled, or swearing about Bligh yet, for in this setting it had no reason to appear. Bligh's goal was to make a ship run like a fine machine. With the humane visions he had imbibed from Cook and others, that meant making its human occupants happy.

If he succeeded, his rewards would be immense. James Cook had been born the son of lowly farm laborers in Yorkshire, and ended up a Fellow of the Royal Society. Bligh's origins had been humble too. With his reputation from this voyage—transporting the crucial breadfruit saplings, showing how effective humanitarian attitudes could be—there was every reason to think he could match Cook's rise to the top.

There were two flickers of what could go wrong. Bligh's official number two, the sailing master John Fryer, was older than Bligh and resented the younger man being in command; he no doubt disliked the even younger Fletcher Christian being promoted to his level. A few months into the Atlantic leg of their voyage, Fryer—possibly to stir things up—informed Bligh that an ordinary sailor, the stockily built Matthew Quintal, 20, had been insolent.

Bligh hadn't seen the event, but by the basics of Royal Navy command structure had to accept Fryer's report. A single day before, keeping the lines of command clear had meant focusing on good rations and fiddle-led dancing. With the word from Fryer, though, keeping the lines of command clear had to mean sudden, vicious flogging. "Until this Afternoon," Bligh wrote, "I had hopes I could have performed the Voyage without punishment to any One." That had to change, and that was when Quintal's arms were tied down and he was flogged.

It seems to have been quickly forgotten (at least by all but Quintal), and for months the ship went back to its previous easy running. But then, approaching the final leg of their nearly 28,000-mile journey to Tahiti—in gentle weather east of New Zealand—probably out of pique, Fryer refused to sign off on the regular bimonthly expenses list that would later be brought to the Admiralty to show that no corners had been cut. That was insubordination of a higher sort. Commands *had* to be carried out, otherwise everything Bligh was aiming to achieve might collapse. He was furious, and called all hands on to the deck. Then, making Fryer stand beside him, he solemnly read aloud the dreaded Articles of War, government regulations applying to all on the ships, and with ferocious penalties attached.

There were clauses threatening death to those who through "cowardice, negligence or disaffection" should "utter any words of sedition"; there also was a particular clause (Article XXXI) threatening those who skipped proper procedure toward the account books with "being cashiered, and rendered incapable of further Employment in His Majesty's Naval Service." That would destroy Fryer's career, and in this era before social security, likely leave him and his family destitute. Fryer couldn't chance it. "[T]his troublesome Man," Bligh wrote, "saw his error & before the whole Ships Company signed the Books."

Once that happened, Bligh relaxed and went back to his easy interaction: having long, gossipy meals with Fletcher Christian and others, treating the deckhands as amiably as before too. "Dancing away," he wrote, "from 4 pm until eight at Night I am happy to hope I shall bring them all home well." All was back to the proper order.

The ship arrived in Tahiti in October 1788, and it was paradise. Tree-covered mountains rose from behind their bay, fresh streams lazed down to a protected lagoon, the beach was rimmed with palm trees. Dozens of canoes raced to the ship; in moments, Bligh and his men were delightfully overwhelmed ("I was so crowded with the natives . . . I could scarce find my own people") for the Polynesian men were bearing food, and the women, beautiful women, were baring their bodies, entirely happy with sharing their favors with these mysterious visitors.

By sunset, the ship was laden with hogs, fruit and textiles; the Polynesian men left, but the women remained, entwined with the sailors in hammocks or on mats. Bligh didn't indulge himself, but understood that "It could not be expected the intercourse of my people with the natives should be of a very reserved nature."

In the next few days, they fell into a new rhythm. Bligh and the ship's botanist made arrangements to collect breadfruit seedlings and grow them in protected regions on land for the half year or so necessary until they would be sturdy enough to be repotted and brought on board. Beyond that, though, after the months of intense work at sea, suddenly there was almost nothing to do.

Bligh watched children play with kites and noted how—just as in England!—they skipped along their paths. He spent hours and then weeks making notes on the plant life and culture and topography; he spent just as long speaking with the local leaders, some of whom remembered him from Cook's last journey (and the wife of the chief, a woman named Iddeeah, impressed everyone with her skill at surfing, wrestling and—once Bligh showed her its use—her accurate shooting with the firearms). He'd picked up some of the language on that last trip, and had studied Tahitian more intensively with the ship's botanist on the trip out this time.

His men, meanwhile, almost all took up with native families, where they were quickly accepted; the majority daring each other to get tattooed (a then nearly unknown habit, even for sailors), to watch or engage in the wrestling matches common in the villages, or—no need to dare here—just stroll the nearly perfect beaches.

In England, the ordinary seamen had been among the lowest of the low; malnourished from a life of poverty, and many disfigured from fights or hard labor; one had "a remarkable Scar on one of his Cheeks Which contracts the Eye Lid and runs down to his throat"; another had "his Left Arm Shorter than the other having been broke"; yet others had axe scars, or scars from scalding.

Here they were as gods.

So long as Bligh and his crew remained in stasis, the contrast with the life they'd left behind wasn't too much of a problem. But the *Bounty* couldn't remain entirely uncared for, and at one point, when everyone was aboard to move it from one anchorage to another one nearby, Bligh realized how much had changed. The lookout was clumsy, and the leadsman (who lowered weighted chains to measure depth) was clumsy, and the men in the scouting boat immediately ahead were clumsy, and soon, somehow, Bligh the master navigator heard the horrible sound of the *Bounty*'s bow scraping against a reef. They were stuck, which was embarrassing enough—several of Bligh's Tahitian friends were on board—then the weather began to change, dark clouds building quickly, and a dangerous swell. If they didn't get the ship off, it would be pushed harder into the reef until it was holed through, and then it would sink.

Bligh did manage to float the ship free, but the episode was dismaying. How could his men have let this happen? That was in late December, and soon all order began changing. On January 5, late in the night, three of the crew deserted, dragging an entire arms chest with them. They were tracked down easily enough, but the officer of the watch had slept right through it. Bligh lashed the three deserters when they were brought back. Even though he stayed well below the maximum number of strokes called for by the Articles of War, it was still a severe punishment. He was just as angry at the officer, putting him in irons for over a week.

Then Bligh found out that no one had been bringing the spare sails out for regular airing. That really was unforgivable. Every one of his officers— every one of the ordinary sailors too, for that matter—knew how crucial that was. They'd need those sails for the near year of sailing to get back home, yet they had mildewed and were beginning to rot. "Scarce any neglect of duty can equal the criminality of this," Bligh wrote.

He realized they had to get off this blasted island before matters got worse, but the weather and breadfruit preparations kept them anchored. His exasperation grew. Before they left, he'd ended up giving one sailor twelve lashes with the fearsome cat-o'-nine-tails for "insolence"; another got twelve lashes for letting natives steal under his nose. He'd even had the innocuous young cook's assistant tied down and lashed for neglecting his duty; then the ship's butcher just as viciously flogged for "suffering his cleaver to be stolen."

Where had the considerate Bligh gone? Perhaps he had never been there. What he'd cared about was his mission, plus showing that a calm, scientific approach could work. The sailors were means to that end. Treating them well made perfect operational sense for as long as the ship remained in a stable equilibrium—Bligh extending fairness and generosity, the sailors responding with good cheer and hard work. Tahiti, though, had ushered in a downward spiral: the traditional one that Cook and Bligh had wished to change, a feedback loop in which sailors were sullen, producing officers who were harsh, which made sailors more sullen, which made the officers even harsher, and on and on.

As we saw with Starrett and the construction of the Empire State Building, a strong and street-smart personality can sometimes shift a whole community's style of interaction—but Bligh wasn't equal to the task. All his tensions came out, like parents screaming at their children for not becoming the prodigies they were supposed to be. The balance that Hillel's questions would have sustained—focused on his mission, yet also considerate to others—was gone.

Eventually, Bligh's men loaded the sufficiently grown breadfruit saplings on board. When they finally weighed anchor on April 4, 1789, Bligh knew he needed to get the ship operating as well as it had before. They would be crossing half the planet to get to the Caribbean, with just one stop at Cape Town on the way. He had the men practice hard, raising and shortening sail on the masts; he switched them to strict shipboard rations, knowing the fresh stock they'd brought from Tahiti would be needed later.

This was little different from what he'd done on the Atlantic run, but the near six months in Tahiti had changed the men in ways that he hadn't expected. Many of them had merely been promiscuous at the start, reveling in this land where, as Bligh noted, where, as Bligh noted, the women "have many other ways as uncommon of gratifying their . . . inclinations. . . . The allurements of dissipation are beyond anything that can be conceived." But as time had gone on, most had settled with just one woman. They'd made friends, had village children to play with, and delectable, abundant food. Several pregnancies were under way.

Within a week at sea, Bligh had ordered another flogging of a seaman whom he charged with neglect of duty. Normally he could have expected his officers to support him without any hesitation, but something was different, notably with Fletcher Christian. Why was he not the same man as before? The reason was that Christian had spent almost every night on shore and was leaving behind a woman named Mauatua he'd been close with, now pregnant with their child. Bligh hadn't settled down with any woman, and if he'd had affairs, they had been brief, always secondary to the mission.

His frustration poured out, and he cursed his men, and perhaps mostly the loss of his friendship with Fletcher Christian. "Whatever fault was found," one of the crew remembered, "Mr. Christian was sure to bear the brunt of the captain's anger."

Christian hated it, begging Bligh to stop, but Bligh was past listening. "Such neglectful and worthless petty officers I believe never were in a ship as are in this," he wrote. Some "condign" punishment, he went on—brutal punishment, even of the officers—might be needed. Possibly Bligh was also defending himself against the lures of this island where naval hierarchy had disappeared and the visions of research that could lead to the Royal Society were meaningless.

The conflict reached breaking point when they were nineteen days out.* Coconuts were an important source of fresh water, and Bligh had stored a huge pile between the guns on the top deck. The officers were responsible for guarding them, but then, on the morning of April 23, Bligh noticed that the pile had shrunk.

Who had been stealing? One after another, the officers said they had no idea. Clearly, however, one or more of them did. They were defending each other against him! Bligh started swearing. "God damn you . . . I'll sweat you for it. You can all go to hell!" He was no longer a calm Captain Cook, understanding that men will be men and need to be judiciously guided. He was bewildered at this disobedience, and then earthbound and furious. Sensible procedures had worked perfectly on the voyage out. Why couldn't they continue that way?! Fletcher Christian tried to intervene, but that just made Bligh angrier, and finally, he stormed to his cabin.

---

* Details of the mutiny and subsequent events are taken from a mix of journals, government inquests, court transcripts and later memoirs—see the reading guide.

According to the carpenter, William Purcell, Christian was in tears. "What is the matter, Mr. Christian?" Purcell asked.

"Can you ask me, and hear the treatment I receive?" Christian answered.

Purcell tried to console him, saying that he too had suffered Bligh's tongue-lashings. But that missed a difference between the two men. As a carpenter, Purcell was protected by an Admiralty warrant that kept him from being flogged. Christian was only an acting lieutenant, and his actual rank of master's mate meant that he *could* be flogged.

That would be a humiliation Christian couldn't bear to imagine. His brother was a Cambridge don! "If I should speak to [Bligh] as you do," Christian told Purcell, "he would probably break me, turn me before the mast, and perhaps flog me . . . [It] would be the death of us both."

The tension seems to have built up—details are sparse—but five days later came the mutiny, led by Fletcher Christian: Bligh was grabbed from his bunk at 5.30 in the morning and dragged on to the deck, his hands tied behind his back; he was sent off in the ship's small launch, with eighteen crew members the mutineers didn't trust. Bligh was defiant, but also disoriented: "I demanded of Christian the cause of such a violent act." When one of the men in the launch tried to take a flintlock with him, it must have been with great gratification that Matthew Quintal, the young sailor Bligh had flogged in the Atlantic, grabbed it back.

The final moments were wild. The mutineers had been drinking rum, muskets were being waved around, and they were yelling down "Blow the bugger's brains out!" Bligh had been yelling back, and was livid. "For God's sake drop it," he called out to Christian. "You have danced my children on your knee." But it was no use. "You know, Mr. Cole," Christian calmly said, addressing the boatswain who was going on the launch, "that Captain Bligh has treated me like a dog all the voyage. I have been in hell."

Bligh still tried to fight back, but to him—the man who had begun this reign of flogging and abuse—Christian couldn't give in. He must have felt some guilt, for he gave Bligh a compass and containers of fresh water— without which he definitely would have perished—but beyond that, he couldn't go. When Bligh demanded that the uprising end, Christian held the bayonet to his old friend's chest. "If you attempt to make the least resistance, you will be put to death."

There was no choice. The mutineers were going back to Tahiti, and in their mood were liable to turn the *Bounty*'s cannon on the launch. Bligh had his men row away, and they watched the *Bounty* recede, topgallant sails rising to catch the breeze.

And then the equilibrium shifted once more.

Bligh's goal—his own desires—had never changed. It was to show that calm rationality could work, bringing a shipload of men around the world on an important mission. In the circumstances of the journey out, this had led to kindly behavior, never more so than when his men were under stress in the horrendous weather at the tip of South America. The structure of command was in order, and Bligh did all he could—encouraging words, extra food, warm feet—to work with that structure to help the men be efficient.

In the changed circumstances in Tahiti, and then back on the *Bounty* afterward, the structure of command had weakened. The exact same desire came out in floggings and tongue-lashing; Bligh trying to force the sailors and officers back into line so this sensible rationality could work once more.

Now, floating adrift in the launch, the structure of command automatically reappeared—and it wasn't down to anything Bligh did, but the new circumstances. Everyone in the boat knew that only Bligh had the capacity to navigate their way to safety, and with that, his personality instantly flipped back. In this setting, there was nothing to block his desire to show benevolent rationality could work. "As soon as I had time to reflect . . . I found my mind most wonderfully supported, and began to conceive hopes." Home was 12,000 miles away. Get there, explain what happened to the Admiralty, and he could start again.

The Japanese artist Hokusai understood this dynamic in the human heart. His famous woodprint *The Great Wave off Kanagawa* stands out for the threatening wave—one carrying a power like "muscle sinews," as he put it— which is about to crash down from the left. But there are also human beings in a boat, approaching from the right. In between is the stability of Mount

Fuji. Only the artist can see that full perspective: the staggered humans in the boat cannot.

It's a constant of world art. Life pours down on us, but how do we respond? Often we have a choice as to which part of our past, of our selves, we bring to bear. Some of us have a greater inclination to fairness than others, but even so, some situations bring this out more than others.

Bligh's first task in the launch was to get food, and he knew of a small island not too far from Tahiti. This started out well, for although it had steep cliffs, within days of leaving the *Bounty*, they were anchored in a rough cove. But in exploring for food, they saw a vine dangling from one of the cliffs, so convenient for climbing that they realized it must be man-made.

Soon natives started approaching Bligh's men, friendly at first, but when they realized there was no supporting ship at sea with deadly cannon, their mood changed. One group of natives stood in position to pull the launch's line back onto the beach, even as the men Bligh had left in the boat were working to keep it in the shallow, frothing water. Other natives collected big stones—"from two to eight pounds weight."

Bligh was in his element again. How to protect his men? He sent word for those in the boat to get ready and stay as close to shore as was practical despite the surf. Meanwhile, he kept the native leaders distracted, calmly writing in his journal at the mouth of a cave further inland. The native who seemed least hostile was named Nagatee, and a bit before dusk ("if we must fight our way through . . . we could do [so] more advantageously at night"), Bligh gripping his cutlass hard, "I took Nagatee by the hand, and we walked down the beach, everyone in a silent kind of horror."

There were even more warriors there now, ominously clacking the stones they were holding. Bligh and the carpenter were the only Englishmen still on shore. Suddenly Nagatee broke free, and with that, events exploded. Polynesians waiting higher up the beach hurried forward to attack, while Bligh and the carpenter started running through the surf toward the launch. The men were at their oars, but other natives were tugging on the stern rope now, holding the launch tight. This was when the quartermaster, John Norton, leaped off the boat to try to free it. He was knocked down, even as Bligh and the carpenter were being pulled onboard. When they looked back, he was surrounded by men with the hefty stones.

Norton was one of the men who had sailed with Bligh before. He had chosen to be with him again, and Bligh loved him for "his worthy character." He was probably still alive, fallen in the surf, but there was nothing to do. That's when Bligh made his decision. The locals still "[had] hold of the stern rope, and were near hauling us on shore, and would certainly have done it if I had not had a knife in my pocket, with which I cut the rope."

And so their journey began. The nearest European settlement was Dutch Timor, over 3,000 miles distant. ". . . We bore away across a sea, where the navigation is but little known, in a small boat, twenty-three feet long from stem to stern, deep laden with eighteen men; without a chart, and nothing but my own recollection and general knowledge of the situation of places, assisted by a book of latitudes and longitudes, to guide us."

Nothing could have been better. Bligh encouraged the men to tell stories about their past, as he did about his; at night, he led boat-wide singing. Bailing was exhausting, so along with joining in as much as anyone, he also worked out an ingenious way of stretching taut cloths above the launch's edge, raising the sides by several inches to help keep at bay the Pacific waves constantly foaming in. He taught the junior men how to count seconds evenly to help measure speed; whenever the rains let up, he plotted their progress on the few blank pages they had and showed everyone where they were.

Food was limited, and crucial to share fairly. He ensured their main supplies were safely locked in the carpenter's chest, and created scales from coconut shells to weigh it out. Not only did this guarantee fairness, it also drew out the procedure so that the meals seemed longer. When a large bird was caught, he cut its stomach open and had the men share the delectable, barely digested cuttlefish and small flying fish inside.

Bligh even ingeniously helped the men sew a raggedy Union Jack flag out of scraps of signal flags found at the bottom of the launch. It was a reminder of home, and a way of pumping up their confidence. They would need it, he said, to properly identify themselves when they reached port.

It worked well. After weeks of storms and these constantly low rations, the men heard a strange roaring sound, which Bligh realized meant they were almost upon the Great Barrier Reef, and needed to find an opening. The crew was unified enough to act in automatic harmony, steering and rowing the launch parallel to the reef as fast as they dared, until suddenly they saw what looked like an opening and turned hard to cut through it. Soon they were in calmer water, and then there was an island again: free from natives, it seemed, and so they put ashore.

And there, safe, discipline quickly broke down—and the helpful, encouraging William Bligh became a furious man again.

It's not that he wasn't provoked. It was crucial to be careful with any fires, in case dangerous locals located their camp. Almost immediately, one sailor started a fire, on his own, which blew out of control, starting such a huge grass fire that "on a sudden the island appeared all in a blaze," making them visible for miles. It wasn't possible to escape right away, for the tide was surging in, so Bligh—recognizing they needed fresh food—sent a party out to hunt for turtles. When they came back empty-handed, he noted—and you can almost hear his sigh—that "This did not surprise me, as it was not to be expected that any turtle would come near us after the noise which was made at the beginning of the evening in extinguishing the fire."

There was more, lots more, at that island and other brief stops nearby. At one point, after Bligh had insisted they share all the food they found, one man went hunting for himself, and Bligh beat him when he found out. Then the carpenter came back from a lengthier foraging expedition and insisted that what he had found was also going to be for him alone. Bligh remonstrated. The carpenter counter-remonstrated.

More words were exchanged, and that was when Bligh grabbed his sharp weapon. "[Since] it was not possible for me to judge where this might have an end, if not stopped in time; I therefore determined to strike a final blow, and either to preserve my command, or die in the attempt: seizing a cutlass, I ordered him to take hold of another and defend himself." That's Bligh's version; in sailing master Fryer's telling, he was almost crazed, and when the men tried to call him off, threatened Fryer with death if he intervened.

Luckily the carpenter gave in before anyone was killed—and then, once back in the launch, everything flipped back again. No one had the possibility of starting unapproved fires, no one was going to secretly search for their own food—and everyone depended on Bligh to get them back. Although there were a few complaints at how low their food supplies were, no problems more serious than that arose, even in the critical accounts by Fryer and others. The entire launch went back to singing and storytelling, with Bligh encouraging his men and tenderly taking care of those who fell ill.

Until, that is, they finally arrived in the safely populated island of Timor, with its large European settlement. There, after a few days recovering, Bligh arranged with British government emissaries to have enough funds advanced to start back home. Once on the way, he and his men began arguing again, so much that Bligh ended up having Fryer and the carpenter arrested at bayonet point, and held in irons for almost a month.

So who was Bligh? All of us change. Some of the triggers are general, as with the internet's anonymity bringing out the worst in otherwise law-abiding people. For Bligh, as we've seen, the triggers were any breakdown in order, as well as being ignored. At other times, even when his men were under duress, so long as a clear command structure was in place and it was obvious what everyone had to do—when there was sleet freezing the sails off South America or seas near-swamping their launch in the Pacific—he was the kindest of helpful captains. When that broke down, as in the incident with the mildewed sails in Tahiti, so did he. The traits that made him compassionate in one setting, in a different setting led to the *Bounty* mutiny. With his wife and friends at home he was always stable, but here it was easy to switch.

Once Bligh got back to England, his different parts flashed out again. He'd failed in his mission of getting the breadfruit trees to Jamaica, and he convinced the Admiralty to fund a second mission. This time he didn't only make space for a hyper-modern nursery. He brought together two ships, and took eighteen armed marines with him. It was a private bodyguard under his direct control. The marines would have no social relations with the sailors, and ensure there was no mutiny.

He led this small flotilla back to Tahiti, and since the presence of the marines meant he felt safe, everyone noted he was as reasonable and helpful as he'd been at his best before. On the island, he kept his men busy with sailing maneuvers while the cuttings slowly grew to reduce the chances of distraction. After the requisite months of waiting, he loaded his cargo ship with the seedlings and small trees he'd sworn to get, and then, barely three years late—having traveled nearly two circumferences of the planet—finally delivered, as he might have humbly put it, the goddamn breadfruit to Jamaica.

The British authorities on the island were speechless, and awarded him a vast cash payment, making Bligh rich. He arrived back in England on August 7, 1793, and wrote in his log, content, "This voyage has terminated with success."

And the other mutinies later in his career? They too show that Bligh couldn't be called simply good or bad. The one that took place on the *Director* a few years later in 1797 came when dozens of ships from the North Sea and Channel fleet mutinied, to a great extent over pay that hadn't gone up since the previous century. Most of the sailors were so polite in asking officers to leave their ships that even Nelson remarked, "for a mutiny . . . it has been the most manly that I ever heard of, and does the British sailor infinite honour." Bligh may have been brutal in settings when he felt his mission was being threatened, but here he was just one of the many officers asked to leave; he wasn't singled out.

The arrest in Australia in 1808, where he'd been sent as governor-general of New South Wales, was even less Bligh's fault. British Army forces there had become corrupt: smuggling rum and forcing women into prostitution. Bligh's efforts to stop it were what led to the troops turning on him. Only the vituperative language that the Admiralty noted Bligh using to insult a near-crippled Second Lieutenant Frazier on the *Warrior* in 1804 can be held against him. There he really does seem to have been a dick.

Some people shift action easily. They're the ones, as the English philosopher Mary Midgley put it, who "spend a lot of time and ingenuity on organizing the inner crowd." It's as if within their own minds they "have to hold a meeting every time [they] want to do something." Others, by contrast, have inner standards so strong that only extreme differences can make them shift.

The balance can only be estimated. John Kenneth Galbraith, head of price control in America during World War II, concerned with gasoline rationing and much else, used to say that perhaps 10 percent of the population would always be considerate, about 5 percent would always be selfish, and the rest—the 85 percent great majority—could go either way, depending on what they saw others doing.

Even so, there might be circumstances extreme enough to break the virtuous 10 percent or redeem the 5 percent—and as for the 85 percent, what is the lesson of William Bligh? A superb sailor and navigator—and often a superb captain—as a commander he has to be reckoned, ultimately, a failure. We need to be judged by the difficult moments in our life, for generally, they're the ones with the greatest consequences. Had he controlled himself in those first weeks on the *Bounty* after leaving Tahiti, the mutiny might never have happened.

This is why it's wise to be aware of the varying potentials within our selves. That means being on guard against circumstances that will bring out our worst aspects —while seeking out, where possible, environments that will shift us toward our better selves.

These shifts can be substantial. Back in the 1940s, Strom Thurmond from South Carolina ran for president on a platform that supported lynching. Yet a few decades later, he was senator for South Carolina, sustained in office by a great number of Black votes. Those voters weren't deceived, for they liked the man they now saw.

How did this happen? One reporter, dumbfounded, asked the then-elderly senator. Thurmond smiled. "Ah changed," he said.

The issue is one we all face, and was caught with especial clarity by Dietrich Bonhoeffer, Lutheran pastor and hero of the German resistance, writing from prison in the spring of 1945, shortly before his execution.

Who am I? They often tell me
I stepped from my cell's confinement
Calmly, cheerfully, firmly,

Who am I? They tell me
I bore the days of misfortune
Equably, smilingly, proudly,
like one accustomed to win.

Am I though really that which other men tell of?
Or am I only what I myself know of myself?
Struggling for breath, as though hands were compressing
    my throat,

Thirsting for words of kindness,
Tossing in expectations of great events,

Who am I? This or the Other?
Am I one person today and tomorrow another?
Am I both at once?

Who am I?

They mock me, these lonely questions of mine . . .

II

THE TEST

BLIGH HAS BROUGHT us to the pivot on which this book turns. We've asked whether it's possible to succeed without being a terrible person, and the answer was "Yes, though it's difficult." That's because the fairness one needs to apply is an art, not a science; always dependent on experience and hard-to-acquire judgment. The case studies gave a head start for acquiring experience in one pillar of human activity after another. The abstract koans summarized some of their general principles, providing guides for how to turn tentative judgments into action.

It's impossible to lay out any more detailed instructions than that, however, for even with experience and judgment, one needs to be stable enough to see plans through. Bligh couldn't quite manage that, while individuals like the pilot Bill Haynes or the guerrilla fighter Ursula Graham Bower could. That's why it was to them rather than the Leo Durochers or Frank Lorenzos of our stories that the advantages available from being decent toward others accrued: the clear listening, creative networks, gratitude and wide buy-in we've seen.

None of that means their victories are guaranteed. The more selfish or conniving sorts we've seen received their own type of advantages, from bullying, cheating and the rest. Each approach has its strengths, each faces obstacles.

Each lies in wait for the other.

Now, though, the biggest question. How far can our exemplary stories go? What Türeci and Şahin created in their vaccine development was impressive, but far from being the real world. Large construction sites, and even the world's largest tech companies, only cover restricted domains too.

It's time to test our insights about fairness's role in the largest, most extreme situation that can be imagined. For this we'll turn to the era when democracy was last under as strong attack as today, and focus on two opposed individuals from that time: Joseph Goebbels and Franklin D. Roosevelt.

For almost a decade, Goebbels seemed likely to prevail. The forces on his side—the worst of human nature—really do have great energy. By seeing him using the reverse of all our positive principles, we'll better understand their underlying nature. Yet we'll also see how Goebbels's distortions produced a degree of blindness and resentment that gave Roosevelt and others the chance to defeat him.

The struggles occured on a global scale, involving immense, unfettered powers. There were book burnings that appalled a continent, invasions and the destruction of entire cities.

Yet through that all, the individual decisions both Goebbels and Roosevelt made before their periods of great power—in the quiet years when they were working out who they *wanted* to be—turned out to be crucial. This is how their distinctive approaches to peace, and then to war, were formed.

PART FOUR

PROPAGANDA MASTER

CHAPTER 8

YOUNG MEN IN TRANSITION

Joey and Elsie
("Reverse the principles, and fail")

NUREMBERG, GERMANY

September 12, 1936

[Italicized text below is from an unknown German journalist, writing in the Official Report of the Reich Congress Rally]

. . . It is just before 7.30 P.M., and the shadows are getting long. Nuremberg's towers are glowing red in the dusk. It's hard to make out the 90,000 men and children in the stadium.

Suddenly:

A floodlight has now shot heavenward! Its beam reveals more than 200 enormous swastika flags! Instantly we realize the colossal size of the field. More lights illuminate the flawless white marble platform. It is an unforgettable sight. It is beautiful!

Orders are blaring from loudspeakers, hurried automobiles
dash, then the voice of Dr Ley comes over the loudspeaker: "Attention!
The Führer is here!" More blue spotlights surge upward, hundreds
of metres, forming overhead the most powerful cathedral that mortals
have ever seen.

There, at the entrance, we see the Führer! He stands for sev-
eral moments looking upward, then walks past the columns of
fighters at his side. An ocean of Heil-shouts and jubilation sur-
rounds him.

Reich Labor leader, Dr Ley, takes the microphone:

"My Führer! My Führer, you believed in us at a time when
all were in despair. [Thunderous applause.] No one besides you,
my Führer, can take the credit for having saved Germany!" [More
thunderous applause.]

Everyone was joined in overwhelming joy.

The Führer now spoke!

"My party comrades! [A storm of applause.] We have fought
for the souls of millions of our citizens. And we were successful!"
[Enthusiastic jubilation.]

Our Führer continued!

"I make this prophecy to you: Jews will learn that Germany
is no place for them! [Thunderous shouts of Heil.] This Reich:
this Reich will grow in the coming centuries! Heil Germany!" [An
enormous wave of jubilation fills the dark field.]

AT NIGHT, IN the darkness, in the vast crowd these words were impossible to resist. What they had been taught to think of as the *Lügenpresse*—the "lying press"—has for the past three years been scorned and safely neutered. Only the leader told the truth. There was no habit left, accordingly, of looking anywhere other than at their leader on his spotlit plinth, no habit of bringing in distracting judgment or memory or standards from their life before to weigh what he said.

These views had been spreading widely. Across the planet, in the 1930s, globalization had stopped working. Traditional jobs were disappearing, and conventional politicians had failed. Citizens looked for help.

But what would it be?

By the time of Hitler's 1936 rally, two main solutions were on offer. One was Franklin D. Roosevelt's approach in America, attempting to bring a country together by including as many citizens as possible; aiming, at least in theory, to help foreigners too. The second approach was the one taken in Germany, where division was the aim; where the then-new media of radio and newsreels were used to help select subgroups for attack, with minorities and foreigners to be vilified, and independent news sources scorned. Understanding how it almost succeeded—for by late 1941, Germany had one of the largest empires Europe had seen—is an ideal way to get even greater understanding of how each approach works.

Many people were involved with Germany's success, but the career of Joseph Goebbels is especially illuminating. As head of the Reich Propaganda Ministry, his name is, justifiably, a watchword for evil. To a great extent, Goebbels simply reversed the principles we've seen so far, configuring them to bring out our worst side.

It might have seemed improbable that he would end up in such an important role. The Nazi movement was proud of strong bodies, and it gloried in violence. Yet Goebbels was a slight man, just about 5 foot 4 inches, with a twisted clubfoot that meant he could only walk with a severe, hobbling limp. The Nazis were also, of course, anti-Semitic, and not only had Goebbels, in his mid-twenties, applied, with great politeness, for a job at a Berlin newspaper owned by the Mosse family, known for its Jewish philanthropy, he'd also had a Jewish girlfriend for well over a year ("Many a sweet lovers' tryst with Else I love her more than I thought").

That background was crucial in what he did next. At a critical moment, he was tempted by the generous side of his nature, but he hesitated, he wavered . . . and ended up crushing it all. That was painful for the young woman who'd trusted him. But combined with his years of being mocked for his disability, this gave him an unfortunately profound insight into the basest of human motivations. It also enhanced an inner coldness, a calculation, that let him use those insights for the worst of ends.

Today, the medical problem Goebbels suffered from is understood as coming from a shortened Achilles tendon, and is relatively easy to fix. In the small industrial town of Rheydt in western Germany where he was born, however, his parents—his father a factory clerk, his mother an uneducated farm girl—could only think of exercise to make it better. That was the worst possible thing they could have done. "I remember a long family walk to Geistenbeck one Sunday," Goebbels wrote in a private memoir later. "The next day on the sofa my old foot complaint returned . . . Excruciating pain."

The hospital diagnosed him as "lame for life." Since he couldn't run, when he was mocked, he couldn't get away, and he certainly couldn't punch back. He had two older brothers, but it's unclear if they helped him much.

In the few memoirs of disabled children that survive from that era, it's a world of cruel nicknames and slurs, of jeering mobs bonded by their exclusion of the weak; incessant, and impossible to forget. "My youth from then on was pretty blighted," Goebbels wrote. "I wasn't popular with my comrades."

In a later autobiographical novel, he described a character just like himself, even down to the damaged right leg, to whom he gave the pseudonym Michael. This Michael, he wrote, was "a strange boy. You did not need to know him to see it when he opened his big, gray eyes wide." Other children "were not fond of him. He was harsh and rude to them. If anyone asked him to do them a favor, he just turned away with a laugh."

Yet in fact, Goebbels wrote, "Michael" hated the isolation; it made him "hard and bitter . . . [and] he was in despair most of the time." As a result, Michael developed a "tyrannical tendency." In the novel, Michael was not going to stay unknown, in a small Rhineland town. "His ambition was to become a great man one day."

By the time Goebbels entered high school, he had developed a quick wit, so that it was dangerous to get on the wrong side of his mocking. He also had become an impressive student, at least by the standards of provincial Rheydt. When he graduated in 1917, most of his contemporaries were drafted straight into the army. He chose to go on to college, and his parents didn't object.

Life there, however, was not what he had hoped. German society was highly stratified, and everyone looked down on the lower middle classes, a category in which a boy from Rheydt, whose father was a mere factory clerk, was most emphatically placed. Being Catholic could break through some of the distinctions, and Goebbels joined the Catholic fraternity at the University of Bonn. But it wasn't prestigious, and in private notes, he revealed how this troubled him: "I'm a poor devil. Money troubles. Social differences. Big calamity."

He tried working as a tutor to get extra cash and buy himself the better clothes that would help, but others seem to have made fun of his limp. Finally he managed to make friends with a fellow student, Karl Heinz Kölisch, who had two sisters, Agnes and Liesel. Throughout his life, Goebbels was desperate to impress girls. His physical presence wouldn't be enough to interest the sisters, he knew only too well. He was "pale and thin," he lamented, and his handicap, he once wrote, was simply "disgusting." His foot would often painfully swell up, even if he was sitting perfectly still. The metal splints he used to try to keep his leg steady inside his boots never worked well.

When physical prowess can't be counted on, one needs to become skilled in other domains. He charmed Kölisch's parents, and listened to Kölisch's sisters, interjecting the compliments and jokes he knew they'd delight in; so skillfully that despite his appearance and lack of sturdy physique, his greatest dream came true.

"Agnes in Bonn," the teenage Goebbels remembered. "A night with her. For the first time she is really good to me." If a certain amount of skill at understanding how to manipulate a woman had brought him this far, why stop there? He seems to have persuaded Agnes that they needed to stay quiet about what had happened—"lied afterward," he explained—and that allowed him, surreptitiously, to move on to the other sister. "Liesel in Bonn . . . A night with her in [a friend's] room. She [performs] a good deed that gives me a kind of satisfaction." Just to be sure though, he registered afterward for a lecture on "Venereal diseases, their causes and prevention."

Over the next few years Goebbels read widely—Cervantes, Ibsen and Tolstoy for fiction, probably contemporary social critics like Weber and Simmel—and his writings suggest he tried to be mysterious and superior. When he decided to do a PhD in literature in 1919, he resolved it was to be at Heidelberg, one of the most respected of old universities in Europe.

The distinguished poet and literary historian Frederich Gundolf was on the faculty, and the young Goebbels flattered him into agreeing to supervise his thesis. Gundolf was a genius, he wrote, a master. Goebbels raced through the work, and by 1921, at 24 years old, he had the thesis done. Gundolf had been "extraordinarily kind." With this recognition, clearly his career was assured.

But was it? Despite Gundolf's help, the outside judges had given Goebbels's work—on an obscure nineteenth-century dramatist—only a minimal passing grade. He'd written so fast that he'd skipped much of the requisite research, let alone any thoughtful analysis.

The low grade ruled out an academic job, but Goebbels's growing resentment saw that differently. Academics were "narrow-minded pedants," he now decided, and anyway, he had greater aspirations. Geniuses like Goethe and Dostoevsky had created their own fame. He could do the same. "My ideal: to be able to write and live off it."

He'd worked on a few dramas and other manuscripts before, but now added to them, pouring out novellas, poems and other works. To our ears, they seem a bit overwrought:

> Many a night I sit upon my bed
> And listen.
> Then I count

How many hours may remain

'Twixt death and me

Unfortunately for Goebbels, the editors at Germany's main publishing houses and newspapers found them excessive too. Other writers were thriving in Berlin, but his work kept being turned down.

He ended up, in his mid-twenties, living back at home in Rheydt, not at all the "great man" he'd hoped, crammed in with his parents and big brothers and little sister, just as he had been in his stultifying high-school days years before. Everyone he'd known at university had automatic entry to middle-class jobs, middle-class networks. Goebbels felt he was "the outlaw, the revolutionary," but to everyone at home, he was "the only one who can't do anything, whose advice is never wanted, whose opinion isn't worth listening to. It's driving me crazy!"

What made it worse was that Goebbels believed none of this was his fault. The problem was with the economy, or perhaps it was with capitalism as a whole—he hadn't had time to work it through yet—but there was one thing he did know. Throughout history, it had been "people with the most brilliant intellectual gifts [who] sink into poverty and go to ruin." He loved Hermann Hesse's first novel *Peter Camenzind*, where the young hero yearns for escape, but at the start has no idea what form it would take. "All I felt was that life was bound to spill some wonderful piece of luck at my feet, fame of some kind, [a] lover perhaps . . ."

And then, probably through mutual friends, he met her, Else Janke. She was in her twenties like him, which was nice, and Jewish, which was curious, and a schoolteacher, which was excellent; bringing him nearer a social class above his parents, as well as his brothers and their friends.

They were hesitant at the beginning—she addressed him as Dear Herr Doctor in their first notes—but soon they became Joey and Elsie. She didn't mind about his limp, and was polite enough to sit for hours gossiping with Mrs. Goebbels. But she also was full of ideas, and when they'd go out to meet her friends—who he liked—Rheydt, suddenly, was no longer the dull backwater it had been before. He could confide in her about his writing dreams in a way he could with no one else. ". . . Walked with E. after the theatre through the clear, cold night. A mist was rising from the darkened meadows . . . Blessed wandering . . . Mute, silent, close to the world spirit."

It was one of those evenings lovers live for, where everything is shared, everything is possible. Better yet, Janke had a good practical sense. How was Joey going to get the plays he had been working on produced if he didn't finish them and then send them out? "Perhaps you are too gentle for these times," she teasingly reprimanded. Together, they would type up his best new manuscripts and make sure they went to suitable theatres in Düsseldorf, Cologne, and beyond.

She got him a new diary to help, and in his very first entry—October 17, 1923—he wrote: "I want to start this right away with her name. What else could I begin today without her?" He resolved to stop sleeping in so late—"Get up at 8!" he wrote—and he would *definitely* exercise more, and above all, he'd finish those plays that would make his fortune.

Something else was going on. The priest at the church in Rheydt had lectured against Jews, and at the university, it had been common to make fun of Jews, but . . . was that really necessary? Goebbels's original thesis adviser, Frederich Gundolf, had been Jewish, yet the kindest of mentors. Heine, the great nineteenth-century writer he admired, had been born Jewish too. The time with Janke had been changing his views. When Goebbels read one too many jeering critiques of Heine, he now wrote to a friend, "You know, I don't particularly like this exaggerated anti-Semitism." It was "demeaning and beneath human dignity."

Goebbels too had been going through the rites of passage described by the anthropologist van Gennep. He'd lived through the first, separation stage, when he left his childhood home to attend the universities in Bonn and Heidelberg. But coming home after graduating had been so great a backward step—to the same place he'd been before—that he was stuck in the worst type of timeless, unconnected stage two.

Janke was offering him a distinctive way out; a world where he might end up as a playwright or cultural commentator, married to this bright local girl his parents liked, a big figure in his small town possibly known for his sharp-tongued satire, but otherwise at ease. None of that happened, however, for when they typed up his plays for submission, and then when he applied again to the distinguished Berlin newspaper owned by the Mosse family, all that came back were rejections.

Janke tried to buck him up to keep him from slipping into depression or anger. Goebbels played the piano well, using a small wedge of wood in front of the sustaining pedal for his damaged leg, or shifting over to use his left foot. She saved up and bought him a collection of his favorite Schumann pieces, but that didn't help.

No one likes being seen in their moment of weakness, yet Janke had seen all his hopes, and now all his failures. He fell back into the familiar embrace of the resentment he knew so well. For wasn't it suspicious how many successful playwrights were Jewish? What if these rejections and failures weren't his fault, but just a mark of *their* closure against him?

He kept his new feelings private at first. After one play they went to, he jotted a note to himself: "All in all, sneering Jewish claptrap. . ."

In fact, the playwright wasn't Jewish, but Janke didn't know this, so couldn't correct him. His resentments got stronger. In his diary, October 27, 1923: "I believe that she loves me very much . . . [but] she is of the wrong race." How could a Jew understand the subtleties of his writing? The idea in his diary is that if she hadn't forced him to send out his manuscripts so early, undoubtedly they would have done better.

He must have blurted something out soon after, for her indignant reply survives. "All that talk about the race question is still ringing in my ears! I believe that in this regard your thinking is absolutely exaggerated." There was one more step she could take. In this era before the contraceptive pill, sex was a greater commitment than now, and for a while, it worked. From

Goebbels's diary on New Year's Eve: "I love Else, and feel myself more deeply connected to her since she gave herself to me . . . "

But even with that, the path she was offering broke down, for good this time. His father regularly complained that he was still living at home and not working like the other sons. "If I could marry you, Else," he jotted to himself, "it would solve a lot of problems . . . Sometimes [I'm] ashamed of myself. I take as much as I can." But money was only part of the problem. She remained, as he noted, "of the wrong race," and there was a new political organization he'd seen discussed in the news, whose leader Hitler was awaiting trial for daring to try to overthrow everything that was holding great souls down.

This leader understood what it was like to feel constrained and tied down; how important it was to break free.

The draw wasn't new. In 1864, Dostoevsky had written, "I would not be the least bit surprised if suddenly, out of the blue, amid the universal future reasonableness, some gentleman of jeering physiognomy should emerge and say to us all, 'Well, gentlemen, why don't we reduce all this reasonableness to dust with one good kick . . . and [live] once more according to our own will!' He'd be sure to find followers: that's how man is arranged."

That's how Goebbels wanted to live. He too had had enough of constraints, and now—seemingly late in 1923, scarce months after meeting Janke—he cautiously went to a meeting at a Nazi branch office not far away. This was bold, for he really was slight, and if the rough men there turned against him, he would be pummeled. But few intellectuals had joined the tiny Nazi party so far, and the men at the local office didn't laugh at him for his small size, but instead saw how his sharp tongue could help them. He was welcomed, invited back; soon granted responsibility as a speechwriter, and then in other important roles.

A new path forward was opening up. He was ready to connect with the world again, but in a manner far from how Janke had imagined. On the high seas, William Bligh's personality had matched the changing fortunes of his ship. Sometimes he was the calm Newtonian type his mentor Cook had managed to be; when that was thwarted, he fell back to the furious lashing master.

Goebbels, for a time, matched that. Through the winter of 1923–4, he continued with Else, whose friends, he knew, brought out the more amiable side of him. But he also was increasingly embarking on this new venture, with men who accentuated quite a different side of his personality. He filled his journal with accounts of what he saw. "Riots of the unemployed here in Rheydt. Desperation and hunger." Else tried meeting with Mrs. Goebbels again, probably to persuade her to shift her son, but neither could influence him.

Finally, he made his choice. His private writings became ever colder— "The Jews are the poison that is destroying the body of Europe"—and by now, as 1924 went on, the rare letters from Janke have changed. He's no longer Joey; it's back, formally, to Herr Doctor.

Whatever they had shared was over.

CHAPTER 9

REICHSMINISTER

Joseph Goebbels triumphant

"First Principle. At all costs avoid being boring.
I put that before <u>everything</u>."

LESS THAN A year after the final letters between him and Else, Goebbels was appointed head of the Nazi Party in Berlin. This wouldn't have been possible in an established political organization, but the Nazi Party was small, with just a few thousand members in Berlin, out of a city population in the millions. Goebbels wrote excitedly about how the party needed his skills. Berlin was the country's most important city. If he could turn around his party's fortunes there, who knew how far the new political movement would rise.

In fact, he succeeded, first in Berlin, then on the widest stage; so successfully ingratiating himself with Hitler, and carrying out the actions his party expected ("Our brave lads pull a Jew down out of a bus," he noted in his diary) that in time, Goebbels's grandest dream came true. From his diary, January 23, 1932: "Boss wants me to be minister for film, radio, propaganda. A huge project!" With his ascendancy over the Nazi propaganda apparatus, from that point on, he had Europe's most powerful nation in his hands, its population nearing 70 million.

What could bring them together?

For him it would be hate, of course: scapegoating. To ensure its success, Goebbels used his position of power ever closer to Hitler to choreograph terrifying nighttime marches, where tens of thousands of storm troopers held flaming torches; he arranged excited live radio broadcasts to carry these spectacles to the nation and the world. He helped write and organize many of Hitler's most significant speeches, and gave numerous speeches of his own, ever more so as the years went on. His ministry poured out newsreels, posters, radio programs, books, curriculum plans, pamphlets; it controlled the theatre and music and movies; it arranged for secret monitoring of public opinion; it had—again through Goebbels's close link with Hitler—the ability to initiate street attacks, and ultimately the encouragement of mass death.

The guile Goebbels had mastered in his life, along with his painfully acquired awareness of how bullying works, guided him throughout. It was instrumental in bringing Nazi Germany to its pinnacle in 1941. His success was founded on the complete reversal of our positive principles. Instead of listening, he silenced opponents; instead of giving, he stoked uncertainty and resentment. He always attacked critics and out-groups with disproportionate force.* How he wove these actions together provides us with X-rays of these very different parts of the human soul. It reveals what decent people of all times are up against.

NOT LISTENING, BUT SILENCING

Because the Nazi Party was still so small when he was promoted to party chief in Berlin late in 1926, Goebbels needed to raise its profile and draw attention to himself. But in this he was opposed by the deputy head of Berlin's police force, a tough army veteran named Bernhard Weiss. Weiss had been awarded the highly respected Iron Cross 1st Class, as a cavalry captain in the Great War. He'd run Berlin's Criminal Police division for years.

---

* A note on chronology. The Nazi Party's support went up and down through the 1920s, and most of the time it was a small, fringe group. Only in the parliamentary elections of 1930 did it first receive more than 10 percent of the national vote. Goebbels's success in Berlin had been a big part of that. Hitler was appointed chancellor in January 1933, and soon took complete control, though his party's share of the vote was still under 40 percent.

In the summer of 1927, after the government banned Nazi assemblies, Goebbels ordered over four hundred Berlin brownshirts and SS members who had been at a rally in Nuremberg to return en masse to the main Berlin train station. He expected that would be enough to intimidate anyone, but Weiss simply had his armed police take up positions near the arriving trains and arrest every one of Goebbels's men.

Goebbels couldn't fight back directly, but he ran a newspaper now, *Der Angriff* ("The Attack"), and he used it to undermine Weiss with the mockery he'd employed so often in his life before. *Der Angriff* stopped speaking of Bernhard Weiss, for that was too respectful. Instead, Goebbels now mockingly began calling him "Isidore" Weiss. "Isidore" was a common Jewish name, and using it now suggested not just that Weiss was Jewish, which he was, but that he'd been hiding it and must hate anyone mentioning it.

In fact, Weiss had let everyone know he was Jewish. He was proud of it, and the Prussian interior minister who'd appointed him had remarked on how good it was to have a Jewish man with Weiss's skill so high in the police force.

But there was no space for Weiss to get that across, for Goebbels swamped him with the label, repeating it day after day, week after week, hundreds of times; in the pages of *Der Angriff*, and then at big open-air rallies, where the initial, relatively small crowds of committed Nazis loved this, hooting and chanting their acclaim.

Ordinary Berliners became confused. With that label so constantly repeated, sometimes just mock-teasingly, sometimes with venom, might there really be something untoward going on that Weiss *did* want to hide?

At first, Weiss tried to ignore the attacks as too juvenile to respond to. When he finally did try to object—even taking Goebbels to court—it was too late. Nobody would listen. Goebbels knew what he was doing. Shakespeare had spoken of "right perfection wrongfully disgrac'd," and that's what was working here. "Isidore is [now] a type, a mentality," Goebbels noted. "Not a person or an individual." The humiliation—even just the battles about whether it was humiliation—was also an excellent way to distract attention from the fact that at that time, Goebbels and the entire Nazi Party had only the vaguest of practical policies to offer.

The technique of giving his opponents mocking nicknames worked so well that Goebbels went on to repeat it wherever he could. In his paper's pages, and in his numerous speeches, the main workers' party in Berlin was no longer the Social Democrats; it was "The Deserters" (even though their leaders had in fact served the nation faithfully in the Great War). Here too the label was attached over and over again. When the Social Democrats' leader demanded an apology, Goebbels simply read the insulting name aloud again, pretending to be confused as to why it offended. The fact that Goebbels hadn't served in the war, even in a supporting position, was lost to attention.

When the German president, the retired general Paul von Hindenburg, was blocking Nazi plans, he got a label too. Hindenburg was no longer a retired war hero. He was a lackey of the "crooked government," Goebbels said; he was engaged in "crooked politics." Hindenburg's supporters knew this wasn't true. But Goebbels could be engaging when needed, and even be funny: he ran humorous cartoons lampooning Hindenburg, and *Der Angriff* wouldn't let up. Again, casual observers were perplexed. Was the nation's president in fact crooked? Hindenburg's supporters took Goebbels to court, and he was fined 800 marks, but shrugged it off. "A first class funeral for Hindenburg," he jotted in his diary, content.

Goebbels was perfect at this. He knew, from bitter experience, how children choose exactly the labels that will hurt most. Having been scapegoated so often, he also knew that choosing a label for someone puts you in control. Whether it's accurate or not doesn't matter. It simply drowns out the conversation, making it harder for anyone on the receiving end to be heard.

"What drives a [new] movement," Goebbels noted at a party rally in 1927, is "not a matter of knowledge, but of faith." This, he said, was where rationalist Jews were wrong, and intuitive geniuses who understood the *Volk* (the "people")—something German nationalists had long insisted no outsider could achieve—were right: "Christ did not offer proofs of his Sermon on the Mount," Goebbels wrote. "He simply made assertions." Goebbels could inform people of anything, for their "own" thoughts were in fact "just a gramophone record, playing back." He would create that gramophone record. What they heard often enough, they would take as true.

The idea was easy to carry along into radio. In his parents' generation, the idea of such invisible voice transmission had been inconceivable. Even when Goebbels had been at school commercial radio didn't yet exist. Since it was so new, there were no mechanisms in place to correct what was transmitted; no easy way, as there was with long-established newspaper outlets, to check that the information given the individual listener was false or true. The enthusiastic responses from the crowd added to the broadcasts' appeal.

Of all the critics to be slurred, the most important was the press, for they could show that what Goebbels was saying was wrong. That's why they had to be criticized in a special way. They weren't the "inaccurate" press. Someone could be inaccurate by accident, and in any event, accuracy is a matter for scientific evaluation. Nor were they the error-prone press. Instead they were the *Lügenpresse*: the *lying* press.

That was better, for lying isn't something you do by chance. Lying is an emotional act, and something you do intentionally, willfully, maliciously. In the church sermons that Goebbels no longer quite believed, the charge wasn't that the Jews had merely disagreed with the apostles about what happened in Galilee and Jerusalem. They had willfully lied about it. Here, in twentieth-century Berlin—far from religious texts, everything transposed to the cut-and-thrust of politics—it was the press he declared to be lying—just as willfully, just as maliciously, suppressing the truth about transformative events that were happening right now.

A personal element may have helped here. Although most of the press in Germany was owned by Lutheran or Catholic families, or by companies that had no particular religious feeling, the Mosse press that had turned Goebbels down was owned by a Jewish family, and the most distinguished newspaper in Berlin, the *Vossiche Zeitung*—the rough equivalent of Britain's *Guardian* or America's *New York Times*—was also owned by a Jewish family.

The fact that they had excellent reporters and were popular among educated people across Germany didn't matter. Goebbels encouraged his supporters to jeer at every mention of these papers' names, to intimidate reporters directly. If his supporters paraded outside their offices, calling out taunts, that was fine with him.

The charge of *Lügenpresse* was compulsive, it was relentless, and soon it became hard to remember a time when his enemies *weren't* the lying press. Their reporters were no longer experts able to weigh evidence, fluent in policy detail or foreign languages and other skills they needed. They were, as he repeatedly said, "enemies of the people"; malicious and untrustworthy—and not to be listened to. All their comments could be ignored.

Goebbels's distortions are a reminder of what the opposite—the careful, open listening of an Al Haynes or Danny Boyle—is all about. Their goal was to be open to reality. Goebbels's goal was to close access to reality and make people believe whatever he wanted them to. He could get away with it, at least for a while, because the catastrophes this would lead to for Germany were as yet still far away.

There's a pleasure attached to believing in the type of conspiracies he exposed. Without conspiracies to blame, we're buffeted by mindless fate, by chance, stuck alone in a large, uncaring world, amidst "the eternal silence" that so terrified the philosopher Pascal. Conspiracy, however, is right here, right among us—secretive plans that have been purpose-built to affect our individual lives. And who knows if they might not be true? Goebbels's charges against the press gave him a confidence the masses came to love.

NOT GIVING, BUT UNDERMINING

Get rid of the "lying" press and you have one less constraint. Get rid of *every* institution that keeps the current government in power—undermine the checks and balances in the Weimar Constitution—and you'll be entirely free. Hitler needed that, and Goebbels, sharing that need, was his perfect instrument. This was the opposite of giving, and here too helps clarify the mechanism of its proper working from our first chapters.

The institutions Goebbels attacked wouldn't feel gratitude toward him—they'd resent him—but that didn't matter. He didn't want their help. Instead, he wanted to break them into a series of isolated individuals, and so entirely at his whim.

A first target was the legislative branch of government, embodied in the parliament, or Reichstag. Much of the country's institutions had been designed by the famed sociologist Max Weber, a notable figure at Goebbels's old university of Heidelberg for many years. But how could an academic know anything? The legislature was incompetent, Goebbels and his agents insisted; it was slow and it was backward-looking, and it didn't *deserve* to be listened to.

The attacks began with the mocking nicknames, and then went further. The legislature was loaded with Deserters, obviously, and no doubt with Jews, and if there were legislators who were neither Social Democrats nor Jews, yet still disagreed with Nazi policy—well, who was to say they weren't secretly controlled by the forces of international finance, which everyone knew—for Goebbels had informed the nation of this many times—was basically Jewish? The fact that most of the main banks in Britain and France and America snobbishly kept Jews out (and in Britain and America often excluded Catholics too, for that matter) was not going to be brought to anyone's attention.

Just as the press could be undermined by pretending they weren't merely wrong, but malicious, Goebbels didn't say the country was following a misled democracy, or an inefficient democracy, or a democracy that needed to be reformed. There was a better, more overwhelming term, and in his newspaper, *Der Angriff*, Goebbels underlined it. "We oppose a fake democracy," he proclaimed. Who would wish to be limited by the established rules of an institution that was fake? Populist voters like to think the establishment is just a charade. Nor, because it was fake, was there any chance his party would be corrupted once they got elected and joined the legislature. When it came to "the marbled halls of parliament . . . [W]e do not want to join this pile of shit. We are coming to shovel it out."

Slamming opponents in the judiciary was important too. Even when Nazi representatives began to enter the Reichstag, a few judges who respected the Weimar Constitution tried to block the worst of their acts. Goebbels turned the full force of his name-calling and public derision on them. He knew that the weak points in any constitution are the people who have to enact it. Judges who insisted on fairness were taunted for being unpatriotic, and—even if they'd been born in Germany, even if their parents and grandparents had been born in Germany—for not being properly German.

Occasionally, courts succeeded in going against what the Nazi Party wanted, and then they had to be humiliated. In 1935, a court in Saxony convicted officials of the Hohnstein concentration camp for attacking its inmates. The minister of justice—a conservative, but at the time no Nazi— said that the decision should be allowed to stand. Hitler immediately gave a pardon to all the accused, and Goebbels started laying in to the local judge and to the justice minister: It was *they* who were in the wrong for going against the will of the people. How dare any official so insult Germany? "While making his decisions," Goebbels declared, "a judge is to proceed not by consideration of whether a judgment is just or unjust, but whether the decision is expedient."

A number of other brave civilians tried to fight back. Just as Hitler was taking power, late in January 1933, the young Lutheran pastor and theologian Dietrich Bonhoeffer prepared a talk for local Berlin radio. He was going to explain the dangers of the path his country was taking, with so many people accepting their new leader as an idol, believing that Hitler alone could solve their problems, and that it was fine to destroy other institutions which held him back.

Bonhoeffer even managed to settle at a microphone and begin his talk, but was almost immediately cut off. Goebbels's staff had been watching him, and these words could not be allowed to go out. (Although Bonhoeffer later left the country and found a safe position in New York, when war began, he returned to Germany to continue his pastoral efforts and work underground to help bring Hitler down.)

Along with threatening legislators and courts, controlling the universities was important too. That was easy, for students and many faculty had long been some of the most enthusiastic Nazi supporters. In 1933, Goebbels found great support there when he personally directed a propaganda masterstroke against the very concept of critical, rational thought.

On the night of Wednesday, May 10, books were going to be burned across the nation: ones by Jews, of course—Einstein and Freud were especially hated, while Schnitzler and Zweig were in there too—but also books by Jack London, Thomas Mann and any others who supported moral standards opposed to the new Nazi plans. His once-admired Heine would go on the pyres too.

Tens of thousands of these books were dragged from libraries and private homes and bookshops, in university towns and Berlin too. Goebbels had helped plan the nighttime spectacle. There would be solemn oaths in front of the fires, bands playing, and addresses by government officials and—in the university towns—by excited professors and students alike.

Pride of place was reserved for Berlin, where Goebbels stood in the big open plaza facing the city's opera house, fires crackling before him, men dragging or heaving books into the ever-larger bonfires. These synchronized burnings, Goebbels declared on a national radio hookup, showed that "the era of exaggerated Jewish intellectualism is now at an end." His family in Rheydt—as well as Janke in her own home—were no doubt listening in, but Goebbels wasn't done. The nation was smart "to entrust to the flames the intellectual garbage of the past." The goal was no longer to be "a man of books." It was, he declared, to be "a man of character."

No trusted questioning of authority was going to come from the professors after that. No trusted questioning was going to come from anyone. In 1930s Germany, with legislatures, courts, universities—and "lying" newspapers—undermined, on what basis could the leadership's decisions be put in doubt?

International organizations remained potentially independent sources of authority, and so they had to be undermined as well. The League of Nations, with its pathetic concern for minority rights, was wrong. The International Red Cross, with its pathetic concerns for emergency aid and public health, was wrong too. International free-trade organizations and organizations for journalists' rights and the Nobel foundation with its lauding of independent scientific voices—all those were wrong, and constantly to be mocked too.

NOT DEFENDING, BUT ATTACKING

Wherever his actions produced resistance, Goebbels helped encourage violence to keep getting his way.

Where our third positive habit involved defending to the right measure, Goebbels attacked without any sense of proportion. For his whole life, Goebbels had been weak. In elementary school, he'd been a target for every bullying child in Rheydt. He'd also been weak in his early twenties, back home and with his girlfriend Else Janke, unable to obtain the positions his artistry merited. Even now, his body was still feeble. But having left Janke and her encouragement behind—as if it meant anything when she so irritatingly asked him, gently, "Have you applied for another position?"—now he could surround himself with super-bodies; an impregnable exoskeleton: the eager-to-fight young men drawn to the Nazi movement at its start.

Through them, finally, he could dominate. Whatever ideal of fairness toward everyone had existed in Germany before, he was now going to remove it.

At a rally early in his time in Berlin, a heckler in the audience called out against Goebbels. Earlier in the speech, Goebbels had explained, with a wink and a nod, that hecklers were to be "politely manhandled out of the building." As a result, the man was now grabbed, beaten and then—to speaker and crowd's delight—flung down a flight of stairs. A few minutes later, a journalist was discovered in the same hall—and everyone knew what Goebbels made of journalists. With just a nod from on high, this man too (in fact from the not entirely unsympathetic Scherl publishing house) was beaten and—again to speaker and crowd's hurrahs—heaved down the stairs.

Goebbels often made a point of being indirect in his instructions, but that wasn't a mark of caution. Rather, it was a way to produce a deeper connection, as with the pleasure we get in understanding a joke. Everyone was sharing the same illicit thought—which this speaker, boldly, was identifying for them all. The encouragement of violence behind it was the ideal way to activate the worst traits that lurk within.

When he told supporters to put up political posters, for example, Goebbels would mock-seriously caution them that "If overzealous party members post them on the walls of empty houses, garden fences, or perhaps on the windows of Jewish businesses," that would be "very regrettable from a moral point of view." But then, going on, he would note that if, however, opponents tried to tear them down—and here again the wink and nod, sharing the feeling with his audience—"Lecture him until he sees the error of his ways, [and] do see he doesn't get hurt."

It was especially pleasing when women could be attacked. Educated or well-dressed women were best, for they clearly had been raised in settings that his own family in Rheydt had missed out on. He regularly encouraged gangs of toughs to roam Berlin's elegant shopping street, the Kurfürstendamm, and find Jewish-looking women to threaten. These young men would begin by standing ominously near, and even though he ever so carefully told them they must not harm anyone, he later mused that "the masses do not understand these finer nuances. They grab anyone they can get hold of."

In reality, the women would be knocked down, beaten, kicked in the face. Men were treated the same way. Goebbels shrugged it off. It was possible, he said, that a few Jews "found [themselves] getting slapped in these outbursts." But who was he to force it to stop?

There's no speech or article where Goebbels expresses guilt about these attacks on women like Else—indeed, attacks which could have been on Else herself, if she and her friends had managed to save up enough for a grand shopping trip to Berlin. But as we've seen, he once admitted, "Sometimes [I'm] ashamed of myself" about Else. In a private diary entry from this time, he records "a strange dream" where he was in a school being followed by a crowd of rabbis who kept calling out to him. "I was a few steps ahead, shouting back at them. It went on for hours. But they never caught up."

Rallygoers looked forward to the taunting hints Goebbels would give. "Compensation for riot damage starts at four hundred marks. I need say no more!" He had to keep his more intense feelings for smaller gatherings— "String 'em up, string 'em up!" he jotted to himself—but enough of his followers understood his message to achieve what he wished.

Why was this so attractive? Joined with a crowd, you're stronger than any single individual outside it. Many people shared Goebbels's resentment at how the recent years had turned out: the loss in the Great War, despite years of valiant fighting; the mystifying inflation; the on-again/off-again foreign occupation; the way globalized trade was undermining traditional industries. In daily life, they couldn't do anything about it, and certainly couldn't get back at those who were doing better. But in the midst of an excited rally?

In 1927, Goebbels's favorite author, Herman Hesse, published the novel *Steppenwolf*. Hesse was no Nazi, but his main character expressed a mood Goebbels shared, and which was spreading through the nation: "What I always hated and detested and cursed most inwardly was the contentment, the healthiness and cosiness, the carefully preserved optimism of the middle classes . . ." Dostoevsky's jeering man was coming alive.

Goebbels was showing a way to act that out; a way that guaranteed his supporters would be powerful and superior for once. Even vicariously this can be attractive. The present-day wrestling journalist Steven Johnson once observed that "People don't come to see someone win. They come to see someone get whipped." Living out that superiority through assaulting those weaker than yourself can be intoxicating. A journalist who observed the beatings on the Kurfürstendamm realized, shocked, that for the groups of young men Goebbels was sending out, "[it was] becoming these youngsters' normal entertainment."

The startling attacks had a further purpose. Goebbels knew he had to keep the populace's attention, and that meant constantly being on the front foot—pushing, harrying, never standing still. In one of the first conferences he gave after officially taking over the newly established propaganda ministry in March 1933, he assembled several hundred broadcasters and candidly explained the approach that needed to be taken.

"First principle," he said. "At all costs avoid being boring. I put that before *everything*." In other settings, he was just as emphatic. "Berlin needs [fresh] sensations . . . This city lives off them, and any political propaganda that fails to recognize this is bound to miss its target . . . When technology is advancing [we] must find new ways and methods every day."

This meant constant fresh news; the more, and more varied, the better. Fairness was left far behind.

One of the easiest ways to achieve his goal was to keep changing the topic. When it came to who was responsible for the Kurfürstendamm events, Goebbels nimbly shifted ground. "[If] Jews behaving arrogantly really had been beaten up there," he said, that was because Germans "had learned at first hand what it means to live under Jewish oppression." The fact of what had taken place there was put into question, and the conversation was shifted to who was responsible, and what degree of resentment was allowable.

Another technique was to constantly change policy, and justify it with such complete lack of concern for what had been said before, that people were bewildered. The events of June 1934 are instructive. Through all the years of Hitler's rise to power the SA—the paramilitary group organizing the storm troopers—had been central to Nazi survival. Its long-term head was Ernst Röhm, and Goebbels had supported him from their first meeting. "He's very nice to me, and I like him. An open, straight military type," Goebbels noted.

In April 1934, Goebbels had the national press—now under his control—laud a speech Röhm gave to the diplomatic corps. The country was reminded what a great man he was. He was, indeed, one of the only individuals so close to Hitler from the early days that he addressed the Führer with the informal "Du." Then, in June of that year, Hitler had Röhm and a number of his supporters murdered, worried they were getting too powerful.

Goebbels went on national radio the next day to broadcast to the nation what had happened.

Röhm, the hero and defender of the state, was not a hero. Goebbels had a smooth voice, surprisingly deep for such a tiny man, and radio and loudspeakers carried his words from the North Sea to the Alps. Röhm had been engaged in "disgraceful and disgusting sexual abnormality." There were indications he had been conspiring to overthrow the government too.

This made no sense. Up until the moment of those June attacks, everything Goebbels had promoted made Röhm out to be a pillar of the state. Now, though, the new line was that he'd always been an enemy. Yet the very fact that it made no sense had "advantages"—at least for someone as guileful as Goebbels. And to further understand fairness' great power when used well, we'll continue with this look at how its dynamics can be twisted to the reverse, this promised X-ray into the different possibilities within the human soul.

What Goebbels gained from insisting that nothing was certain, and nothing could be trusted to remain constant, was that all eyes had to be turned ever more on the propaganda minister and his master, from whom these cascades of disorienting information arose. Goebbels achieved the same disorientation when he pushed multiple press and newsreel and radio reports announcing that Poland was no longer an ally but an enemy; when Russia went from being Germany's greatest enemy to suddenly in 1939 becoming an ally that could not be questioned, until—with Germany's invasion in the summer of 1941—it became the greatest enemy again.

Even on a smaller scale, constant, misleading shifts were central. To create effective propaganda, Goebbels once explained, you need "a skillfully formulated series of apparently unmotivated mental leaps." One day in May 1933, he told a gathering of the film industry that they didn't have to worry, the government had no intention of curbing artistic freedom. Two weeks later, however, he created a Reich Chamber of Film, which would make sure there was no artistic freedom.

That summer, the Berlin Philharmonic conductor Wilhelm Furtwängler, who wasn't Jewish, said he was worried about persecution of his Jewish colleagues. Goebbels let it be known that there would be no such persecution. Furtwängler and many other Germans were relieved. Almost immediately afterward, however, in another reversal, Goebbels ensured that Jewish musicians began to be attacked and fired again. The musical world was at sea, unable to make any plans, and dependent now on what Goebbels did next. "That worked well," he wrote in his diary.

Everyone had to look toward him, and Goebbels loved it. He relished praise and could never bear criticism. Sowing chaos was the ideal way to ensure that continued. Carl Jung spoke of subconscious wounds that never heal, never age; the modern commentator Charles Blow notes that "concealment makes the soul a swamp." As with other authoritarian sorts we've seen, after Goebbels's painful earlier life, no amount of esteem could be enough.

From the beginning, he would lie about the size of the crowds. For one embarrassingly underattended address on the big Wittenbergplatz in Berlin, the still-independent *Berlin Lokalanzeiger* newspaper estimated the crowd as possibly 5,000; Goebbels insisted it had to be 20,000 at least.

He bragged about his speeches too; incessantly to others, and in his private diaries. "My greatest feat of oratory yet," he jotted about one talk in 1929. "Despite my depression, concentration beyond belief!" Later, after his first radio broadcast: "The speech makes a fabulous impression. I'm in top form. Brilliant press reaction today."

This continued even when, as propaganda minister, it was his staff terrorizing newspaper editors that guaranteed the positive coverage, not to mention the ministry producing laudatory newsreels of its own. A radio speech from this time "made a very deep impression on the nation," he noted; while as to another of his public addresses: "During the whole war there surely hasn't been a speech made in Germany that has been quoted and commented on so much throughout the world." When it came to the Winter Olympics, held in Germany in 1936, "Everybody is praising our organization. And it certainly was brilliant."

Other people were declared good if they backed this. They were enemies, or at the best weren't noticed, if they didn't. Everything was about him. For a long time, he'd derided the king of Bulgaria as "sly and crafty . . . double-faced." But after the king invited him for a private audience and explained that "the articles I write in the *Reich* are part of his everyday reading," Goebbels instantly reversed. "The King shows the greatest understanding . . . He follows what I do with such alert interest. He is a real people's king [and] sympathetic."

In the combined 32 volumes of his diaries, Goebbels made scarcely any comments about the feelings of his wife Magda (a younger woman he met at his office and married three years after the final letters exchanged with Else). A very few times he remarked on her tiredness, as when she'd had a cold on a day when they were supposed to be touring Athens. Otherwise, she's only mentioned for how she affected others' view of him, such as formal receptions where he was pleased when people complimented her ("She's more beautiful than all of them," he wrote).

When his wife once tried to raise her own public profile, however, through backing a Nazi fashion design office, he slapped her down. "This won't do . . . She causes me nothing but trouble."

Within his own ministry too, Goebbels needed to be the center of attention, and would undermine his staff at random moments to ensure it. A few of its most junior members were safe, for they posed no possible threat. At any level above mere secretary-typist, life became harder, as Goebbels would shift from being friendly with them one day to making an insulting "joke" about them the next.

For his most senior staff members, the undercutting was more serious. They tried to forestall it by bending and complimenting him to an embarrassing degree, emphasizing the honor—the incredible honor—of serving under his awe-inspiring direction. In response, more than once, Goebbels fulsomely complimented an adviser back, then almost immediately let the press know that man was being expelled. If the adviser was lucky, he would avoid prison and only be forced to take on hard, industrial factory work. After a few weeks or months away, he would then be allowed to return, now as disoriented—and powerless—as the general public. Because of these constant assaults, the repeated demonstration that he was surrounded by incompetents, it was clear that if anything went wrong it was their fault, not his.

Everyone had to be attacked: those senior staff, old supporters like Röhm, a too-independent wife, the very notion of truth itself. "The aim of our movement," Goebbels explained, "[is] to mobilize people for the national ideal . . . If the aim has been achieved, then critics can pronounce judgment on my methods if they wish; that is a matter of complete indifference to me."

NOT INCLUDING, BUT EXCLUDING

There's more to be seen by looking at the reverse of decent action, so resonant today. Goebbels hated inclusion, and pushed to create divisions. To this end, he insisted there had been a golden age just a few years in the past.

Germany had to get there again, but enemies had got in the way, enemies who infiltrated and preyed upon loyal citizens.

Naturally, those enemies had to be identified and separated. Once that happened, good Germans would be on the inside. Enemies, the non-members now, would be on the outside. The more those groups were despised, the better everyone else automatically became.

There was resistance. Secret observations by Goebbels's propaganda ministry showed that a large number of non-Jews in Germany didn't want to turn against Jewish citizens (or if they did accept the general principle, they'd want to make an exception for a favored Jewish neighbor or shopkeeper). Goebbels realized he had to break any links of gratitude.

First of all, Jews were constantly labeled with insulting, dehumanizing slurs. They had to stop being considered ordinary people; the mix of carpenters and doctors and engineers—and police commissioners—that other Germans knew and lived among. Instead, narrowly, they were now traitorous Jews, or Bolshevist Jews, or vermin-ridden Jews.

Negative adjectives were crucial. As with the nicknaming of Weiss—and with the charges of crookedness against once-revered President Hindenburg—the first few times this was done, it might have seemed excessive and, to much of the population, slightly ridiculous. But Goebbels had it repeated, hundreds of times per week, in old media like newspapers, as well as in the exciting new media of radio and newsreels. Soon individuals who'd never met a Jew, or never thought much about Jews, had these associations at the front of their minds. Even if they didn't go along with all the details, they "knew" that there was one group, called Germans, and another group, called Jews, whose loyalty to good Germans was somehow in doubt, and who were dangerous to have anywhere near.

Because of the long years of vilifying the press, in time there were no independent voices around to criticize this. And because of the years spent undermining the very idea of independent courts, legal challenges couldn't be made against these assertions either.

To further keep everyone off-balance, Goebbels pushed all initiatives in uneven, intentionally confusing steps. When regulations came out with lists of professions that Jews were to be fired from, it was noted that there were others that remained open, along with a proviso that Jewish veterans of the Great War were exempt. Then there was a pause, then the veterans were no longer automatically exempt; then there was another pause . . . and in that way, attention divided, the exclusions would carry on.

Violence was central, and in early November 1938, Goebbels brought it to a head, creating a deranged public theater encompassing the entire nation. He would get as many ordinary Germans as possible to join in the vilification of the Jews. The overall plan was largely his own, though he worked long hours with his staff and others to arrange the details.

Starting on an ordinary Tuesday morning, gangs broke into Jewish shops, beat the owners and staff, broke displays, and then threw merchandise out on to the streets, there to wait temptingly for looters. This was exceptional in an orderly society, yet across the country, as the American consul in Stuttgart was startled to observe, "the police looked on, either smilingly or unconcernedly." That, however, was Goebbels's intention. Crowds were attracted, and once the first looters began to take what was now available, greater numbers joined them.

Other gangs broke into Jewish synagogues (including those in Köln, so close to Rheydt). There too they beat anyone they found, smashed tables and chairs, but then they also poured gasoline and set the buildings alight. Firemen who arrived stood back ("We were ordered not to use any water," one remembered). They waited however many hours it took until the buildings were burned, only using their hoses if they had to wet down houses nearby that might be in danger.

Again crowds gathered, with local Jews often rounded up and made to kneel in front of the burning buildings, their hands above their heads. What the crowds saw were men and women they'd once known as neighbors, shopkeepers or just friends—with their diverse personalities, diverse looks—now transformed into near-identical scared, kneeling beings. They'd become an out-group par excellence, and all those who watched were united simply by not being them.

In the coal-mining town of Dinslaken, 45 miles from Rheydt, a Jewish orphanage was invaded. "Fifty men stormed into the house, their coat or jacket collars turned up; they began their work of destruction with the utmost precision." The director, Yitzhak Hers, was an educated man, well known in the town, but could do nothing. Children who tried to protect their favorite possessions were thrown against walls. Director Hers staggered out into the cold, trying to protect the crying children now clustered around him. A crowd was milling, several hundred strong, and he turned to them for help. "Among these people I recognized some familiar faces, suppliers of the orphanage or tradespeople."

But Hers was no longer a proud citizen. He was merely a victim; bleeding, standing on a wet lawn, without a proper coat in the freezing air, surrounded by terrified, crying children. He glanced up and saw "a heavy cloud of smoke billowing upward. It was obvious from the direction it was coming that the Nazis had set the synagogue on fire." Hers turned to the crowd again. Some had to remember their friendship, he hoped. "Only a day or a week earlier [they] had been happy to deal with us as customers." Now, though, he saw it was different. "They were passive, watching [my orphanage's] destruction without emotion."

Goebbels was exultant. "Reports are now coming in from all over the Reich. 50, then 70 synagogues burning . . . The people's anger is raging now. There's no stopping it." Late that night, he took a break, scanning the horizon. There was "a blood-red sky," he noted with satisfaction. It was the flames from burning synagogues reflecting off the clouds. These events came to be known collectively by the euphemistic name Kristallnacht, from the broken glass through the night. To a Reuters correspondent soon after, Goebbels explained away the entire episode. What he had done was best for the nation; it was "purely about separating Germans from Jews."

"There are no parliamentary parties in Germany any longer," Goebbels noted approvingly two years after Hindenburg was gone. The reason it had been so easy to ban them was that "we had waged a campaign for years that

persuaded people of their weaknesses . . . and disadvantages." This had been
exhausting, but worth it. After that softening up, "they could be eliminated
by a [mere] legal act." Hitler was the new state's main motivating force of
course, but Goebbels at the propaganda ministry had been indispensable.

The resistance that had been everywhere at first faded as the years went
on. The spectacles were exciting. Being amid the crowds was exciting. The
certainty, the unity—the pleasure in being superior to the scorned minority,
as well as the Dostoevskyan pleasure in overthrowing everything—was exactly
what had been missed. Politicians, business leaders and others who should
have known better—and some who later deeply regretted it—drifted to his
side, quietly, often one by one, drawn by the thrill of power, plus the useful
patronage it could give. There also was the pleasure, relief, in not being targeted themselves. Highways were built, and jobs came back. The weakness
of defeat in World War I was gone.

In the autobiographical novel Goebbels had written around the time
when he was first meeting Else Janke, his alter ego "Michael" had the "ambition to become a great man one day." Reality had surpassed that more than
he could have imagined. He had respect from Hitler, which he loved. He had
villas and mansions, exultant crowds listening to his words, trembling fear
from civil servants, arts administrators, and virtually everyone else he met.

If he wanted to hear Beethoven played he could instruct the ever-helpful
von Karajan at the Berlin Philharmonic and it would be done. If he wished
to discuss literature, a phone call would be made and the eager Professor
Heidegger would instantly travel to Berlin. If he wished to sleep with any
actress, the fact that his ministry controlled Germany's film industry made
that a given. Many distinguished families across Europe loved his finally
putting down those irritating Jews, plus the thrilling sense of power that
sharing his presence gave. After Goebbels had publicly exulted in mobs turning on children, grinning when news arrived about how far it had gone, the
constantly starstruck Englishwoman Diana Mitford chose his drawing room
for her marriage to Oswald Mosley, leader of the British Union of Fascists.

He didn't have time to go back to his hometown much, and when he
did he remarked, in his diary, how narrow and dull his old acquaintances

now appeared. It's true that when he did come upon Janke there she resisted, a brave act given that by that time, with the slightest nod, he could have the bodyguards he was surrounded with arrest her and everyone she knew. ("I run across Else. She's curt and clipped. How that hurts. In the afternoon she puts in no appearance. Good!")

But what did that matter? Rheydt had a castle, which had been in ruins for years. Couldn't he be lord of the town? Goebbels gave a single instruction, and ownership was transferred to his name. Architects soon began fixing it up. He could control whoever he wished.

The whole country was equally triumphant. Germany already had world-beating engineering and chemistry, a well-organized civil service and for the military, an outstanding general staff. With the new unity among its non-Jewish citizens, every expansionist desire began to come true. In early December 1941, Britain and Russia were on their knees. (It helped that— albeit through budgetary matters he'd had nothing to do with—the German economy was roaring.) America, across the ocean, was pathetic, weak, riven by factions and squabbling courts and unions. Hitler addressed an exultant Reichstag: "When I decided 23 years ago to enter political life in order to lead the nation up from ruin, I was a nameless, unknown soldier . . . Today I stand at the head of the mightiest army in the world, the most powerful air force . . ."

Germany's might stretched from the English Channel to the outskirts of Moscow; from the Arctic Circle to the Sahara. The army and police followed orders, and in one town after another, mass murders had long since begun.

Who could possibly say that bad people lose? A continent was being transformed. All our positive principles of morality were gone. The worst in human nature was coming out. At the start of December 1941, Germany's domination suggested that it truly might last for 1,000 years.

PART FIVE

PRESIDENT

CHAPTER 10

GILDED YOUTHS

The Ordeal of Franklin D. Roosevelt

(*"Combine the principles, and succeed"*)

"I remember thinking to myself, Do men really behave like this?*"*

BRITAIN IN DECEMBER 1941 was still holding out against invasion, protected behind its narrow sea barriers by the Royal Air Force and the Royal Navy. But it wouldn't be able to strike back on its own. For that it would need help. Russia was, at the moment, struggling too hard to provide direct aid. The answer would have to be America.

And America, in recent years, had not been in any shape to defend the world.

The Great Depression that began on Wall Street in 1929 had hit hard. In 1933, when Hitler had become Germany's chancellor and Goebbels was heading the propaganda ministry, millions of Americans were still unemployed. Since there was almost no unemployment insurance, poverty was everywhere. Suicides had more than tripled since the good years before the Great Crash; factories were closed, huge agricultural regions were being abandoned. The fabled Empire State Building had been completed in record speed, but now stood nearly tenantless, with New York's multitude of unemployed derisively calling it the Empty State Building as they walked by the once-bustling site.

We know today that the 32nd president, Franklin Delano Roosevelt—FDR—turned his country around, preserving capitalism as an economic motor, while reconfiguring it for wider benefit. Along the way, he made use of all our recurrent principles: listening, but without too much ego (though this one he barely scraped through on); giving, yet carefully auditing; defending, but proportionately so—and in a way that naturally brought others in, for it didn't need vicious exclusion to make it work. It's the near opposite of what Goebbels had done, and an excellent way to see how these courses of action can fit together for aims such as FDR's, even today.

Roosevelt wouldn't have seemed a likely candidate for using fairness to achieve these decent goals, as compassion had been far from his horizons at the start. He'd been the quintessential gilded youth: raised in a family with the accumulation of old money that seemingly proves idleness decays the mind. Distant ancestors had made the fortune, but since then, for at least six generations, most of the family had floated along doing not much of anything beyond shooting, riding and—since the trust funds must never, under any circumstances, be threatened—judiciously procreating; a "dynasty of the mediocre," one newspaper accurately called it.

What happened next is a remarkable inverse of Goebbels's life. Goebbels had started out poor and handicapped. After a few years of moderate success in the wider world, everything had collapsed: he'd ended up stuck back at home, feeling he'd hit rock bottom, raging at being the one family member "whose opinion isn't worth listening to" as his family hovered near. A kind young woman had tried to encourage him, but although he followed her path for a while, that failed, and he ended up the skilled monster we've seen.

Franklin D. Roosevelt had started at the opposite extreme, but he too suffered a grave physical handicap and hit rock bottom; raging at being shunted aside and a family that no longer took him seriously. Yet here when a kind young woman encouraged him, he began to draw on more humane aspects of his soul he'd barely touched before. He emerged as the near opposite of Goebbels, ultimately helping drive the alliance that destroyed everything Goebbels had helped create.

The story is instructive for us all. Once again, we all have choices. How do we decide what to do with them?

Although Franklin was an only child, he'd grown up in large part on an estate 80 miles outside New York, where there'd been a butler, a houseman, a personal maid, a housemaid, a kitchen maid, a cook, a cook's assistant, a laundress, a nurse, a nursemaid and governesses (usually European, and thus prestigious); there also were, in the main house or associated buildings scattered on the estate, stable boys, coachmen and many others, who tended the lawns, orchards, meadows and gardens.

The pampering that Roosevelt received as a child wasn't limited to his family's estate. His whole world was arranged to pamper him. When he was allowed into the nearby village, his governess had been instructed by Roosevelt's battle-ax of a mother, Sara, that under no circumstances was he to play with the boys he met there; they were too common, and beneath him.

That might seem enough for rocks to be thrown and insults hurled. But few of the boys dared taunt Franklin, and many of the adults he met touched their caps when he passed. They depended on the family's estate, and couldn't afford to do anything that might harm their jobs.

Roosevelt ended up tall and strong. Yale's football coach described him as "a beautifully built man, with the long muscles of an athlete." He was amiably witty to those of his class. Hit in the stomach with a baseball at boarding school, he wrote home that the line drive was "to the great annoyance of that intricate organ, and to the great delight of all present." He was colder, though, when it came to the masses, insulated by his upbringing and the trust fund which meant he'd never have to work.

Arriving as a new member of the New York state legislature at age 28, the social reformer Frances Perkins—a woman who would play a central role in Roosevelt's later achievements—tried to get his support for a bill that would keep children from working more than 54 hours a week in factories.

Roosevelt brushed her off. "Can't do it now. Can't do it now. Much more important things," she remembered him mumbling. But Perkins knew men like him always objected to new ideas, and for years she had been filling a large red envelope she labelled "Notes on the Male Mind" with ideas for how to get past that.

One of the most effective techniques, she'd found, was to take skeptical legislators on factory visits so they could see how bad conditions were. If she could get the men to climb on to fire escapes or accomplish other dangerous acts, that was even better. When she led one state senator crawling through a tiny hole in a factory wall to peer down a steep iron ladder covered with ice that ended 12 feet from the ground—ostensibly the factory's fire escape—she got his vote for better factory safety. "I remember thinking to myself, *Do men really behave like this?*" But yet it worked.

Yet however much she tried with Roosevelt, nothing succeeded. He didn't know any factory workers, and he'd never heard *his* servants object to the long hours his mother employed them for, so why should he bother? He wouldn't come on any visits to learn more. "I can see [him] now," Perkins wrote later, "standing back of the brass rail . . . his small mouth pursed up and slightly open, his nostrils distended, his head in the air, and his cool, remote voice saying, 'No, no, I won't hear of it!'" He didn't support her bill.

Colleagues found him variously "arrogant," "awful," and a smug "know-it-all"; none of which was helped, Perkins remembered, by his "unfortunate habit . . . of looking down his nose at most people."

An older machine politician was blunter: "He was a patronizing son of a bitch."

Largely through family connections, Roosevelt became assistant secretary of the navy in 1913. He had already told friends that he was going to be president some day: his cousin Theodore had been, and it would be his turn soon. He was already a member of five clubs in New York, and in Washington he added a sixth one, the Metropolitan Club, which famously had blackballed the president of the time, Woodrow Wilson, for being too common.

Roosevelt was married by then, to an equally upper-class woman, Eleanor (who was also his fifth cousin; the top social circles were nothing if not familiar). From occasional camping trips, Franklin knew how to cook, at least a bit, but not only had Eleanor never cooked, she had to explain to him that she didn't know how to *order* food. That had always been done for her too.

They had six children, one of whom died young, and with the interest from trust funds and other family investments (the income running to about $450,000 a year in today's currency), they employed ten servants to help around the house. Once America entered World War I, Eleanor explained to a journalist that the servants were now helping them economize by using less laundry soap than before and being more parsimonious with the servings— some meals were down to three courses—as they waited on the Roosevelts' table at breakfast, lunch and dinner.

Roosevelt's mother had given him an 18-bedroom, three-story "cottage" on an island off Maine for vacations. His children had the run of the island, and took on the same unthinking superiority he'd come to assume. When his eldest daughter's German shepherd chased a flock of sheep into the sea, the family concern wasn't so much for how this hurt the owner, but that somehow the poor dog might be punished.

If there were picnics, the children didn't carry food or blankets to sit on; groups of locals were hired to do that for them. Eleanor kept a large megaphone suspended from the porch ceiling so that she could blare instructions whenever the multitudes of caretakers weren't doing enough.

For the Fourth of July in 1913—Goebbels still a high-schooler in Rheydt, his life "pretty blighted" by the students who taunted him for his limp—Roosevelt asked the admirals in his Navy Department if they would mind terribly sending one of their battleships to anchor off the island for his children to see. If they also could see fit to fire off a 17-gun salute, he wouldn't mind that either. (They did try to resist when he suggested he pilot one of their destroyers through the dangerous straits near his island, but they couldn't resist too hard. With the later famed William F. "Bull" Halsey who was supposed to command the destroyer no doubt biting his tongue, Roosevelt's children got to see their father waving from the helm as he gaily steered the 700-ton behemoth.)

In 1920, he was selected to run for vice-president on the Democratic ticket, again largely because of his family name. Although the Republicans won that year in a landslide, everyone saw that the cheerful young Roosevelt's prospects looked good for a run of his own some day. While he waited, he worked part-time at a boutique law firm and at a large securities firm, where his figurehead positions brought him an additional $350,000 a year in today's money. All he had to do for a few days a month was use his networks to bring in business.

Roosevelt was a fit man, and at the naval yards, he'd easily climbed up the sailors' riggings. But one afternoon in the summer of 1921, age 39, vacationing again on the Maine island, he found himself suddenly feeling tired; much more so than he'd experienced before. To perk himself up, he jogged with his children to a nearby freshwater pond for a dip. But he was still tired when they came back—"I'd never quite felt that way before"—and in the morning, he had a temperature and could barely stand.

Over the next few days his legs got weaker, then he couldn't move his arms or hands, and then he couldn't lift his legs at all. Within weeks, a doctor who'd been called in sent a terse telegram to a Harvard specialist:

ATROPHY INCREASING POWER LESSENING
CAUSING PATIENT MUCH ANXIETY . . .
CAN YOU RECOMMEND ANYTHING . . .

The diagnosis was polio. Along with the shock and humiliation—he'd lost control of all bodily functions—the fast-multiplying virus made any touch excruciating, even the brush of a solitary bedsheet.

After a few months, recuperating first at his New York town house, then at his mother's estate outside New York, some of the symptoms went away. He could use his upper body again, and in a formal examination, doctors noted that his bowel and bladder were now fine, and he could also have normal sexual functions—there were "No symptoms of *impotentia coeundi*," as they delicately phrased it.

But his hips and legs remained paralyzed, with only the slightest glimmers of muscle response.

At first, Roosevelt didn't accept what that meant. In October 1922, he decided he was going to make it into Manhattan to show he could handle an ordinary day at the securities firm (which was still paying him). To get there from his mother's estate, he first had his servants strap braces on his legs, each about 12 pounds of iron, which went "from the heels of his shoes to a clamping that fit against the buttocks." Then he watched as they wrapped padded straps tight around his knees and around his thighs. The servants carried him downstairs, and with his chauffeur's help, he dragged himself into their Buick.

When they reached the office—an entire city block, at 120 Broadway—a young lawyer named Basil O'Connor was in the lobby and saw what happened.

It was hard getting out of the car. When the chauffeur pulled over and got out, then opened the side door and helped twist Roosevelt around to face the building, suddenly there was no seat rest to grip, and Roosevelt slipped backward into the Buick. A car behind started honking. The chauffeur ignored it, pulled Roosevelt up, started to straighten Roosevelt's legs, and then—this was hard, for the mechanism was under Roosevelt's trousers—worked to start locking the braces at the knees into their fully extended position.

By now, a lot of cars were honking. The chauffeur stepped away to yell at them and Roosevelt, this proud, once-so-nimble man, was left immobile, one rigid leg sticking out of their Buick. Finally, the chauffeur got back and helped him up. But before Roosevelt could get a good grip on the crutches, he fell back against the car. The chauffeur grabbed him, but Roosevelt's hat had blown off. They had to wait while a member of the rapidly growing crowd picked it up, tried to uncrumple it, and then put the hat back on him.

Finally, the chauffeur got both Roosevelt's hands on the crutches and stood aside. Roosevelt swayed at first, but then he got his balance. He was supporting nearly 200 pounds of dead weight entirely with his arms and by his armpits. O'Connor noticed that Roosevelt's knuckles went white as he slowly, very slowly, dragged himself forward. He "held his head down, tugging and hauling with enormous care. Already he was soaked with perspiration."

Because his hips were paralyzed as much as his legs, he couldn't swing one leg forward at a time, but had to rotate his entire upper body and build up momentum for his legs that way.

The crowd was bigger now—they were watching a *Roosevelt*, the man who'd just run for vice-president—and he actually made it into the lobby. But the marble floor was slippery, and after just a few more steps, the crutches skidded away. Roosevelt crashed down, hard. A few bystanders started forward, but then stopped.

Roosevelt tried to twist into a sitting position, forcing a smile. But it was hard to get enough leverage from the sprawl he was in, and he finally called up, "Give me a hand there." O'Connor was fit, yet Roosevelt was a big man, and it was impossible to dead lift those 200 pounds alone. Only with the chauffeur and another bystander hurrying over—the crowds staring as all three tugged—did they get him up. They succeeded in supporting Roosevelt to the elevator, but it was clear he couldn't do it on his own. There was no way he could carry on a normal business life.

What to do when your dreams are gone?

Roosevelt tried setting up yet another small law firm, but his heart wasn't in it, for he could only get into the (less public) office through a mix of being carried and pushed along in a wheelchair, which he hated.

His mother didn't want him to even try to get to work. Her own husband had ended up an invalid, and she'd been happy taking care of him, so why couldn't Franklin accept early retirement to their country home? In the months he'd stayed there after his first attack, she'd been delighted that he worked on his stamp collection, just as he had when he was little, that he slept late and gave no complaints when she had servants bring him his favorite breakfasts so he wouldn't have to get out of bed. If he continued like that she could be sure he'd not strain himself.

Eleanor wasn't much better. She'd never much liked sex—confiding in her eldest daughter that it was "an ordeal to be borne"—and seems to have entirely turned against it in fury after she'd discovered a few years before, in 1918, not only that Franklin was having an affair, but that it was with the woman who was her own social secretary; a woman who was tall and slim, with blue eyes and a throaty voice. This would have hurt anyone, but must have been especially bad for Eleanor, whose own mother had told her she was too plain for men to be attracted to, and had always been insecure, wondering if anyone would ever care for her.

She did everything that was required for her husband when it came to emergency care, but otherwise kept a cold distance. Their son James recalled that by this time, the marriage was no more than "an armed truce."

With little love at home, and national politics seemingly impossible due to his disability—with his old Harvard friends being too unnaturally jovial about his polio when they were around, and no chance of a real job—Roosevelt was at a loss. It was the Jazz Age, of speakeasies and F. Scott Fitzgerald, and witty slim women in flapper dresses. Yet he was no part of it; just a man in his forties, far from love, living off money he'd inherited, waiting to pass time in this "dynasty of the mediocre" until he died.

Throughout 1923, Roosevelt drifted until finally, at a loss, he resolved to leave his established East Coast life behind. One of his old friends from Harvard, John Lawrence, hadn't been as stilted as the others when he'd come to visit. Even better, Lawrence had always liked a good time. They decided that they could rent a boat—no, they could *buy* a boat, a houseboat, a big long houseboat, and they could have friends, and invite girls, and if they were going to drift their lives away, then let it be in the warm waters off Florida.

And that is what they did, for months on end: fishing, sunbathing, drinking and cruising in the coastal waterways, starting in Miami, and working down the Florida Keys. They named the boat *Larooco*, in honor of both their names. Franklin's legs were still feeble, but he'd spent months working on parallel bars at home to develop his shoulders and arms. Now, on the *Larooco*, he was able to get around with agility. In the corridors below decks, he would reach up to the crossbeams, and—supporting himself entirely by his arms—swing himself forward where he wanted to go. Friends would wait at the end with his crutches ready, and he'd let himself down to continue. Eleanor came to visit once, but left after just a few days. She didn't like sun, and she didn't like swimming, and she couldn't understand why no one was *doing* anything; be that reading worthwhile books or instructing the servants in what to do.

None of the passengers minded her departure, especially not Franklin, for there were other women available now. One was Frances De Rahm, an old girlfriend, now married and there with her husband, but they all enjoyed showing that their wealth released them from the inhibitions of formal, working America. The men that Roosevelt and Lawrence brought down to the boat were already used to swimming without their clothes, and Frances joined in the skinny-dipping, inking in the ship's log (probably with a reference to her bust size):

> A female went swimming—she was far from a peach
> She was as the Lord made her, so what could she do
> But call herself, gaily, a true 32

There was lots of drinking—another kick against Eleanor, who supported Prohibition—and card-playing, and along with the other wealthy guests, there was a solitary blue-collar passenger (aside from the elderly married couple who cooked and piloted the boat), an energetic professional Roosevelt had known from his law firm and the vice-presidential campaign, a young Irish Catholic woman from a rough part of Boston, Marguerite "Missy" LeHand.

She later became one of the most important people in the country— halfway between administrative assistant and White House chief of staff, making the cover of *Time* magazine—but there, on the houseboat *Larooco*, she was, at least at first, just another ebullient guest, hurrying ashore once to get ice cream with her new friend De Rahm, in a race to see if they could get it back to the others before it melted (they failed).

It wasn't by chance, however, that Roosevelt had asked her down.

Like his lover from a few years before, LeHand was tall, with blue eyes, a throaty voice and a near-constant smile, "a compound of cunning and innocence forever baffling," one admirer wrote. She was bright too, having pushed up from her old neighbourhood of Somerville (known, disparagingly, as "Slumerville" by those in wealthier parts of Boston) to end up working with the Democratic National Committee. Asked to look after the correspondence and contracts left over from the 1920 presidential run, she'd created systems of impressive efficiency to get that done.

A common phrase for having a good time in this period was "Let's cut up," and to honor that, LeHand wore a charm bracelet which had on it a tiny pocketknife with a working blade. When she wished, she'd just flick it open: why not begin now?

Roosevelt was smitten. LeHand seems to have matched her new friend De Rahm's physical ease, for one evening he wrote in the ship's log:

> Grog in midst of glorious sunset
> Almost as poetic in coloring
> As Frances' and Missy's nighties

He didn't care who knew. One friend, back north, wrote to Roosevelt, "I can picture you divanating in local garb, with a mint julep in one hand [and] Missy clad—God knows how—languorously fanning you . . ." When LeHand had been out tanning too long, Roosevelt said, "Missy, if you get any more sun today, we can use you tonight as a port running light."

Yet she and Roosevelt shared a deeper understanding than just drinks and sunsets and friends who swam as the Lord made them. LeHand had suffered rheumatic fever as a youngster, which frequently led to some form of atrial fibrillation. She could swim alongside De Rahm or other frolicking guests, but not for long; she couldn't run along a beach or keep up in a tennis game either.

That made it easier for her to see past the famed Roosevelt, with his inherited wealth and his perfect family—with its holidays on its perfect island—into the man who had to keep up a front. Others had tried. "I tried continually to study him," one wealthy friend reflected, "to try to look beyond [Franklin's] charming and amusing surface into his heavily forested interior.

But I could never really understand what was going on in there." Friends recognized that Roosevelt kept a very slight distance, and that if they ever pushed too hard, a nasty coldness erupted.

LeHand recognized more, seeing into the agony he felt. "There were days on the *Larooco*," she remembered, "when it was noon before he could pull himself out of depression and greet his guests, wearing his lighthearted facade."

Roosevelt loved that LeHand understood him, however unjust that was to his wife. LeHand possessed a "charm of manner," he reflected later, that was "inspired by tact and kindness of heart . . . She was utterly selfless."

They often stayed behind in Florida after the other guests had left, just the two of them on the boat for days or weeks: her helping him onto sandbars or small beaches from the *Larooco*'s launch, swiveling his legs while he used his strong arms to lift himself over the edge; resting together in the sun to gossip and drink the rum they both liked; pausing when huge flocks of geese and other birds shot past. A miniature cocktail shaker ended up on the charm bracelet she wore, alongside the working pocketknife.

Back on board, if it was still light they'd rest together, sunbathing on a big mattress dragged onto the deck. Roosevelt worshipped books, and at his New York town house, had a spacious library. For the *Larooco* too, he'd arranged for crates of books to be shipped down, which he and LeHand neatly arranged and indexed. They'd spend hours reading together, sometimes just thrillers or mysteries, but sometimes more thoughtful works. Afterward, there'd be more drinks and conversations on the cypress-planked deck until dark and beyond; a wind-up gramophone keeping them company. Time seemed endless, and one long afternoon they painted all the wicker furniture blue, just for fun.

They were supposed to have separate cabins on opposite sides of the main below-decks corridor, but the hired couple who cooked and piloted the boat weren't going to check, and it wouldn't be surprising if they consummated their affection. When Roosevelt's 12-year-old son Elliot, on a brief visit, accidentally surprised them in the stateroom, the boy saw LeHand in her nightgown, sitting on his father's lap, Franklin "holding her in his sun-browned arms."

On the surface, Roosevelt and Goebbels should have had nothing in common. Roosevelt had been physically imposing as a young man; he was wealthy and connected. But at a loss after his polio attack, he too had been going through the Dutch anthropologist van Gennep's rites of passage: those stages where you start in the world you're familiar with, move into a very different realm—a limbo that's betwixt and between—and only then, after that period of separation, become able to reconnect with the main world, changed from who you'd been.

The first part of this rite of passage, the separation, had been to leave his mother's Hudson River estate and his Manhattan town house, his wife and children and career, and the entire establishment he'd been immersed in before.

The second part, the free-floating limbo, was his life on the *Larooco*; rambling along the Florida coast with no past or future, just a continuum of sun and salt water, of sunsets and rum and infinite lingering talk. There was no asceticism about it—on the contrary—but asceticism is only one possible way to undergo a rite of passage. Any period of time sufficiently "apart" from your previous life will do.

Wherever there's uncertainty about where to land, this transitional step produces anguish. William Bligh's men found Tahiti the most magical of timeless limbos and hated when their captain tried to pull them from it back to the sharp discipline of a British naval vessel. The result was his men flinging him into the *Bounty*'s launch so they could return to the lustrous, timeless realm they'd experienced.

Goebbels's second stage had seen him, desolate, back at home with his parents in Rheydt, trying first the literary world and then the political world as a way out. Roosevelt's second stage had been his drifting life on the *Larooco*, and that's what he was now tired of. It wasn't as idyllic as it seemed, even though in his letters home he tried to give that impression. But it wasn't doing anything for his polio, and he also was too intelligent to imagine decades more just drifting along there.

The drinks and guests and card games and fishing that filled the time were pointless, and as he was coming to see, it was selfish too. He had gone all the way to the "if I am only for myself" extreme of Hillel's query, with nothing generous left. Roosevelt had a family, but what was he doing for them? His eldest son James, stuck back home, remembered that "those were the lonely years. For a long while we had no tangible father whom we could touch and talk to at will—only a cheery letter-writer, off somewhere on a houseboat." He was lying to his wife and cold to his family. He was wealthy enough to remain that way forever.

But although Roosevelt was ready to find something more, where would it be?

It couldn't be back in the Hudson River estate or Manhattan; not yet, however much he missed his children. Waiting out those years as a "cripple" at home, doing nothing but watch his investments mature, or struggle occasionally to a Manhattan office to earn more money, would be a desolation he couldn't bear. Aside from the state of his legs, his health was excellent, and given the longevity of other relatives, he thought he might survive into the 1960s or even 1970s. Eleanor wasn't going to do anything to help. With tactlessness impressive even for a woman who addressed her children's picnics by megaphone, she'd written asking him to send his extra golf pants for James "as you don't use them now."

This is where LeHand was so important.

Members of Franklin's previous social circle had always been polite enough to their servants but rarely had any understanding of worlds outside their own. One of Franklin's distant cousins was amazed that someone who'd grown up as poor as LeHand could be pleasant and well-mannered, despite having "no background at all." Another relative, the notably acerbic Alice Roosevelt Longworth, professed to approve of his dalliances. "Franklin deserved a good time," she liked to say. "He was married to Eleanor." But that was merely because Longworth had always resented Eleanor. To her, LeHand was just another pleasant affair.

Else Janke hadn't been able to bring Goebbels to the best of the waiting worlds he had available. As a schoolteacher in a provincial town, she didn't have the pull to ensure the manuscripts they sent out to theaters across Germany were accepted. LeHand was more experienced, more connected—and had an easier partner to work with. Roosevelt's body had failed, but his wealth and connections had left him far less tortured than Goebbels. However submerged his confidence was, LeHand could tell some of it was still there.

Even if Franklin was going to enter national politics again, he was in no condition for it yet; she recognized that. But from backstage knowledge he'd built up before in his Navy Department job and in conversation with very many officials during his vice-presidential run, he still had an astute grasp of the play of political force. (He was able, or so rumor had it, to draw a line across the country from east to west, and name each county it crossed.)

Because Roosevelt's popularity had never entirely gone away, a handful of political visitors still came down to the boat, with the social reformer Frances Perkins prime among them. LeHand saw that the political realm was the only place where he was going to find meaning. But to do that, he'd have to be at least a little bit more mobile.

More time away was indispensable. The way Roosevelt's mother had given up on Franklin's recovery was beyond LeHand's comprehension. She knew that exercise made her own irregular heartbeat better, not worse. Polio had damaged Roosevelt's legs, but that wasn't the same as if they had been amputated. The man she loved was desperate to get some function back. Even a slight improvement would help him in crutch- or cane-assisted walking, and avoid humiliations such as that collapse at his Broadway office.

Back at the Hudson Valley estate, before these *Larooco* years, he had actually tried getting on a horse. Although his mother insisted he stop immediately, he'd been able to ride a few steps, gripping the horse's flanks with his knees until his weakened thigh muscles began trembling too much.

On the *Larooco* now, LeHand ingeniously tried settling him in a rocking chair so he could try to move himself by using his quadriceps alone. It was hard to get right. "The tendency at first," Roosevelt recorded, "was to cheat by rocking with the body." But LeHand was persistent. "Within a few days I could rock back and forth by using only the knee and the lower leg and foot muscles." That rocking proved at least some muscles were still able to function. They were weakened and would never be strong enough to support his full weight, but this was much better than nothing.

LeHand was going to see he had more therapy. It would also have to be in an environment more suitable for connecting with policy officials such as Frances Perkins than with the delightfully skinny-dipping Frances De Rahm. LeHand's father had been an alcoholic who abandoned the family; as she'd grown up, her mother had been forced to depend on boarders. That gave her the strength to insist. Roosevelt's life as an invalid was going to end.

There was a resort deep in rural Georgia that seemed a promising start.

Was Roosevelt at this point himself a good person, or a bad one? The question doesn't apply, for he wasn't either yet. He was just floating, stuck, his integration back into the real world only begun. Whether he'd end up generous or selfish was still up in the air.

If he'd continued directly in politics at this point, his polio somehow miraculously cured, he might have ended up as one of those genteel amateur politicians whose rise to the top is aided by a pleasant demeanor and family connections, but whose purpose, once they achieve power, no one can discern.

LeHand had strong hopes that Roosevelt would become something better, even though the resort they arrived at in the autumn of 1924 seemed a depressing change from the elegant houseboat. The hamlet of Bullochville, Georgia, had one crumbling hotel and a handful of guest cottages 1,000 feet up in wooded hills. Neither she nor Roosevelt were immediate fans of Georgia country food. "There we had lukewarm possum soup, and it wouldn't have been good even if it were hot," Roosevelt remembered. In Georgia, they received formal queries of a literacy far from the educated world aboard the *Larooco*, and they had fun composing pun-filled replies (which, politely, they didn't send):

> *Can you walk with a cain or some assistants?*
> I cannot walk without a CAIN because I am not ABEL.

None of that mattered. The hamlet was near the bottom of a long mountain ridge which had millions of pounds of magnesium deposits within it. The water that bubbled out and was led into pools was, accordingly, loaded with that magnesium, making it denser than the ordinary water inside human cells. This meant anyone stepping into those pools weighed less and was buoyed up.

Roosevelt found he could support himself standing even in just four feet of water. Then, more wondrously, pressing his arms against the water in the Bullochville pool, he could, while staying vertical, "walk" across the pool; moving "almost as well," he wrote, "as if I had nothing the matter with my legs." This was a freedom Roosevelt hadn't experienced in years, and would be the perfect way to build up the residual vigour in his legs.

Through a local newspaper interview, word went out that Roosevelt was there. Letters began to arrive, followed by people, dozens, then hundreds of them, polio patients from across the country; as one observer put it, "the uninvited, the unheralded, the hopeful, and the all but hopeless."

One of the first to make it to Bullochville (soon renamed, more attractively, as "Warm Springs"), was a 25-year-old from Pennsylvania named Fred Botts. He'd once had a beautiful baritone voice and hoped for a singing career, but at 16 he'd contracted polio. His family, not knowing what else to do, followed a common practice of the time and shut him up in a bedroom on their farm. The music teacher who'd begun giving him lessons stayed away, for no one in rural Pennsylvania knew whether this dreaded disease might be contagious from casual contact or not.

When Botts heard about this distant resort, he had his younger brother help get him onto a train. He wasn't allowed among the other passengers, so spent almost the entire journey inside a wooden cage in the luggage van. When the train stopped at Warm Springs, he was able to call loudly for help. Eventually a guard carried him off.

And it was through coming to know individuals like Botts at the resort, that the "patronizing son of a bitch," Franklin D. Roosevelt—of Groton and Harvard, as his younger cousin Quentin had been—started to transform.

The philosopher John Rawls once wrote about what he called the "veil of ignorance." If you're going to be inserted into an unknown society but don't know what position you'll have—what income, what class, what talent—it makes sense to try to have that society arranged so that wherever you end up, there'll be plausible opportunities and a decent guaranteed minimum on offer for you.

Aristocrats throughout the ages have responded to variants of that argument with boredom. It didn't apply to them, for they knew very well what position they had: they were on top. It's the attitude of the New York real estate queen Leona Helmsley, who famously explained that taxes were for the little people. She wasn't one of the little people, so why should what was unpleasant for them bother her? The great religions have tried to change that, with prophets, priests, bodhisattvas and gurus across the millennia giving their calls for compassion for other people. Their failure rate has been impressively high, for it takes an exceptional person to honestly feel "There but for the grace of God go I." The young Franklin D. Roosevelt, like most of us, had not been an exceptional person.

Now he was.

Botts looked terrible when he arrived. His parents had scarcely bothered to feed him, and he was bare skin and bones. Roosevelt couldn't grasp this. How could human beings shut away their own family? Surely they had enough money to get help?

Roosevelt made sure Botts got a good meal his first day, and the next morning, after breakfast, led Botts to the pool. Already Roosevelt had gymnastic rings and swing bars suspended just above the pool. Attendants lowered the two in—Roosevelt showing no embarrassment at his own weakened legs—and Botts remembers how Roosevelt made him get to work. "It was 'Catch hold of the bar this way . . . now swing in and out . . . Harder! That's it . . . Now again this way . . .'" Afterward, they lay in the sun together beside the pool.

It didn't stop with Botts. "A message came up the hill," Roosevelt recalled of that time, "and said 'Two [more] people have been carried off the train down at the station. What shall we do with them? Neither of them can walk.' Well, we held a consultation and decided that we would take care of them . . . But before we could put the cottage in order, eight others had arrived . . ."

Roosevelt and LeHand put up wall charts so newcomers with no experience of physical therapy could understand how different muscle groups worked. They devised ramps to make getting into the pool easier, and Roosevelt supervised exercises in the pool for hours on end. One of the worst effects of polio was excruciating cramps in the feet as muscles stiffened, and beside the pool, Roosevelt would patiently massage the feet of those who needed it for hours.

Roosevelt had never intentionally treated people badly. It was just that with his privilege, his wealth, any generous actions he'd taken had been from a distance, without a deep connection. Here, his weakened legs bare, amidst dozens of other people young and old transforming through his help—ones he chatted with and sang with and played water polo with—the worlds of his Maine island and the wealthy *Larooco* crowd were far away. Like many men of his background, Roosevelt wasn't ostentatiously religious, but had been raised to know the King James translation of the Bible very well. The famous lines from the Book of Ruth matched what was happening here now: "Whither thou goest, I will go; and where thou lodgest, I will lodge: thy people shall be my people . . ."

At the main hotel, the resort's able-bodied residents had been just about able to handle Franklin D. Roosevelt sitting among them in his wheelchair. His family was distinguished, he was rich, everyone knew his late cousin had been a heroic aviator. But they weren't going to accept these newcomers, and insisted that the new "polios" be forced to eat in the hotel basement. Years later, Roosevelt's son James could recall his father's "cold anger over this intolerant attitude."

Roosevelt knew that his own suffering had been none of his fault. What his new friends suffered wasn't their fault either. He had LeHand pointedly wheel him into the basement. From now on, they would eat alongside everyone else who was in wheelchairs.

Even so, that was only a temporary fix. There were more complaints from the able-bodied; a feeling that the new patients, many of whom had little in the way of funds, just did not deserve the same treatment as their betters. Within months, Roosevelt decided that there was only one thing to do. He was going to violate the strictest rules of his class and use up his inheritance, almost all of it, to buy the whole resort: the pools, the hotel, and over a thousand acres of the land beyond. He'd build new lodges, excellent ones, and hire trained physiotherapists, and create ramps and training facilities everywhere. Those who could afford would pay, and for the rest, he'd have an extra fund to cover their costs. No snobbish previous residents would be able to say no.

He brought Eleanor down to show her his good works so far and discuss his plans. But she hated rural Georgia. It was too hot and too poor, and as on the *Larooco*, there was also that incessant drinking and singing at night, now with even more people, many from the most inappropriate backgrounds. Despite that, at a quiet moment, Roosevelt went ahead and outlined his vision. It would give him a purpose during his rehabilitation, and help others. He'd computed that the purchase would still leave him with a third of his original fortune. What did she think?

Eleanor told him she did *not* want him to do this. It was a terrible idea, and it was too expensive, and what was he thinking?

Franklin prided himself on his poise, but this was too much. He exploded. From a letter Eleanor wrote a friend shortly afterward, we can sense what he said. "He feels," she said, "that he's trying to do a big thing & that all of us have raised our eyebrows and thrown cold water on it."

A few days later, Eleanor was back in New York. She tried to be conciliatory: "I know you love creative work . . . I'm old and rather overwhelmed . . . Don't be discouraged by me." But the truce their son James had once noticed became even colder. In the four years around this period, Franklin was at Warm Springs or other places away from home for 116 weeks. His mother was with him for two of them; Eleanor for two as well. LeHand was with him for 110.

On picnics, they would stretch out together on a favorite bluff they'd found far beyond the town, 1,400 feet up. In his early years of marriage, that was the relationship he might have been able to have with his wife. But with her rejections of his dreams, that was impossible. Roosevelt and LeHand built a cottage together, and they also spent hours talking over their progress with the patients, trying to work out exactly what kind of encouragement would work for each one. Back in Warm Springs, LeHand would type up their notes. On the rare occasions when they had to be apart he wrote to her as Missy; to her he was Effdee (for F.D.).

Franklin loved driving. On the *Larooco,* they'd sometimes hired a speedboat which he would helm, going fast through shallow lagoons; scanning for the stingrays in the clear water below. Here in Warm Springs, he worked with a car mechanic to attach a series of thin rods to his Model T's pedals and push them up through thin holes cut in the dashboard, thus letting him drive entirely through hand controls.

Once Roosevelt was behind the wheel, friends remembered, "he wanted to show that he could go faster than anybody." He'd drive LeHand along the rutted, red or yellow clay roads, her hair blowing in the open air; occasional hints of the *L'Heure Bleue* perfume she liked floating over to his side. Where the trees thinned out, LeHand knew to brace herself, for he'd weave in and out among the pines.

Almost always they'd pull over in farmyards too, or stop by a general store. "[Roosevelt could] talk to a man who didn't have any education," one farmer remembered, "and he had sense enough to talk to the best-educated man in the world. He could talk about *anything.*"

In a stay of just a few weeks, there's time to pick up local color and a few charming stories. But in a stay of months—and Roosevelt spent almost half of the next three years in Georgia—there's time to go deeper. At first, when Roosevelt heard the farmers lament how it was almost impossible to earn a good living however hard they worked, he thought that with a bit of ingenuity, he could do better. Since corn and cotton were unprofitable, the solution, obviously, was to try something else.

But when he took on some more land and hired local managers, nothing he thought of worked. He tried planting fast-growing trees for paper, but they were too resinous for the local mills to buy. He tried cattle, but they scarcely thrived on the soil, and then he tried apples, which failed too. Even growing peaches didn't make a profit—an embarrassment in what was proudly called the Peach State.

It was a humbling experience. The farmers weren't lazy, and they weren't ignorant. It simply wasn't possible to do well here, not with the poor infrastructure at hand. If there were to be any solutions, those would be better roads, or more electricity, or a state-wide purchasing agency; improvements that only larger organizations could provide.

Patients were coming from across the country, and it was in this period that he learned more about city life too. After an afternoon with a young man from the New York slums, "Franklin told me he admired the patience of people under unbearable tenement living—sometimes one water faucet for a whole house—and in some cases the properties were owned by wealthy people who left the care to agents who had no interest but exacting rents."

This wasn't news to LeHand, not after her Boston "Slumerville" upbringing, but it was to Roosevelt. Polio had flung him into a world of limitation and dependence, of vulnerability and curtailed power. It's what finally made him see that others had been there all along.

Dietrich Bonhoeffer, the German pastor, had asked:

> Who am I? They tell me
> I bore the days of misfortune
> Equably, smilingly, proudly,
> Like one accustomed to win.

But also, questioning his innermost identity, he had gone on to wonder, *Am I really that which other men tell of?* Roosevelt, in his own rawness, had finally been forced to question that too: for himself, and from that for others.

Roosevelt had learned compassion. The false bonhomie he'd used to keep so many others at bay wasn't the only way to act. From the large range of potential "personalities" we have within, this is the one that had come to the fore.

That's where we can see Goebbels and Roosevelt shift to such different paths. For Goebbels, the family home in Rheydt, plus the encouragement of

Else Janke, wasn't enough. He'd tried to be more widely generous—"You know, I don't particularly like this exaggerated anti-Semitism"—but he'd had too much resentment from his youth. The claims of fury, of brutality, which radical politics so deliciously could bring out, were too much for him to resist.

Roosevelt was different. Although he'd been cold to those outside his caste, that had only been a part of him. He'd always had layers of decency, and this is what the time in Warm Springs—combined with the encouragement of LeHand ("Missy is my conscience," he liked to say)—brought out.

Frances Perkins had now met Roosevelt several times since his selfishness over the 54-hour bill. The first few times that she'd seen him act more warmly—"more amiable more slaps on the back"—she hadn't been convinced it was sincere. She felt he'd "learned to be nice to people," and that was it. But as the years of polio continued, and especially after the move to Georgia, she felt that a better part had finally come out.

"It's a dreadful thing to say," she admitted later, "but knowing the streak of vanity and insincerity in him, I don't think he would have [become kinder] unless somebody had dealt him such a blow between the eyes."

That's why transitional states are so powerful. In his letters home from the *Larooco*, Roosevelt had been having a fine time, but he also was educated enough to realize it was meaningless. That's why he was ready for what he experienced in Georgia.

Van Gennep's third stage, integrating back into the world, was complete. "There had been a plowing up of his nature," Perkins recalled. "[Roosevelt] emerged with new humility of spirit."

The question was what to do with it. In the early days of his rehabilitation, the few political events he was dragooned into attending had been excruciating. At the 1924 Democratic Convention, asked to give the speech nominating Perkins's mentor, Al Smith, he'd barely been able to make it to the podium. With his left hand gripping a crutch, and his right clutching his son James, "Outwardly [Father] was beaming, seemingly confident and unconcerned, but . . . his fingers dug into my arms like pincers . . . His face was covered with perspiration." When James transferred a second crutch to his father to make the final steps on his own, it got worse: Roosevelt desperately dragging his legs along, the thousands of delegates breathless as they watched.

He did give a superb speech once he made it, but he'd been unable to wave to the audience or make the smallest gesture, having to clutch the podium with both arms to keep from toppling over. Frances Perkins was at that convention, in the front row, and saw how much his hands were trembling from the strain when he was done. She also realized that no one had prepared for his exit. "I saw around him all those fat slob politicians—men—and I knew they wouldn't think of it."

Perkins hurried up, bringing another woman with her, and they stood so they would seem to be congratulating Roosevelt. That way they blocked the audience's view of his struggles until a wheelchair was finally brought up and—still blocked from sight—he could be taken away.

The years at Warm Springs didn't cure his polio, but even slight improvements were always satisfying. Once, when a secretary brought a check for him to sign where he was sitting, he said, "Wait a moment. I want to show you something." He gripped the crease on one trouser leg, lifted hard, and ended up with one leg crossed over the other, looking perfectly normal. "Now," he said, beaming, "what do you think of that!"

By 1928, Roosevelt's ability to walk forward with canes—cautiously, carefully—was so much better that everyone realized what this could mean. Al Smith was planning a run for president, and his team wanted Roosevelt to help the ticket by running for governor of New York.

LeHand didn't think he was ready. "Don't you dare," she said, as they were driving back from the first meeting where this had been mooted. "Don't you *dare*." But he knew it was time, and before long she was convinced too.

He did run, and the race was so close that when he left campaign headquarters at New York's old Biltmore Hotel, he thought he had lost. Only Perkins and his mother remained when the news finally came through, nearly at dawn, that he had won. His administration was successful, and when the Democrats were looking for a presidential candidate in 1932, he was a natural choice. The incumbent, Herbert Hoover, had once been lauded as a great engineer and humanitarian, renowned for his skill in bringing relief to victims of the great Mississippi flood of 1927. But he'd been discredited by his failure to bring the Depression to an end, and his seeming lack of concern for those suffering. Roosevelt was the Democratic candidate in 1932 and won in one of the greatest landslides in US history.

It was a perilous time. America's economy had collapsed, and the social fabric was coming apart. "This country cannot continue to exist as a democracy with 10 million or 12 million people unemployed," one of Roosevelt's closest advisers said at the time. "It just can't be done." To fix that, jobs, employment and social trust would be crucial. The same Frances Perkins who'd seemed so unbearably plebian long before—a woman concerned with the world beneath his class—was, Roosevelt now recognized, exactly the sort of person he needed to fix that. There had never been a female Cabinet secretary, but he'd broken enough precedents to get this far—there had never been a "cripple" in the White House either.

In February 1933, he invited Perkins to his New York town house to offer her the position of secretary of labor. For a brief moment, forgetting what she was like, he might have imagined it would be a polite, pro forma interview. But Perkins wasn't there as a supplicant for secretary of labor: rather, she had questions for *him*.

Her problem was how to be sure that a busy president-elect would keep his word on what they agreed to. Her old red envelope's "Notes on the Male Mind" gave her the needed guide. She realized from it that she'd have to bring a written summary of what she wanted, then state what was on it, list what actions the man she was speaking with would have to authorize, go through the difficulties that were likely to arise, and finally, most importantly, have him repeat what he'd agreed to. It was a technique, she once explained, that worked well with eight-year-old boys.

Here at his town house, she read Roosevelt her list. On it she had items that would be taken for granted by subsequent generations, but at the time were the wildest of heresies: a minimum wage. Maximum hours. Retirement benefits. Unemployment insurance.

"Nothing like this has ever been done before," she concluded. "You know that, don't you?" Then she remembered what her father had taught her: If you have anything to say, say it definitely and stop. So that's what she now did.

When Roosevelt had first met Perkins in the New York state capital, he hadn't "heard" anything she'd said about improving conditions for people in hard times. Warm Springs had changed everything.

There was silence in Roosevelt's until, finally—not looking down his nose at anyone—he nodded agreement. "I'll back you," he said. His inauguration was coming up soon. LeHand was going to be in the White House, and now Perkins would be with them. They had a lot to do. The first hundred days of his presidency were about to start.

CHAPTER 11

NEW DEALER

Hitler's White House Invitation

"We were not against industry making a profit . . . But we were
damned sure they were not going to make an excess profit."

GOEBBELS AND HITLER paid close attention to Roosevelt's election, and at first thought there might be something positive for them there. The affinities between the two countries went deep. Generations of Germans had grown up with the Wild West novels of Karl May, in which a determined German immigrant found America a wonderland of opportunity, ever-expanding into lands occupied by tribes of inferior military technology. In the very first book in the series (several hundred thousand copies of which Hitler saw were later distributed to the German Army):

> "Can you shoot?" asked my companion suddenly.
> "Fairly," I said, not so much, I am afraid, because I was modest as because I wanted to have the fun of letting him find out that I was a crack marksman.

More than five million Germans had settled in America over the years, and it was the American Treasury that had pressured France and Britain to ease back on World War I reparations, thereby boosting the German economy. Everyone knew America's industrial potential—its glamorous skyscrapers—and trade between America and Germany was strong.

Both countries were looking to powerful leaders to help them out of the Depression. Roosevelt took office on March 4, 1933, just weeks after Hitler was named chancellor, and almost immediately invited him to the White House. "I am very interested in developments in America," Goebbels declared on the radio, its shortwave broadcasts reaching the world. "I believe that President Roosevelt has chosen the right path. We are dealing with the greatest social problems ever known."

Most of all, in Goebbels's eyes, more recent similarities were auspicious too. American legislation enshrined the inferiority of selected racial groups. There were strict penalties for sexual relations across those lines, and rules were in force almost everywhere keeping Black and Native American people in their place.

In recent years, racial tensions in America had become stronger. Immigrants from Eastern Europe were mostly blocked from entering the country. Lynching was increasing, with organized mobs of thousands often gathering to watch. In forward-thinking circles, it was a matter of pride to forcibly sterilize individuals deemed to be weakening the genetic pool, with California alone arresting and sterilizing about 1,000 "undesirables" each year in the 1930s. In Virginia, one state official remembered, "Everyone who was drawing welfare then was scared they were going to have it done on them. They were hiding all through these mountains, and the sheriff and his men had to go up after them . . . They'd run them down in cars to Staunton [the state hospital] so they could sterilize them."

When it came to Jews, matters also seemed encouraging from the perspective of Germany's propaganda ministry. Opinion polls showed the majority of Americans didn't think Jews should be granted equal rights (and in one Roper poll, 10 percent thought they should be expelled from the country). Top universities such as Harvard and Yale officially restricted their numbers, and when a propaganda official from Nazi Germany visited Harvard the year after the inauguration he was greeted with acclaim.

Roosevelt hadn't come out and attacked Jews in his inaugural address, but he had disparaged bankers, which experts in Germany considered a promising sign that he would go further.

All of this was a misreading. Roosevelt was fundamentally different from what Germany's new authorities thought. He and LeHand were especially repelled by the public book-burning Goebbels had organized in May 1933, just two months after his inauguration.

For a moment, Goebbels tried to finesse that, having his ministry lie about the burnings, saying that they'd been spontaneous acts by a handful of students. One of the authors whose work was burned was the deaf and blind Helen Keller, much beloved in America for her work as a suffragist, anti-racism campaigner, and advocate of birth control (when that was still largely illegal). When she wrote an open letter to German students criticizing the burnings—a letter that ran on page one of the *New York Times* and in numerous other American newspapers—Goebbels had his ministry add that none of her books had been burned.

This made no sense. Everyone knew Goebbels had organized the burnings; his own ministry had bragged about it. Hundreds of witnesses had seen Keller's books thrown in the fires, and again his propaganda ministry's own cameramen had filmed it. Although that tactic of reversal worked well at home, in America, it just led to ridicule. Before long, Goebbels realized that Roosevelt wasn't going to encourage the trends in America he and Hitler liked. If anything, Roosevelt was diminishing them. The offer Roosevelt had made for Hitler to be honored at the White House was never taken up, and Goebbels began to shift the propaganda ministry's line to a new message: It might be true that America's past business success had been impressive, but that was an empty shell.

Goebbels made sure that Germans saw how impoverished America was. Pictures of people forced to live in shelters made out of oil drums—and in the Depression, these weren't hard to find—were distributed everywhere. He also explained, repeatedly, that instead of there being one sensible, streamlined authority running everything— as Hitler and the new Nazi elite would efficiently run Germany—America showed its weakness through democracy's typical failed mix of squabbling authorities: unions, state legislatures, big business, independent professional associations and the like.

As the years went on after Roosevelt's 1933 inauguration, the differences seemed only to get greater. Not only were glorious new roads built in Germany, but the work was carried out immediately, unquestioningly, as soon as the leadership ordered. Courts in Germany did what the government told them, while Roosevelt couldn't even overturn rulings of doddery old men on his Supreme Court.

Nor could Roosevelt create anything resembling an army, the fundamental currency of national strength. By the end of 1939, America was able to support perhaps five full army divisions in the field; Germany was on track for 136. American equipment was so sparse that, in large-scale maneuvers which the promising Colonel Dwight Eisenhower was helping run in Louisiana, troops often had to use wooden sticks to simulate rifles (and trucks with large brooms strapped on top to simulate tanks). Many of Germany's divisions, by contrast, were equipped with the latest tanks, and ready for fast *blitzkrieg* assaults.

This weakness was only to be expected. America, Hitler insisted, was "a half Judaized and Negrified society." In a sarcastic article entitled "The Cross-Examination of Mr. Roosevelt," Goebbels explained that Roosevelt wasn't really running America. He was merely a mouthpiece for "the pious nonsense of the Jewish-led plutocracy." It was unconscionable "that such a man has the impudence to judge us."

Goebbels's propaganda ministry went on to hint that Roosevelt hadn't been weakened by polio, but by syphilis. He was being sucked dry by Jews around him. He was soft, wasting his time with feminine ideas about fairness and decency and kindness. He had even appointed a woman to run crucial homeland policies—Frances Perkins—and another woman—LeHand—was known to be a crucial Oval Office gatekeeper.

How could such a man turn a mongrel nation around?

Goebbels's was a typical underestimate of the strength that decent sorts can have. Roosevelt's experiences hadn't made him weak. On the contrary, they'd made him strong. The years in the wheelchair, when his only interaction with others had been through words, had boosted his determination. "You go in there and see FDR wanting to tear him apart," one senator remembered. "You come out whistling Dixie."

In every respect, they were now fully different. Goebbels had emerged from his transitional stage stuck at home in his twenties as a man who relished violence and tried to exacerbate divisions in Germany. But when Roosevelt emerged from his *Larooco* and Warm Spring years, he was insistent on following all the approaches to enhancing fairness we've seen, with their surprisingly powerful "constraints" included. As Roosevelt wove the main pillars of action together, the best of our koan-style guides were back. This is telling for our own world, where similarly big resets to shift society in a fairer direction are so desired.

NOT SILENCING, BUT LISTENING

Goebbels destroyed Germany's independent press. He wanted information to pass in one direction only: outward from those in the Nazi innermost circle, whose insight it was forbidden to question. In the White House, by contrast, at the start of each day, propped up against his pillows in bed, Roosevelt liked to skim through his country's independent press: the *Herald Tribune* with its grand pedigree, but also the *New York Times*, the *Wall Street Journal*, the *Washington Post*, the Chicago papers and others.

This took a thick skin, for most newspaper proprietors feared what he was doing, and the editorials they pushed in their pages generally matched. He didn't, however, charge them with being part of a *Lügenpresse*—a lying press—nor did he surround himself with yes-men who agreed that every critique was wrong. Why would he blind himself that way? It was important to know what opponents were thinking. In any event, their actual reporters often disagreed with their proprietors, and the news pages were filled with observations and facts he needed to know. He had aides prepare a daily package of clippings from yet more papers, again with instructions not to spare him from negative remarks.

In person, Roosevelt was easy with journalists, bringing them in to sit casually around his desk each Wednesday and Friday in the Oval Office and having informal conversations with ones who were especially well traveled or knowledgeable. He was also famous for listening at length, his welcoming smile putting guests at ease, to the great range of people that LeHand and others led to the Oval Office (even if he drove them to distraction with his vagueness in actually following up on what they thought he'd agreed to).

He knew he needed to be supremely well informed. Jump-starting employment across an entire continent was going to be no easy task. It was, as one adviser put it, "As if the Aztecs had been asked suddenly to build an airplane." Keeping a sharp eye on Germany and Japan's expansion—and not falling for biased, pro-Communist reports coming out of Moscow— also needed multiple, independent information sources. Roosevelt wouldn't possibly jeer at experts as Goebbels and the rest of Germany's leadership automatically did.

The key was to be confident enough to ask questions. After one briefing, he said he was still confused and couldn't grasp why there was such a difference in how old versus new mortgages were being treated; could somebody fill him in? Another time, after listening to a phone briefing about an economic issue, he mumbled agreement, then hung up, thought about it, and quickly called back. "I don't understand it yet."

The one time Roosevelt did fall into an authoritarian reflex and try to shut down an institution simply because it opposed him shows how much those temptations exist. The Supreme Court at that time was deeply out of date. One of the justices, James Clark McReynolds, had been born before the Battle of Gettysburg; four others were of the same vintage. They'd grown up in a world of privilege and hierarchies, several serving as corporate lawyers, and they hated anything that threatened what they knew. McReynolds, for example, would never mention Roosevelt's name, but just refer to "that crippled son-of-a-bitch in the White House."

When the justices blocked one too many New Deal initiatives—including laws that protected 15-year-old girls from being exploited in sweatshops— Roosevelt decided that they could use some upgrading. He proposed a bill to expand the court's membership, thereby diluting the reactionary votes.

The temptation was understandable, but that way dictatorship lay. It was precisely because the court might take decisions opposed to the executive that the Constitution had made it a separate arm of government. Roosevelt's bill was slapped down in Congress, and although he sulked like a child—wasting political capital trying to defeat congressmen who'd opposed him—he finally accepted the rebuke, and never strayed that way again. The fact that he was used to self-restraint in his own life helped. These are the circumstances that keep us in one channel or another. America luckily was spared seeing what he might have become, unfettered by such restraints.

NOT UNDERMINING, BUT GIVING

Next for the generous giving that others, from refined Ursula Graham Bower to the crotchety contractor Paul Starrett, were so good at. Roosevelt knew he needed a lasting system to protect workers from the worst fluctuations of the market. In the city of Chicago, the visiting writer Edmund Wilson was startled to see hundreds of old people, many who'd clearly spent their lives working hard, reduced to scrabbling through garbage dumps to get enough to live on ("digging in with sticks and hands . . . [even] in hot weather, when the smell was sickening and the flies were thick"). But what would the new system be, and how to get it enacted?

Useful guidance arises when someone sees a new opportunity opening up, and has a sensible understanding about how to use it. Elites and much of the middle class in America in the 1920s had been locked into the belief that raw capitalism was best. With the Depression, however, the country was adrift, vulnerable, briefly open to change.

When Roosevelt had been in that same state in his first years on the *Larooco*, LeHand had helped him. What he wanted to do now was transfer that on to his entire country, shifting it in a more generous direction. Various forms of social security had already been put in place in Europe, and aspects had even been tried out in the USA by distant cousin Theodore a quarter-century before. Roosevelt didn't explicitly lay out a goal to "modify social security so it could spread more widely in America," but that was at the heart of his thinking. Frances Perkins would be the natural choice to carry that goal forward.

On the surface, that might have seemed straightforward. When Perkins had been an investigator with New York State's industrial commission, she'd stood up to rock-throwing strikers, and even went undercover to break up a group that had stockpiled dynamite to use in their fights. "You sure had your nerve," a sheriff of New York County told her when she emerged. "It was risky business." Not a lot fazed her. The White House was different, however. When the first meeting was called, four days after the inauguration, FDR hobbled in on crutches, then with help settled at the head of the table. Perkins, as labor secretary, was all the way down at the far end.

"I could see that they were all looking at me," she remembered. No woman had ever served in the Cabinet before. "I kept perfectly still." The conversation started up. The Cabinet officers reported by order of seniority on the state of their departments. Perkins was last, and when it was her turn everyone looked to her.

And she couldn't say a word.

Her whole life had been building up to this. The night after she'd met Roosevelt in February to get his sign-off on her goals, she'd cried in her bed, terrified at what the publicity would do to her teenage daughter. Perkins's husband had spent much of their married life in and out of mental asylums, and in that era, she'd had to keep this a never-whispered secret. Even without that she was being criticized—by men and women alike—for daring to focus so hard on a career.

Here, in this attractive Cabinet room, the sun coming in through oval windows, she knew she had to go ahead, that if she didn't speak, she'd be letting everyone in her life down. "I had been taught long ago by my grand-mother that if anybody opens a door, one should always go through . . . The door might not be opened to a woman again for a long, long time." But this was such an intimidating setting. The senior Cabinet officers continued star-ing at her. "I think some weren't sure I could speak."

The silence went on.

It's always wise to give nervous subordinates some easy success to begin with. Roosevelt understood that if there was one certainty, it was that Perkins would be prepared. He'd certainly been on the receiving end of her lengthy listings of injustices before.

Here, in the Cabinet meeting, as she recalled later, he smiled her way. "Frances, don't you want to say something?"

It was the opposite of Goebbels crushing his own staff, sending them off to prison when he was dissatisfied with them, or even when he was just toying with them. With Roosevelt's encouragement, finally Perkins was off. She was working on plans for a federal employment service, she said, and now confidently laid out the data for them to consider. Vice-President Garner, a Texan most suspicious of females in power, puffed away on his cigar while Perkins spoke, all the facts and statistics now pouring out. He was gruff in her presence, but later admitted to his wife, "She said it loud enough so I could hear. She said it plain and distinct."

It was a good start, but Roosevelt knew that always being encouraging is just as unhelpful. Creativity doesn't come from constant encouragement. It comes from *selective* encouragement, and that means blocking what's wrong. In one of the next Cabinet meetings, Roosevelt stopped Perkins cold when she started listing construction projects in New York to support. She had to realize those projects were never going to get political approval, he said. Interior Secretary Harold Ickes flinched at seeing a woman treated this way—he was hard on her—but for Roosevelt, it wasn't personal, merely the pointer he needed to give if she was to get anything done.

His guidance was needed several times more. Perkins was experienced in the necessary skills of political infighting, but Roosevelt by this time had become an expert. This especially came out in what was going to be the centerpiece of the new administration's accomplishments: a social security system that would help the aged, the poor, the unemployed. Two of Perkins's specialists on this complex topic, the stately, dark-haired Edwin Witte and the glamorous, red-haired Berkeley economist Barbara Armstrong, had strong disagreements about how to proceed.

Witte was convinced Armstrong didn't know what she was talking about. He said so. Armstrong felt Witte didn't know what he was talking about. She said so too: repeatedly, vigorously, and—where possible—using leaks to the press to let others know. The fact that she began to call him "half-Witte" delighted reporters.

Roosevelt knew Perkins had to stop this, but his blunt instructions to her in Cabinet about construction projects hadn't been typical. He didn't want to hurt her feelings, and, to be honest, remembering her firmness back in New York State—pushing child labor laws, marching into rough factories he'd avoided—he was still probably a bit scared of her. He often tried to have others deliver difficult news on his behalf. On one occasion, Perkins remembered, chatting with her after a Cabinet meeting, Roosevelt ever-so-casually asked, "Did you hear from my missus?"

"Yes, it's bright of you to communicate with me like that," Perkins answered. Cabinet officers aren't supposed to be sarcastic to their president, but in cases like this, he deserved it. Roosevelt had asked Eleanor to deliver a difficult message about strategy to Perkins.

"I meant to tell you myself," he stammered, "but the more I thought of it, the more I didn't see how I was going to do it."

Finally, though, Social Security was ready. Perkins outdid herself in constructing it so that workers felt they'd personally paid for the benefits by a tax directly on their wages. Roosevelt appreciated that ingenuity. Payments that go only to the poor can easily come to be rejected by the majority. But payments that in principle go to everyone are more deeply embedded. Perkins and Roosevelt hoped it would future-proof their bill, undermining appeals to go back to more coldhearted, winner-take-all times. And since the benefits felt deserved, not a handout, in 1935, Social Security passed.

It was one of the high points of American civilization: ending extremes of poverty, and soon underpinning a stable middle class that endured for nearly half a century. Roosevelt knew he was lucky enough to have a majority in both houses of Congress, but he also was skilled enough to take advantage of that for the widest possible good. Without both in operation—the setting and the skill—any noble sentiments would have faded away.

Perkins wasn't going to abuse Roosevelt's trust, but it was important to recognize that others might. Here he had an excellent head start, for in his years at the Navy department in World War I, he'd dealt with a tremendous number of crooks, drawn by the sweeping profits available on warship contracts, and he'd come to recognize their type. He relished such stories as the one about the Texan poker shark who leaned across the table and said to his mark, "Play the cards fair, Reuben. I know what I dealt you." Now, in his own presidency, he knew skillful auditing would be indispensable, and to his pleasure, soon found an administrator who was a master of that art: the tall, slender Iowan Harry Hopkins.

One of Hopkins's friends described him as combining "the purity of St Francis of Assisi . . . with the shrewdness of a race-track tout." This was not metaphorical. "Many of his important staff conferences . . . were held in automobiles en route to or returning from the Maryland race tracks."

Hopkins knew that the smell of billions of fresh-printed dollars, in the Depression, was going to be near impossible for local political machines to resist for long. Roosevelt had given him the general guidelines he needed to go ahead, but how best to carry them out? He began, like the Empire State Building managers, by sending out auditors to check funds weren't being diverted, and then sending out independent auditors to check the original ones.

Then, in reflective breaks at his racetracks, he came up with better ways. The greatest weak spots were in buying equipment for the workers on the New Deal's many construction projects, and then in actually getting salaries to them. Well, why not piggyback on the payment networks which the Veterans Administration (VA) had in place? Those were already tried and tested. And for that matter, when it came to buying construction and other equipment, why wait for a myriad of state officials to do the procurement when hundreds of nice, ripe army warehouses were waiting across the country, stuffed with useful equipment already?

Hopkins's staff were delighted. They'd been drawn to government to help others, and now they had the chance. The army's Lieutenant Colonel John C. H. Lee, studying Hopkins's office while this was going on, saw that there was none of the yelling and screaming from on top he'd taken for granted on army bases. "Assistants address Mr. Hopkins fondly as 'Harry,'" he wrote, his surprise still clear. "There is no rigidity or formality, yet he holds their respect, confidence and whole-souled cooperation."

All Roosevelt's generous acts came back to help. Great numbers of army officers and VA officials had already seen how his programs had been helping the country, often the very neighbourhoods or rural districts they'd come from. They were only too happy to help Hopkins in return.

Since Roosevelt had been temperate in his interventions to fix the economy, as war neared, top businessmen were happy to join the government. But although he and Hopkins loosened regulations—so that, for instance, investment in machinery could be offset against tax—they also listened to experienced military auditors as the contracts were given. "We were not against industry making a profit," the general Roosevelt appointed to run the negotiations said, "but we were damned sure they were not going to make an excess profit." None of this would have worked if Roosevelt hadn't set the right model from the top. At the time of Hopkins's death a year after the war, although several hundred billion dollars of disbursements had gone through his offices, the personal cash savings Hopkins had totalled $15,000.

Roosevelt himself put all his own money in a blind trust, and when news came out that his son James had been using a White House position and the family name for personal gain, he insisted James release his income tax returns, and saw to it that he was not employed in any way at the White House again. According to William O. Douglas, who first delivered the news, Roosevelt bowed his head in sorrow for a long time at his desk in the Oval Office when he heard how his son had fallen.

NOT ATTACKING, BUT DEFENDING

From the time Roosevelt first took office in 1933, he knew America was caught in the most dangerous of situations. As one of his supporters remembered, "Revolution is an ugly word to use, but I think we were dangerously close at least to the threat of it."

It didn't help that part of America's ruling elite, including many people Roosevelt grew up with, had always looked down on the masses. "This country should be governed by the people who own it," John Jay, first chief justice, famously said. And when Roosevelt's programs did start putting people back to work, *Fortune* magazine sniffed, "It creates for [its recipients] the fiction that they are still useful citizens."

There were riots and sometimes shooting as people fought against corporations that used mass unemployment as an excuse to lower wages even more; against sheriffs and sometimes national guardsmen who tried to enforce the sale of farms to banks that had scooped up distressed mortgages. Ever more armed troops were brought out in the Midwest, in San Francisco, in steel towns.

It wasn't only in Goebbels's Germany that one could find individuals eager to bring out the worst that lurked within. Potential Caesars like Douglas MacArthur were on the loose, along with demagogues like Huey Long from Louisiana and the popular fundamentalist Gerald L. K. Smith. "I'll teach them how to hate," Smith said. "Religion and patriotism: keep going on that. It's how you get them really het up." On the Capitol steps, double lines of police stood guard, carrying rifles; the sole way that Congress could safely meet. America needed to be protected, reconfigured so those dangers wouldn't get worse, and the economic problems that triggered them were brought to an end. But even in those emergency defenses, Roosevelt insisted on proportion.

Goebbels had criticized financiers as a conspiracy of blood-sucking vermin. Bankers in America were similarly little-loved (especially when, after creating the conditions for the Wall Street Crash, they asked the government to rescue them). On the one hand, Roosevelt knew that he had to stop their excesses. He pushed to end insider trading, and set up agencies giving homeowners time to catch up on mortgages and other debts that could make them lose their properties. Since the worst frenzies had begun when investment houses started gambling with ordinary account-holders' money, he encouraged Senator Glass and Representative Steagall in introducing legislation that blocked investment banks from scooping up retail banks to pilfer.

But that was as far as it went. Bankers weren't bloodsuckers. They were human, and their jobs as worthwhile as everyone else's. "Capital must

be invested in enterprise," Roosevelt said. Making a fair profit while doing
so was good for everyone. It's just that it was to be done "[without] the
manipulation of professional gamblers" from now on. Because Roosevelt's
instinctive habit was to be proportional, it was easy for him to open gateways. Bertrand Russell once said that if you declared all Englishmen were
fools, you'd be attacked by an irate nation. But if you said that 90 percent
of Englishmen were fools, then everyone in the nation would comment on
your perspicacity; how had you managed so well to recognize the idiots
they were surrounded with?

By not insulting businessmen as a category in the early years of the
New Deal, Roosevelt had avoided making the heads of America's greatest
corporations feel they were pariahs. Die-hards would never be persuaded,
but there were many waverers, including the chief executive of General
Motors, who were won over.

Roosevelt had also known it would help to get the backing of at least
some Republicans. This too is the opposite of Goebbels's approach, where
turning on anyone who isn't fawningly on your side is always right. He'd
justified Hitler's murder of the storm troopers' leader Ernst Röhm in large
part on the grounds that Röhm might become a political threat. In the very
period of Roosevelt's first months, numerous German political leaders and
union officials who resisted Hitler's new government were arrested and sent
to the newly created Dachau concentration camp.

There were plenty of voices in America that wanted to do the same.
Huey Long had been broadcasting on the dangers of leaving opponents
on the loose. Roosevelt, however, took the most public possible way to
show he was at ease with Republicans who weren't blindly obstructionist:
he appointed three of them, from the Republicans' moderate wing, to his
Cabinet. (Eisenhower, elected as a Republican president two decades later,
similarly appointed a prominent Democrat to his first Cabinet; John F.
Kennedy, his successor and a Democrat, selected two Republicans for his
Cabinet as well.)

This wouldn't work in all circumstances. Sometimes people who dislike
you are never going to change, and Roosevelt knew when only force majeure

made sense: against enemies such as Germany; against the most recalcitrant of big-business lobbyists and their paid-for congressmen.

Justice McReynolds of the Supreme Court—the one who would only refer to the president as "that crippled son-of-a-bitch"—hated Roosevelt's civility. He disliked the very idea of trying to bring Jews, Blacks or women into the category of those who deserved to be treated fairly. One year McReynolds cancelled the official photograph of the court when he realized that he might have to sit next to Louis Brandeis, who was Jewish. When a Black attorney, the brilliant, Harvard-educated Charles Houston, was arguing before the court, McReynolds turned his chair around to show he wasn't going to listen to him, either. Whenever a woman was pleading a case, he would walk out.

Reconfiguring a Supreme Court is an intentionally slow process, dependent on existing justices dying or retiring, and then a presidential appointment approved by the Senate. Luckily, in the issue of McReynolds's behavior, although sections of the right-wing press encouraged him, even the Murdoch-like owner of *Time* magazine recognized such closed views were wrong, and the resulting social pressure moderated him a bit (as photographs of McReynolds sitting, albeit unsmiling, near Brandeis in later years show).

Roosevelt's reflex was to be implacable when necessary, but otherwise almost always offer redemption. In his time, there were a great number of settings where it worked, even at home. His wife, for example, had been a bigot when she was younger, once saying she wouldn't read a particular book because the author "was such a loathsome little Jew"; another time writing about a luncheon guest that he was "an interesting little man, but very Jew."

Franklin was not impressed with those views, yet instead of rebuking her directly, he let her get to know that luncheon guest a little better. It was his friend Felix Frankfurter, Harvard professor, stalwart of the New Deal (and later, to McReynolds's further distress, outstanding Supreme Court justice). Spending time with Frankfurter, Eleanor, to her credit, changed her attitude and in later years became a great advocate for those downtrodden in life.

When the Daughters of the American Revolution (DAR) refused to let the Black American contralto Marian Anderson sing at Washington DC's

Constitution Hall, Roosevelt didn't attack them as out-of-date elitists either. Although he defended Anderson—helping arrange for her to sing at the Lincoln Memorial instead; inviting her to the White House during an official visit from King George VI—when he later addressed the DAR, he made his points with a humor they could join with. How curious it was, he said, that both he and they were descended from immigrants. But none of them should be ashamed, it had happened "through no fault of their own."

What he was saying, in the gentlest possible way, was that if it wasn't their fault their ancestors had been on the *Mayflower*, it certainly wasn't something they could take much credit for either. He wasn't weak in doing this—he ensured Anderson sang, and at the most glorious of venues. But here again, the door was open for those who'd opposed him to switch.

There was a further wisdom here. Each time Roosevelt told a joke at his own expense, or protected a singer like Anderson, he was giving himself solid practice—a miniature navigational fix—in the way he wished to act. That's how we get habits to lock in. It was a good model for his nation too.

. . . AND INCLUDING

Finally, there was Roosevelt's use of the powerful corollary to skilled defense: widening, universalizing, including. Instead of Goebbels's rallies with screamed-out threats against enemies, almost immediately upon taking office, he'd begun a series of quiet fireside chats delivered over the new national radio networks.

His tone was easy, relaxed, inviting. "My friends," the first radio speech began, "I want to talk for a few minutes with the people of the United States . . ." By itself, that could simply be an effective way to deliver propaganda, but the content of what he said was different. There was no resentment against mysterious opposition forces, no cascade of abuse and vilification. Everybody was going to be brought inside.

Religion was as great an issue then as now. Along with bringing political opponents into his Cabinet and treating bankers as fallible humans, Roosevelt happily told one interviewer that " . . . in the dim past [my ancestors] may have been Jews or Catholics or Protestants. What I am more interested in is whether they were good citizens and believers in God." In the most extreme possible rebuke to anti-Semites, both German and domestic, he selected numerous Jewish advisers; in a rebuke to racists at home, he appointed America's first Black district judge, and had Black advisers regularly visit the White House.

Roosevelt was far from perfect, and often gave in to the great number of Democratic congressmen who abhorred racial mixing. His liberal supporters were appalled when he stayed neutral as Southern Democrats in the Senate ensured that a bill to block lynching never passed. There was no ethical basis for his inaction, simply power politics. He needed the votes of those racists to get the bulk of his New Deal legislation through.

The point about the power of fairness when skillfully applied held again: every nation—just like every individual—has different potentials waiting inside it. In America of the 1930s, great racism still existed. When the Black Olympic star Jesse Owens came to New York one week, for example, he was forced to use a side entrance at the luxury hotel where he was staying. But great openness also existed: Owens was in the city because of a ticker-tape parade in his honor, where he had been cheered on by hundreds of thousands of New Yorkers, Black and white alike. Goebbels aimed his ministry to bring out the worst in his people, but Roosevelt was aiming to bring out the best: not a single, favored in-group, but a nation that could widen to encompass everyone.

The idea is one Roosevelt knew well from his intimate knowledge of the Bible. A covenant arises when different parties come together and agree to share a task—possibly a lifelong one—yet in it none crush the others. Marriage, famously, is a covenant; a business with genuine esprit de corps approaches that too.

The United States was designed to be a covenant as well (the word "federal" coming from the Latin "foedus," which in the Latin Bible translates the original Hebrew word that is rendered in English as "covenant"). It's an excellent solution to Hillel's paired questions, of how to get the balance between oneself and others right. Roosevelt was aiming to restore that balance in a grievously divided America, widening inclusion in a way everyone could support. As with Nadella's much later turning around of Microsoft, there's growth that way, but it's a harder path than the one Goebbels chose, of simply pressing the button of mocking others, of insisting that every relationship is zero-sum.

Again it didn't always work, even when the ideal was there. Roosevelt had wanted New Deal money to go equally to everyone who needed it, in addition to being used to raise standards. But once Southern Democrats in Congress saw that Hopkins was serious about enforcing the minimum wage rules, they rebelled. Their price for keeping the New Deal going, they said, was to end the nonsense that Black Americans in their states should be included in the same regulations as everyone else. Roosevelt, to his shame, again gave in.

He also underwent a William Bligh-style shift after Pearl Harbor. No doubt boosted by fury at the damage to his beloved fleet, he overruled his FBI director J. Edgar Hoover, who explained that Japanese Americans presented no threat. Instead, Roosevelt ordered that all Japanese on the West Coast be arrested and detained without trial far away in the Western deserts, even if they were US citizens subject to Constitutional safeguards. Nor did he quickly change course when any immediate threat of Japanese invasion had ended. Although some individuals were allowed out—especially volunteers for the US Army, or farmers needed for harvests—he stuck to this misguided policy almost to the end of the war.

Luckily, such actions were rare. Roosevelt could be cantankerous, and had those very flexible notions of keeping his word. But aside from socialites who considered him a class traitor, and the portions of the business community that never accepted profits couldn't come first, almost everyone felt with reason that here, finally, was a president on their side. Despite his partial surrender to Southern Democrats, Black Americans shifted their traditional support from Lincoln's Republican Party to Roosevelt. One millworker explained the feelings shared by many: "Mr. Roosevelt is the only man we've ever had in the White House who would understand that my boss is a sonofabitch."

.   .   .

Watching from Germany, Goebbels found America's efforts laughable. When war began in Europe—America still on the sidelines—Germany had more modern planes than all its enemies combined. The Reich's labor leader, Dr. Ley, issued commands, and Germans followed them. Everyone knew what would happen to those who resisted.

America had no such central authority as Ley. When a new factory for military aircraft near Detroit put out a call for workers, for example, one Kentucky woman wrote to the managers explaining why it wasn't for her. "I am very sorry I dident get to work in your plant. But Sir I was up their alone and dident know no one. And dident have eny Place to stay. Even for the one night. So I cam back home . . ." Elsewhere, there were sit-down strikes, top executives refusing to work with the government, and even some so hating Roosevelt that they preferred to invest in German factories helping the Nazis instead.

Here too Goebbels was wrong in thinking this only meant weakness. The strikes carried information about what was acceptable and what wasn't. When working conditions were modified to take that into account, the workforce became more productive, not less.

That particular Kentucky woman couldn't find housing, but only because production was expanding so quickly. In 1940, the site, called Willow Run, had been a maple tree farm. A year later, one of the world's largest factories was standing in its place, tooling up to produce heavy bombers, the manufacturer having been limited to carefully audited— albeit substantial—profits. As with the efficiencies in Hopkins's offices, this maximized the funds available for the other new factories and shipyards being built across America.

Most of all, Roosevelt prepared for war by ensuring inclusion. Procurement of machine tools and other resources was to adhere as closely to the original goals Roosevelt had laid out for Hopkins as possible. Partly from guilt at what he'd let happen with the minimum wage, he pushed hard to get Black workers and Black-owned companies treated equally with everyone else in the new wartime contracts. As a result, one ethnic group after another saw their lives transformed for the better. What they contributed shot up.

"More important than the vast works of strategic importance built," one of Hopkins's closet friends wrote, ". . . were the things saved from obsolescence within the workers themselves." That was the ever-widening covenant's heart: the richness an "injection of fairness" can achieve.

All of us are shaped by our companions, yet we usually have a choice in who those companions are going to be. Goebbels preferred the thuggish volunteers in his local Nazi party over the friends of his Jewish sweetheart. Roosevelt ended up with Harry Hopkins—a gentleman to the tip of his fingers—living in the White House as his closest adviser. Even in the earliest auditing, Hopkins had instructed his staff going around the country to "Go talk with preachers and teachers, businessmen, workers, farmers. Go talk with the unemployed, those who are on relief and those who aren't. And when you talk with them don't ever forget that but for the Grace of God, you, I or any of our friends might be in their shoes." Goebbels hadn't cared that he was unfair to the people he attacked in such vast numbers. Hopkins's wider application of fairness would have meant nothing to him.

LeHand was living at the White House too, and was the same good soul she'd been on the *Larooco* and in Warm Springs. Indeed, she and Roosevelt often made a point of visiting Warm Springs together, a respite from dealing with the calculating politicians of the capital. Roosevelt knew that he'd draw sustenance from this refuge which had brought the better side of his nature to the fore. In Washington LeHand was busy—the "Swiss Army Knife of the White House," one biographer put it—engaged in supervising Oval Office communications, as well as who had admission (in honor of which, she'd added two more charms to her bracelet: a tiny diary, and an equally tiny mailbox, with working door and flag).

She and Roosevelt swam most mornings, and after the 7 P.M. drinks with others, they would often end up together. The importance wasn't just whatever physical intimacy they shared. It was their values. Although LeHand was a devout Catholic and Roosevelt at most an occasional Episcopalian, both had wanted the Bible at his first inauguration to be opened to 1 Corinthians 13: "And now faith, hope, charity, these three; but the greatest of these is charity."

They believed that those words of Paul to the Corinthians, along with the world's other great moral traditions, were constraints no mortal should dare to break.

PART SIX

WAR

CHAPTER 12

HOW GOOD PEOPLE SUCCEED

Payback

("To sow, is to reap")

"The Dutch are the most insolent people in the entire West! . . .
Their bishops . . . incite the people to open opposition."

BY DECEMBER 1941, the differences between these two worlds were coming to a head. Here's where we'll see Roosevelt's reflex of decency and resultant fair approach working, and Goebbels's opposite approach—despite its initial successes—finally imploding.

At the start of that month, Goebbels, as we've seen, had everything an unemployed doctoral graduate could have wished for. He controlled almost all newspapers, films, theater, newsreels and radio in Germany. With typical immodesty, he gloated at his success. "Film production is flourishing almost unbelievably . . . What a good idea of mine!" Since Hitler was giving fewer speeches, Goebbels had progressively taken over that role, regularly addressing the country, to massive, enthusiastic acclaim.

In the west, his country's troops were safely dug in on the Atlantic coast. In the east, German reconnaissance patrols had advanced close enough to

Moscow apparently to see the towers of the Kremlin through their binocu-
lars. Goebbels's home was a palace by Berlin's Brandenburg Gate, designed
so that he only had to take a single set of stairs to the vast propaganda
ministry alongside.

He would "trip up the steps like a little duke," one of his secretaries
remembered, "through his library into his beautiful office." He wore "suits of
the best cloth, and always had a light tan. He had well-groomed hands—he
probably had a manicure every day . . . Sometimes his children came to visit
with the family's lovely Airedale. They were very polite and would curtsy and
shake our hands." We've seen how people can pivot in different domains. To
his children, he was warm and considerate. His references to them are pretty
much the only entries in his diary where he shows warmth to anyone. But
that's perhaps understandable. The children—and the lovely Airedale—were
already under his total control.

Most satisfyingly—for he really had come to hate Jews—Goebbels
had been able to keep a lid on news of the work German troops, police
and local auxiliaries had already accomplished during their advance. Any
sentiment he'd felt for Janke or her family was long since forgotten. Even
before the largest battles on the Eastern Front, an officer Goebbels knew
well had organized a mass killing of Jews near Riga. Crowds who'd received
his propaganda helped a bit, making sure that children and those who
were disabled couldn't be hidden away, but most of the work was done
by armed men, indoctrinated for years by Goebbels's smooth, deep voice.
They forced groups of Jews together and shot at them for fun while leading the rest, terrified, into the forest, then systematically killing thousands
in vast pits. Several women managed to get out—half-naked, wounded,
begging for mercy—but, to Goebbels's satisfaction as he read about it, they
too were then killed.

There were a few difficulties he had to keep an eye on. The army's cen-
sors were letting through too many letters from front-line troops complaining
of the cold outside Moscow. That would have to be stopped. There also were
continuing reports of Russian and Ukrainian partisans attacking German
supply trains. Stern measures would have to be taken there. But England

was weak, and Russia was now weak, and America, run by that ridiculous Roosevelt, was not even in the war.

And then, in just seven days, everything Goebbels was so proud of began to collapse.

On the night of Thursday, December 4, German sentries in the bitter Russian winter outside Moscow began to hear an ominous noise. Unbeknownst to them or their officers, the Soviets had managed to transport eighteen divisions of fresh Siberian troops across the country. The new troops had proper winter clothing, often camouflaged white; they were backed by tanks and aircraft and—the Soviet specialty—rank after rank of heavy artillery. The noise got louder until these troops attacked out of the night and ended up breaking through the German lines, threatening the entire army with encirclement.

The following Sunday, December 7, the largest fleet Japan had ever assembled attacked America's naval base at Pearl Harbor, deep in the Pacific. The US immediately declared war on Japan.

What was Germany to do?

There was no treaty forcing Germany to back Japan (and the German government had little problem ignoring treaties that weren't to its advantage). Churchill recognized how precarious the situation was, and he always said the next few days were among the most anxious of his life. America's attention was on Japan, and there was little popular support for declaring war on Germany. If the US did indeed devote all its effort toward the Pacific, Germany would have a chance to regroup in Europe, and then, after dealing with Russia, could turn its full might again on Britain.

The world's experienced foreign correspondents all understood that. They were telexing in or broadcasting their reports. But Goebbels's insistence that any paper that disagreed with him was the *Lügenpresse*, the "lying press," meant that once he obtained power in 1933, he had closed down his country's independent newspapers.

It was an extraordinary act—willfully blinding an entire nation—and then he'd gone further, making it illegal even to listen to foreign broadcasts, and above all the BBC. The edict applied to everyone, government ministers included. He knew that a few officials would try to get around that, but he was ready to block them. "It is really amusing," Goebbels wrote in his diary, "to see how ministers now approach the Führer, asking his permission to listen to foreign radio stations." He ensured almost all those requests were blocked.

It was satisfying to hold back information the army might need. "I am permitting," Goebbels noted in his diary, "only two copies of the [monitoring service] transcripts to go to the Armed Forces Supreme Command." There was one ministry that would be granted an exception, naturally enough— his own propaganda ministry—"but that is nothing to worry about, since I indoctrinate [staff] daily, and there is no possibility of their becoming gradually infected."

Since so few people outside his ministry had any independent sources of information—and for those who did, Goebbels's vicious tongue meant they were scarcely going to say anything—it was natural, when he met with Hitler on December 9, to privately agree on what had to be done.

Germany was going to declare war on the United States.

This was a catastrophic choice, but Goebbels had helped create a world-view where Hitler's decision made sense. Everyone "knew" that America was run by Jews, and Roosevelt was just a front man. Goebbels's propaganda ministry had promoted that line after all, non-stop, for years. But although Jews were all-powerful and omnipresent, they were also, Goebbels and his ministry had insisted, weak and enfeebling. That mix had gone all the way back to his *Der Angriff* editing days, slurring the Jewish military veteran Bernhard Weiss in the Berlin Police. No country that the Jews ran could, accordingly, be fundamentally strong. When Roosevelt had spoken about multiplying America's output for the war effort, he had been deluded.

In blinding the nation, however, Goebbels had blinded himself. Two days later, on December 11—a week after the counterattack outside Moscow—Hitler stood before the huge metal eagle relief in the Reichstag and announced to the world that Germany was now at war with America.

"What can the USA do faced with our arms capacity?" Goebbels sneered. "[Roosevelt] will never be able to produce as much as we, who have the entire economic capacity of Europe at our disposal!"

He was about as wrong as it's possible to be. As the businessmen who ran Roosevelt's war production boards (most taking a nominal one dollar as pay) and others worked their magic in America—as women joined the labor force and contracts were skillfully audited for corruption; as Italians and Scots and Hungarians and Irish came together in factories and shipyards, and underemployed engineers were brought back to work, and great numbers of those previously scorned Black workers revealed their skills in factories and as production foremen—the resultant production dwarfed what Goebbels could have imagined.

The Battle of Britain in 1940 had been fought in aerial combat between a few dozen or at most a few hundred planes at a time. Total available aircraft reserves were about a thousand fighters on the British side, and perhaps twice that with the Germans. In contrast, the US constructed 47,000 military aircraft in its first year in the war, and once forces of that quantity were brought to bear, the entire air war would inevitably shift balance. By 1944, the US was producing more planes than Germany, Japan, the UK and Russia combined. Shipyards that, prewar, had typically taken in the region of 200 days to complete a cargo ship now turned them out in under a month, and when working around the clock—full construction teams with arc lights above them—in under two weeks. (And although America's prewar army had been weak, its navy was one of the strongest in the world.) The Willow Run factory outside Detroit was also in full operation now, producing vast B-24 bombers, at its peak a finished one appearing every 63 minutes.

Goebbels had constantly mocked Roosevelt's talk of trust and love as weak. But in these most important matters, when worker commitment and wide buy-in was needed, then—once skillfully channeled by Hopkins and others—the effects of Roosevelt's approach were overwhelming.

In the spring of 1943, Germany had over 200 U-boats in the Atlantic, and was sinking about half a million tons of merchant shipping a month. Most of the submarines' successes took place in a large mid-ocean gap, outside the reach of conventional shore-based planes. To counter this, sixty B-24s—less than half a week's output from Willow Run—were modified for ultra-long-range flight and sent to help deal with the problem. These behemoths were able to cruise for 18 hours at a stretch, carrying hundreds of depth charges, and a dozen heavy machine guns. At this period, before the development of usable snorkels, submarines had to spend most of their time on the surface. They were also slow: submerged, the submarines traveled at the pace of a man walking; on the surface, they could go as fast as a bicyclist. Once the planes' massive searchlights and radar were switched on, any submarine caught on the surface was going to be overwhelmed. This strategy successfully complemented other defensive measures, to the extent that in May, Admiral Dönitz withdrew his entire U-boat fleet from the North Atlantic, leaving the route clear for Britain's resupply. And Willow Run was just one of very many factories across North America.

One by one, the principles that had brought Goebbels up in the world began to destroy him. The feedback loops—whose consequences he'd so long scorned—were closing in.

When unjust people lose, this is how it happens.

He'd amused himself thinking up scurrilous nicknames to mock Jews, and relished it when that helped force them out of the country. But more than half the German scientists who'd been awarded Nobel Prizes in the years since World War I were Jewish. When he'd forced Jews abroad, he'd shunted many of his country's best scientists and engineers into the hands of his future enemies.

Ernst Chain, for example, was a patriotic 27-year-old German biochemist who'd been so brutalized in Berlin for being Jewish that he fled to Britain. While Goebbels was managing to sustain a mood in Germany that led to Chain's mother and sister being murdered, Chain himself, working in Oxford with a dedication one can only imagine, was playing a central role in the creation of penicillin: a drug that saved lives in the British and American armies, not the German one. Nor was it only Jewish scientists that Goebbels's vituperation forced away. The Italian Enrico Fermi, a lapsed Catholic, was the gentlest of men. But when he saw how Germany's racial attitudes were spreading—and from a dislike of bullying, as well as to protect his Jewish wife Laura—he moved across the Atlantic, first to

New York's Columbia University, then Chicago, and then Los Alamos in the New Mexico desert. There, he and his students were central to the construction of the atomic bomb. Other European scientists, following similar paths, created breakthroughs for the Allies in radar (including types the submarine-hunting B-24s used), in metallurgy, in aerodynamics and other militarily useful fields.

Goebbels couldn't see the link. As the war went on, he knew that German submarines were failing ever more at sea; that countermeasures against British and American aircraft were failing too. In 1943, the chairman of the German Physical Society explained to him that this was because "Anglo-Saxon physics has completely eclipsed us." "The report is very depressing," Goebbels wrote, when he received the study. But what had caused this eclipse? A brave official in the education ministry suggested it might have been "the continuous public attacks on science, especially by the Party." Goebbels would have none of that. "I don't regard this objection as well founded," he jotted, before turning to other matters.

Goebbels had also delighted in creating division. He and other pure Germans were on the inside, everyone else was on the outside: weak, inferior, deserving only contempt. In preparing Germany for its invasion of Poland, for example, he piled on the abuse in speeches, newsreels, articles; Slavs were dirty, brutish, far inferior in energy and intelligence.

This was spectacularly misjudged. Goebbels and Hitler had destroyed Germany's once-great science departments in Göttingen, and it was Poland now that had the world's finest centers of mathematics. Logicians in Warsaw were creating concepts which would help lead to modern computers; the school associated with the great mathematician Stefan Banach in the city of Lvov developed the functional analysis used in the quantum mechanical calculations integral to constructing the atomic bomb; younger mathematicians at the University of Poznań had started working out the secrets of the Enigma coding machine.

Where once that might have helped Germany—the two countries had engaged in a number of alliances in recent years—now all Poland's surviving skills went to Britain, France and America. The Enigma work famously was passed on to British intelligence and helped jump-start Britain's code-breaking complex at Bletchley Park. Experienced Polish flyers trained their new RAF colleagues and downed over 200 German planes in the Battle of Britain.

Goebbels's glee in mocking outsiders also helped ensure his country's occupation of Europe went badly. For what did Germany have to offer the countries it occupied? In the view he'd promoted so skillfully for years, the world was in Darwinian struggle. Relations between nations were zero-sum. For one group to rise up, another had to be forced down. It was important to remain suspicious, guarded, untrusting; always ready to treat others as mercilessly as you would expect them to treat you. This was not a recipe for lasting support. Yet Goebbels was surprised at the resultant ingratitude from occupied countries and neutrals alike. In his diary for just a few months in the middle of the war:

> . . . The Swedes sent us an exceedingly insolent reply to our last note . . . The commentaries which appeared in the Swedish press about it outdo each other in impudence!
> . . . Events occurred in Copenhagen that are more than shocking. Acts of sabotage against Wehrmacht barracks and communication installations increase day by day . . .
> . . . The Führer did not succeed during his talk with [Hungarian regent] Horthy in convincing him of the necessity of more stringent measures. He continues to resist every effort to tackle the Jewish problem!
> . . . According to reports from Norway, now even the Nasjonal Samlng [the avidly collaborationist Quisling government] has become obstreperous . . .
> . . . Within [occupied Poland] conditions are in some respects quite chaotic . . . Assassinations, acts of sabotage, and raids by bandits are on the increase . . .
> . . . The Slovenes are now in open rebellion. They have gone almost entirely over into the camp of the partisans.

> . . . The Dutch are the most insolent and obstreperous
> people in the entire West! Their bishops have had a pas-
> toral letter read from the pulpits, in which they incite the
> people to open opposition . . .

And even, in unimaginable miscomprehension:

> . . . Lapper sent me a summary of conditions in
> the Ukraine . . .
> Our officers there have not succeeded in spurring the
> Ukrainian people on to collaborate with us . . .

Goebbels had nothing to offer Germany's main allies either, aside from the chance of military spoils. Once that became less likely, their fervor disappeared. He had shown them his solution to Hillel's questions—he was choosing maximum national selfishness—and they, quite fairly, were choosing no gratitude back.

A year after the declaration of war on America, for example, German troops deep in Russia were struggling to take the city of Stalingrad. Their flanks stretched for hundreds of miles, and depended on Romanian, Hungarian and Italian troops to defend them. But those allies knew the Germans despised them. They also were far from home, it was astonishingly cold, and armed partisans who hated them were everywhere.

It didn't help that they had also seen what Germans, indoctrinated by years of Goebbels's ministry, did to women before they killed them. One Italian artillery lieutenant, appalled, felt this "disqualified them in my eyes from membership of the human family." An Italian general who understood his men wrote that 99 percent of them "not merely expected to lose the war, but fervently hoped to do so as swiftly as possible."

The Soviet general who'd led the counterattacks in Moscow the year before now repeated a similar maneuver on the flanks far outside Stalingrad, sending yet more Russian divisions rushing in from the wind-howling terrain, aimed at these foreign troops.

"We ceased to be an army," the Italian artillery lieutenant remembered. "I was no longer with soldiers, but with creatures obedient to a single animal instinct: self-preservation."

The Romanians collapsed; deserting when they could, surrendering en masse when they couldn't. The Hungarians and Italians fell apart. The German Army, which only held parts of Stalingrad, was left isolated, with the bulk of its forces soon either killed or captured. Few of them left Russia alive.

Goebbels was disgusted with his allies, the Romanians, the Hungarians, the Croats, the Slovakians and most of all the Italians. "The only thing certain about this war is that Italy will lose it!" he'd written. "We always were too accommodating." All those nationalities were incapable of demonstrating the valour a true martial race possessed.

This too was wildly incorrect. Italians weren't going to fight for Germany, and many had mixed feelings about Mussolini. In America, however—under a president who had declared to the Daughters of the American Revolution that "All of us, and you and I especially, are descended from immigrants"— they would fight, and famously so. The US Army was weak at the start of the war, yet a fearsome weapon by the end. And who composed it? Of a total of 12 million GIs, an estimated 1.2 million—a tenth—were Italian Americans: crushing Germany's once-vaunted armored forces in France, and then across the Rhine.

Germany's problem was one inherent to empires built on race as opposed to ones built on potentially wider covenants, where agreements can be willfully selected. Germany's allies were ingrates in Goebbels's view. But as with the occupied lands, they'd been given nothing to be grateful for: they could not be allowed "inside" in any way at all.

Norway, for example, was ostensibly run by one of the most fervent of regional collaborators, Vidkun Quisling. But when Quisling's supporters in Norway proposed calling him a *Foerer*—the Norwegian cognate of Führer— Goebbels slapped that down. "There are certain terms that we must absolutely reserve to ourselves!" he declared. The label Führer was "not to be applied to any other person than the Führer himself."

For the same reason, no other state could call itself a Reich. "The whole world must in future understand," he wrote, "that by Reich is meant only the *German* Reich."

The US alliance with Britain was the opposite. The two countries squabbled as might be expected—a planet wouldn't have been large enough for some of their generals' egos—but they shared deep, universal values. Goebbels's delight in bullying was no part of it.

When Harry Hopkins was Roosevelt's emissary to Churchill in the dark, early days before America's official involvement in the war, he finished a dinner toast with the same lines from the Book of Ruth we've seen before: "Whither thou goest, I will go; and where thou lodgest, I will lodge: thy people shall be my people, and thy God my God." Then he added, very quietly; "Even to the end." One can't conceive of emissaries from Hitler and Goebbels's Germany wishing that to any foreign leader they had to ally with. Nor could one imagine them collaborating on weapons development with their allies, as Britain and America so famously did.

There are yet other ways to succeed, of course. Stalin's Russia took an entirely different path in foreign relations, in treatment of occupied lands, in brutality toward its own troops. The point again is merely that different ways often are possible—and Germany's way, for the deep reasons we've been seeing, in the end did not prevail.

As Goebbels and the Nazis stuck to the harsh principles they'd used on their way up, they lost out on what Roosevelt and many others had gained. Goebbels was typical of the regime, in addition to being a driving force. If he'd wanted to bring back any of the more decent principles we've examined, it was too late. Instead of listening, he'd closed down the sources of information he would later need—that left him blind. Instead of giving anything to those beyond his limited core constituency, all he'd done was grab: possessions, freedom, where he could, life itself. And instead of defending himself proportionately, fairly, he'd always lashed out to excess—stirring up resentment and repelling possible allies.

It's possible he could have acted differently if there had been some institutions to correct his errors, to push him back toward competency, even within his demented goals. But Goebbels had already done everything he could to help Hitler destroy those institutions. The independent courts, independent legislators, independent universities all were gone.

Through it all there was his hatred of wider inclusion. Instead, constantly, he loved creating divisions through violence, crushing those he could exclude and seeing them squirm. In his rise to power, this lashing out had been delightful, satisfying, often thrillingly fun. (This was when he had written "String 'em up, string 'em up!'" with such glee in his diary.) But it was attractive only because his early targets had often been weak: women out shopping, an elderly orphanage director near Rheydt, at worst a group of trade unionists to be fought by a storm-trooper mob.

Lashing out at the Red Army was a different matter.

The German General Staff was exceptionally competent, but had roused an entity it couldn't stop. The setback at Stalingrad was just the start of the catastrophes. The next year, 1943, still on Russian soil, Germany engaged in the largest tank battle in world history. They lost; Russian soldiers—each of whom knew what Germany had done to their homeland, and now had ever more skillful leadership—won. Even at that point, some form of stalemate might have been enforced on the Eastern Front. But in 1944, Russia's improved staff launched Operation Bagration: 1.4 million hardened men, along with 5,000 tanks. It was one of the decisive battles of all time. Russia's force faced Germany's Army Group Center—the anchor of the Eastern Front that protected the most direct path to Berlin—and annihilated it.

"At the moment, things look very bad on the Eastern Front," Goebbels had once written in his diary. "Troops lost a lot of equipment Our retreats are no longer orderly." He noted that a success "would considerably brighten the scene," but had to admit that wasn't likely. "It gives one the creeps to look at the map and compare what we had under our dominion about this time last year with the distance we have now been thrown back."

His reflex at every defeat was to attack his generals. During the earliest setbacks outside Moscow, his diaries record, "I talked at length with

Martin"—Goebbels's liaison to the Army High Command—"and asked him to inform me of all officers who are guilty of fostering defeatism, and to make a written report on them!" This didn't do much to help the army, and merely led to Heinz Guderian, Germany's most skilled tank commander at the time, being removed from active service. Later, Goebbels had some hope when the Grand Mufti of Jerusalem helped organize an SS detachment of Muslim volunteers, but soon even he had to admit those volunteers were ineffective in combat.

And then, first from over the horizon, then ever closer, the "Judaized and Negrified" Americans, along with British and Canadian and, before the end, most-determined Free French forces, began to move in from the west. The Soviet–German battles had been titanic, but on their own might just have led to a stalemate. Western supplies—and these vast armies, along with years of bombing—did much to tip the balance.

All of this was Goebbels's nightmare come true. Mongrels, subhumans, were destroying his Reich! Some of the fighter pilots shot down turned out to be Negro-Americans. How were they operating highly complicated machinery? There were pilots with Polish names and Italian names as well, many of whom had destroyed one German plane after another in the air. How could these inferior humans too fly so skillfully? Then remorselessly, as the ongoing technical breakthroughs in Britain and America made it harder to bring down the fighter planes, ever more bombing raids were getting through: massive flotillas of vehicles high up in the sky, while Goebbels couldn't remain outside even to glare at them. When he took shelter, "the pressure was so strong that even our bunker, though constructed deep underground, began to shake . . . Air raids hang over us like fate."

What he discovered was what we've seen before: that reality bites back, that what's happening in the outside world can be blocked for a while, but not held off indefinitely. The consequences of our actions swirl around to come back. Bonhoeffer had described

> Struggling for breath, as though hands were
> compressing my throat.

For him, that pressure had come from forces he comprehended, and knew he was greater than. To Goebbels, flailing, it came from a terror that made no sense. Always before, he had been able to insist that reality was what he said it was. But now that failed.

Each time he emerged from his bunker, the damage was worse. "Fires have broken out again in many places," Goebbels recorded, "so that Berlin is still ablaze . . . One can hardly pass through the streets, so deeply are they covered with debris." The whole world was going up. "Last night it was Frankfurt's turn to suffer heavy attacks." Far away in the Rhineland, Rheydt's textile factory and surrounding homes had long since been destroyed.

Under the stress, Goebbels fell back on all the approaches that had served him so well before, applying them with greater desperation. What other tools did he have? There were more attacks on underlings, more complaints that everyone else was letting him down, more attacks against outsiders. The implication of not blaming others—the very idea that he could have been at fault—was impossible to bear.

Sometimes he would rummage in his files for memories of his old *Der Angriff* time and reminisce about those days of his first, unexpected success. There were more speeches and radio events and—when pauses in the bombing raids allowed—public spectacles; more calls for the destruction of the Jews and pleasure when he heard they were being killed. He had to get everyone to understand. "[To] ask why are there any Jews in the world . . . is exactly like asking why there are potato bugs." The image of parasites was pervasive. Every species of creation, political broadcasts insisted, was always trying to replace its enemy. Fall behind, and they will replace you. "[Only] the nations which first saw through the Jew are going to take his place in the domination of the world. There is no other recourse for modern nations than to exterminate the Jew."

This also explained his enemies. To Goebbels, Roosevelt was a secret Jew, patently, and as to Britain, "The English are a very peculiar people. They are obdurate to a degree that gets on one's nerves in the long run." The reason was now obvious. "They are the Aryans who have acquired most of the Jewish characteristics."

To distract the population, Goebbels tried changes of attention, just as he had before. At one point, he led a crowd of thousands at Berlin's vast indoor sports palace in a call-and-response speech where he thrilled them by asking, "Do you want total war?" He paused for a moment to drag out the suspense, pressing his hands behind his back as if he were thinking it through. Then he picked up, leaning forward. Fast now, more emphatic: "If necessary, do you want a war more total, and more complete, than anything you could possibly imagine?!"

None of it worked. Although Goebbels had been proud when the last Jewish children in Berlin had been rounded up to be killed, even here his satisfaction was incomplete. Some humane habits in others kept on coming out. "Unfortunately our better circles, especially the intellectuals, once again have failed to understand our policy about the Jews. In some cases they have even taken their part! A lot of Jews slipped through our hands. But we will catch them."

Nor was the bombing getting any lighter. "War in the air is become more and more bitter . . . Conditions in the city are pretty hopeless," he jotted again in his diary. His own home was still standing, but almost all the windows and doors were gone. "I get up at an ungodly hour with my head throbbing, but there's no heat or water." Having once prided himself on being so perfectly manicured—shaved and besuited as he strode into work—now he had to scuttle into the ruins of the propaganda ministry to find a place to shave and wash and change. "The last raid on Essen causes complete stoppage of production in the Krupp Works . . . We are learning to accustom ourselves to a primitive standard of living."

After the D-Day landings, Goebbels was promoted once more. Along with running all propaganda, he now was in control of the entire economy, as Reich Plenipotentiary for Total War. He bragged as always, having one of his newspapers declare that "Reich Minister Dr Goebbels is the soul of our defensive operations." But it wasn't going to make a difference.

Germany's military production had more than doubled since the start of the war, and Britain's tripled. America's, however, had gone up twenty-five times. The numerous strikes in American factories—something inconceivable in Germany—had turned out to help, not hinder. Roosevelt and Perkins had pushed through legislation which ensured that workers and managers had to meet, with compromises enforced on both sides.

In those negotiations, pay went up, but not so much that owners couldn't still make good profits. The strikes were also often about poor working conditions, and when those were fixed, the outcome was the positive motivation which skilled managers—such as the Empire State Building's Starrett earlier—always elicited among their workforce. The nation's structure was becoming one where the best in human nature could come out.

That's what the New Dealers' approach to industrial growth produced. Germany, by contrast, was herding great numbers of foreigners into their factories, sometimes as forced "volunteers," often as slaves. Terrorized by their foremen, and hating their overlords, they worked about as enthusiastically as one might imagine.

Nothing in the German domains matched Willow Run, which by the late stages of the war had upped its B-24 production yet again. Hundreds of shipyards were operating, with the largest of them producing big, ocean-going cargo ships seemingly nonstop. LeHand had passed away by then, her heart condition leading to a series of strokes (after the first of which Roosevelt rewrote his will, giving her half the income from his estate; he hated seeing her so weakened). In 1944, Roosevelt too was very ill, and had only one more year to live.

It didn't matter. The supplies America poured out were fed efficiently into the Allied fighting forces. All American logistics for Western Europe were under the control of the man who'd learned so much admiring Hopkins at work: once lieutenant colonel, now General J. C. H. Lee. America had provided the RAF with 13,000 fighters; it was also providing half the aviation fuel used by the Soviet Air Force, and over 300,000 fast, sturdy trucks with which the Red Army was hammering in from the East.

Occasionally, Goebbels did grasp what was going on. "Morale among the masses is so low as to be rather serious." But what was the reason? "I am somewhat confused . . . We were so great and resourceful in [propaganda] at the time of our struggle for power! Why can't we achieve mastery in this art now? . . . We simply must do something to offset this American munitions propaganda."

Less than seven years before, when Goebbels had initiated the November 1938 attacks against Germany's Jews, he had taken a break, scanned the horizons, and noted with satisfaction "a blood-red sky" from the synagogues burning. Now, in his diary, he described looking up again. It was war all right: War more total, and more complete, than anything he could have possibly imagined. "One industrial plant after another has been set on fire. The sky above Berlin is bloody, deep red . . . I just can't stand looking at it. What a life we are leading!" Shortly after, just days before the war's end in Europe, Goebbels killed all six of his children before committing suicide himself.

THE REPAIR OF
A BROKEN WORLD

OUT OF THE rubble, out of the ruins, America and Britain could have imposed a conqueror's peace in the West: taking what they wanted and leaving their enemy bereft. That has been the way of most great powers through history.

But the western allies created a different world.

The fairness Roosevelt had worked to increase under his presidency became the model for the postwar system. There was the General Agreement on Trade and Tariffs (subsequently the World Trade Organization), under which small nations could take stronger ones to court, and win. There was the Marshall Plan for postwar reconstruction—the quintessence of generosity, building on the opposite of zero-sum suspicion. There was NATO, a potent guarantor of defence without aggression, the World Health Organization, and much more.

The ideals were far—very far—from being always fulfilled, but on the whole, the result was decades of prosperity, safety, trust. Nations that had been at each other's throats found resentment sliding away, with gratitude for what could arise from working together taking its place.

That, of course, is over. Life is askew, and the world is far from the right way up. Much of that was inevitable. Public memories usually last only about as long as a single long life, so it's no surprise that the safety mechanisms Roosevelt put in place began to be lifted away.

A half-century after his time, protection from the more unscrupulous of financial manipulations was taken away, then even later—over seven decades after Roosevelt's death, into the 2020s—the alliances between democracies on which postwar safety had depended were left to weaken too.

What had been happening on the personal level matched that. Jobs became ever more insecure, as indeed increasingly did relationships, neighborhoods; trust more generally. It was the world Thucydides once described, where "The strong do what they can and the weak suffer what they must." In this setting, many of the worst traits we've seen will succeed. The sort of person drawn to the opportunities which that opens up—Dostoevsky's "gentleman of jeering physiognomy," eager to "reduce all this reasonableness to dust with one good kick"—never goes away.

Yet along with those lurking dangers, all the strengths we've seen remain available too, however battered our societies have become, be that from economic turmoil or dangers from the natural world. This is what's consoling. There are plenty of terrible people in the world, as always, but they're in a minority. Far more are neutral, swayed by whatever appears successful. When systems are set up to make life harder for the worst sort—and what they hate most of all is seeing their unscrupulous or ineffective actions revealed—then everything positive we've seen can pour out: the transmission of accurate information, extra gratitude to wield, fresh sources of creativity, enthusiastic alliances.

Doing that takes skill; to find the middle way Hillel so eloquently highlighted. It's hard in times of stress, and as noted, the details will always need to be worked out afresh. Disagreements on what's desired will inevitably remain. That's the nature of human society, and why this is an art not a science; why the self-mastery to ensure we don't let our personalities shift as much as Bligh did is crucial too.

But the stories we've looked at—from Türeci and Şahin's comforting tea to Roosevelt's soul-changing reflections at Warm Springs—show us how to begin.

READINGS AND
REFLECTIONS

THE CHAPTERS IN this book build on a multitude of thinkers who've reflected on the questions that the simple term "fairness" opens up: what it might be, and what it's been thought to be, how it's been achieved, and how it's been blocked. This guide is for readers who might want to explore some of those topics in greater depth. I'll mix that with a few of the background sources for particular chapters; I'll also go over some of the decisions I made about putting this all together. (And even though I'll try to keep the numbers down, I'll **boldface** a baker's dozen that readers might especially enjoy curling up with.)

Many of these discussions hinge on whether we think humankind is good or bad. The Bible, of course, is majestic in exploring both sides, with accounts such as the story of King David (start at Chapter 16 in the First **Book of Samuel**) revealing how this tears apart even the individual soul. Such duality is at the center of much later literature and memoir, extending into a prison camp's depths, as with Solzhenitsyn's *The Gulag Archipelago*:

> If only it were so simple! If only there were evil people
> somewhere insidiously committing evil deeds, and it were
> necessary only to separate them from the rest of us and

destroy them. But the line dividing good and evil cuts
through the heart of every human being.

That's what the recognition of ambiguity in the introduction picked up on; the entire Bligh story at the pivot of this book in Chapter 7 as well.

Classical authors were fond of writing life stories that encouraged us to land on the better side of this line, and Plutarch's *Lives* was yet another model for this book, with its ingenious pairing of biographies; with the way he reveals character not through abstract descriptions but through recounting deeds. The failure, alas, of such guides over the millennia—on to the many Renaissance handbooks of manners they inspired—has, as noted, been impressive to behold. Despite these setbacks, the more optimistic of our modern social scientists have continued showing how deeply aspects of decency are available both within us and our societies, and there's much to be inspired by in Adam Grant's *Give and Take: Why Helping Others Drives Our Success* (2013), Nicholas Christakis's *Blueprint: The Evolutionary Origins of a Good Society* (2019), and Rutger Bregman's *Humankind: A Hopeful History* (2020), with its terrific account of a real life *Lord of the Flies* that turned out not at all as the novel of that name suggested. (Throughout these notes, I'll focus on readily accessible recent books. Their bibliographies, plus online sources, can quickly bring readers up to scratch on the earlier literature.)

A complication is that what authors such as Plutarch counted as noble wasn't necessarily what their soon-to-be-invaded neighbors did. A Roman emperor might be considered magnificent for expanding the state's frontiers; we today are just as likely to consider the villagers on the other side of the frontier who were killed in that expansion. The questions that raises about the possibility of finding a universal standard also fill countless shelves. Who's to say when one person's gain outweighs another's loss?

Jonathan Wolff's *Introduction to Moral Philosophy* (2018) examines philosophy's amassed literature here in a refreshingly lucid way. It goes nicely with his *Ethics and Public Policy* (2019), where he shows the sense in seeing ethics not as a set of axioms to be put in tidy order, but tools to engage the world with—in other words, more like medicine than like physics. Amartya Sen's

The Idea of Justice (2009) is similarly pragmatic, calmly showing how much we can care about injustice, even when we're not quite sure what perfect justice might be. It's the approach I took in this book as well.

Isaiah Berlin was warier in what he thought possible, and since he had a brilliant mind—plus dictated most of his work—his published writings are charmingly readable. His *The Proper Study of Mankind: An Anthology of Essays* (ed. Henry Hardy and Roger Hausheer, 1997) makes about as strong a case as possible for never pushing too hard for social reform in any one particular direction. But yet, the limitations of a largely cloistered existence come out in comparison with a man whose life was far rougher, yet whose voice is the very definition of well-based decency: George Orwell. In a way that's hard to pin down, Orwell's own collected *Essays* (ideally the Everyman's Library edition, selected and introduced by John Carey, 2002) are more realistic than those of Berlin or a number of similar thinkers. In the course of Orwell's essays, faith in the common man—on which the quest for fairness depends—isn't a cold, logical premise. It's what life itself reveals. That feeling stretches across William Blake's simple, haunting *Songs of Innocence and of Experience*—a work which, along with Plutarch, also helped my structuring of this book. There are many books on Blake and his times, but Tracy Chevalier's 2007 novel *Burning Bright* outdoes almost all in—as much as anyone can—getting into that extraordinary visionary mind.

Even after a plausible goal is set, a gap is likely to open between what's intended and what ultimately takes place. Partly that's simple psychology. We have a great capacity for calm, logical reasoning, yet an equally great capacity for utterly ignoring what our fine minds suggest. A further, emotional source is usually needed to push us forward. The idea spans world literature, from Dr. Seuss to Alexander Pope's *Essay on Man*—"On life's vast ocean diversely we sail, Reason the card [compass], but passion is the gale." It's become increasingly central in social science research, for which Daniel Kahnemann's *Thinking Fast and Slow* (2011) is a catchy, highly readable starting point. Maximilien Van Aertryck and Axel Danielson's short documentary *Ten Meter Tower* (2016) goes well with that. Short-listed for an Academy Award with good reason, it's a 16-minute look at different people trying to jump off a high diving board, compulsively capturing the instant when each is trying to overcome their fears. (Here and throughout, videos or documents without a specified source are readily available online.)

Another reason goals frequently elude us is that actions at one level rarely translate directly to the same quality of action at a higher level. The point is often associated with the eighteenth-century Anglo-Dutch writer Bertrand Mandeville, whose *Fable of the Bees* described a world where preening bees worked so hard showing off to each other that their hive ended up active and prosperous. When the bees became more decent and restrained, it weakened and began to die. The idea is that what seems selfish on the individual level—such as the drive for profit—can turn out for the good, if it unleashes an initiative that in a larger society benefits everyone. Later conservative thinkers often took that to mean all efforts at political reform would fail; FDR's teams, such as Labor Secretary Frances Perkins, responsible for Social Security, simply concluded that it meant legislation had to be constructed carefully so that such second-order effects could be taken into account.

To make the underlying logic clearer, I arranged the first few chapters of this book to be ones where direct effects could dominate, thereby letting the inner dynamics of listening and of giving be seen in nearly pure form, what Max Weber would have called their ideal type. By the time I reached the Graham Bower story, however, more complex moral twists were building up—here whether her actions were needed at all, given India's near-inevitable independence—and by the Microsoft chapter, the problem of judging couldn't be avoided. If a large corporation is on the whole good, then someone who helps it can be judged as equally good; if the corporation is not, then—our cigarette company examples—those who help it are not. As with the question of universal standards, when does a consequential goal make up for a local injustice? It's a core topic in artificial intelligence ethics these days, for highly targeted bots are similarly not designed for taking into account anything but their preset goals, something a certain sort of old-style corporations have long demonstrated.

These are the trade-offs that Machiavelli was so concerned with. It's a shame I only had the briefest space for him, as the Machiavelli of history is far from the monster that selected quotations can suggest. Erica Benner's *Be Like the Fox: Machiavelli's Lifelong Quest for Freedom* (2017) has great detail on this complex man pondering his life even as it's taking place, deciding that yes, duplicity and terror might be necessary if it's the only way to keep an entire city-state safe. Alexander Lee's *Machiavelli: His Life and Times* (2020) takes that further, gracefully working in an understanding of the entire era. And Philip Bobbitt's *The Garments of Court and Palace: Machiavelli and the World That He Made* (2013) emphasizes that although the plain reading of some of Machiavelli's more cynical remarks is impossible to escape; in the full context of his life, responsibility always comes back to the individual conscience. There's no prearranged listing of actions we can automatically follow and then say that we're done.

Ancient writings of many traditions have been there before, and I've often thought of the timeless claim, in Deuteronomy 30, about the sort of guiding vision which:

> . . . isn't hidden from you, neither is it far off. It is not up
> in heaven, that you could say, Who shall go up for us to
> heaven, and bring it to us, that we may hear it, and do it?
> Neither is it beyond the sea, that you could say, Who shall
> go over the sea for us, and bring it to us, that we may hear
> it, and do it? Rather the word is very close to you, in your
> mouth, and in your heart, that you may do it.

It's the opposite of the ideas behind the word "disaster," which picks up on Renaissance and earlier Greek notions of fate being written in the stars (the "astres," as in the English "astrology").

There's a deep respect for individuals in that Deuteronomy 30 view, even ones at the bottom of the social heap. It's a topic blurred in many classic utilitarian writings, but dealt with magnificently in Eric Auerbach's *Mimesis:*

The Representation of Reality in Western Literature (original edition 1946; many later editions).

Let me now go through my book section by section.

INTRODUCTION

Harvey Weinstein's trajectory from the top of Hollywood to the ignominy of a prison cell—a fall triggered by his own arrogance, yet needing a shift in society's attitudes to take place—is well charted in Ronan Farrow's *Catch and Kill: Lies, Spies, and a Conspiracy to Protect Predators* (2019), and in *She Said: Breaking the Sexual Harassment Story That Helped Ignite a Movement*, by Jodi Kantor and Megan Twohey (also 2019).

The "What shall it profit a man" question is from the Gospel of Mark, while the assertion that abstract principles can only take us so far—and that beyond this the particulars of each case will take over—is at the heart of Aristotle's work. For readers fond of analytic prose, there's little better than an afternoon with suitable liquid refreshment and that author's **Nicomachean Ethics**, particularly the early books within it, where the intermediate paths which this wise Greek of 2,300 years ago found best in one set of circumstances after another are laid out. There are many guides for steering through his other works, and for a start I'd recommend Edith Hall's crystal-clear *Aristotle's Way* (2018).

Türeci and Şahin's approach matches Aristotle's vision—keeping to key principles while adjusting them as local circumstances required. It also neatly matches the mRNA they worked on, which similarly carries well-constructed yet transitory information to where it can initiate needed actions. The parallels shouldn't be too much of a surprise, given the recurrent patterns in our own thought. It's a running motif in reminisces from two of mRNA's main discoverers: for François Jacob, I'd recommend his intense, meditative *The Statue Within* (ideally the 1995 edition); for the more whimsical Sydney Brenner, see the long series of online interviews with his old friend Lewis Wolpert (start with number 66, on Francis Crick).

For Türeci and Şahin themselves, an excellent snapshot of their world just before the pandemic is the lengthy F-1 prospectus for BioNTech's American IPO in late 2019 (available online); see especially the sections on "Risk Factors" and on "Business." In addition, I benefited from talks with the venture capital community, past employees, regulatory officials, as well as background profiles in the German and international press (where from a strong crowd, Klusmann and Schulz at *Der Spiegel*, as well as Joe Miller at the *Financial Times*, especially stand out). Emilio Segrè's run-in with the abrupt Mr. Lawrence is in Segrè's 1993 autobiography, *A Mind Always in Motion*. The topic of harshness vs. compassion in research labs—and how that links with the human souls behind them—is at the core of Nuel Pharr Davis's *Lawrence and Oppenheimer* (1968). Anthony Fauci's exuberant response to the vaccine results was reported by Ed Yong in *The Atlantic* (Jan/Feb 2021). The promised tutorial is on my website at the page for this book, davidbodanis.com/books/the-art-of-fairness/how-to-design-an-mrna-vaccine-in-60-minutes.

PART ONE: LISTENING

To capture the feeling aboard Flight 232, I'd start with Errol Morris's hour-long filmed interview with Captain Denny Fitch (variously titled "One Hell of a Tale," or "Leaving the Earth"). Then turn to **Al Haynes's revealing talk** at NASA's Ames Research Center (May 24, 1991), while for those with an engineering bent, the detailed report from the National Transportation Safety Board (NTSB/AAR-90/060) reads as an intense, real-life detective story. There are several transcripts of the cockpit communications floating around online, but some of them have been somehow mangled, so do compare them with the above sources, and Laurence Gonzales's trustworthy *Flight 232: A Story of Disaster and Survival* (2014).

The flight has been much discussed in popular and academic literature, with General Stanley McChrystal's *Team of Teams: New Rules of Engagement for a Complex World* (2015) continuing into the more general difficulties of shifting, as he put it, from running a command as a "chess player" to running it as a "gardener." Atul Gawande's *The Checklist Manifesto: How to Get Things Right*

(2011) takes another articulate angle on the humility that leaders of intense teams need. For a full range of parliamentary typologies, see the supremely browsable *Parliament* by the Dutch designers van der Vegt and de Lara (2016).

For the successful Olympic opening in East London, *Danny Boyle: Creating Wonder. In Conversation with Amy Raphael* (2013) is an accurate, lengthy set of interviews (with good explanations of how even the popular newspaper infiltrators were beaten); Boyle's self-criticism quote is on page 138, and dates from the start of the *Beach* debacle, when—in a rare, Bligh-like shift—he stiffed his long-time lead, Ewan McGregor, for the more bankable DiCaprio. For more background, I spoke with a number of regulars at the rehearsals, most informatively Boyle's collaborator and writer, Frank Cottrell-Boyce. The Queen's bold parachute jump can be viewed at 38:00 of the BBC's full video of the ceremony, available online. For what went wrong on the movie *1941,* the BBC's Barry Norman's 1990 interview with Spielberg (available online) is as masterly as those of us who'd come to love Mr. Norman would expect, letting Spielberg mull over the resentments dating back even to high school that emerged on that set. Coe's reminisce of his father's quietness is also available online; it's the third in a series sponsored by Investec, and he's speaking to Clare Balding, who wisely gives him plenty of time to remember.

What good listeners do is reduce the delays that are inevitable when too much information is pouring in, or when we straddle domains that inherently operate at different speeds. This is a subject that economists have explored in terms of information asymmetry; ecologists in terms of Batesian mimicry; in finance, it's the short-termism that regulators so regularly find reason to lament; in politics, it's a commonplace of what entitled, or wealthy, or otherwise protected leaders can get away with before the world corrects them. None of this is new. Gibbon in the 18th century described the emperor Diocletian from the 3rd century recounting, from experience, what a Roman emperor faced: "Secluded from humankind by his exalted dignity, the truth is concealed from his knowledge; he can see only with [his ministers'] eyes; he hears nothing but their misrepresentations." One needs a clear head, plus the habit of insisting on bringing in wider views, to have a chance of breaking past that. For the present day, Abhijit V. Banerjee and Esther Duflo's

***Good Economics for Hard Times: Better Answers to Our Biggest
Problems*** (2019) shows a number of ingenious fixes that can be created by
sensible analysis, at least in the field of public policy.

PART TWO: GIVING

Carol Willis made the architectural historian's discovery of a lifetime when
she came across the original notebook which the Empire State Building's
construction team used. It's reprinted, along with telling engineering and
managerial explanation, in her edited volume *Building the Empire State Building*
(1998). For the great Lewis Hine photographs as the construction was taking
place, along with further context, see *Thirteen Months to Go*, by Geraldine B.
Wagner (2003). Here too I was drawn in by a personal connection: my grandfather and namesake, David Passell, was a steelworker at Youngstown Sheet
and Tube in Ohio while it was forging many of the beams for the Empire State
Building. I don't think he ever visited the New York site, but the memories
he passed down of diverse foremen at the blast furnace made vivid to me
how workers of his time would respond to Starrett's gruffly offered fairness.

Paul Starrett's own *Changing the Skyline* (1938) has the opening scene in
Raskob's office, though where Starrett only admitted saying "not a blankety
blank thing" to Raskob, I took the liberty of filling it in with "Not a damn
thing" (though I would suspect additional adjectives may have been in play).

The subterfuges that the Starretts' workers were tempted by live in
Thomas Kelly's Zolaesque novel of the construction, *Empire Rising* (2005); the
way analogous subterfuges are still attempted, on every scale, is a motif in the
memoir of one of the best American secretaries of defense of recent years,
Ash Carter's ***Inside the Five-Sided Box: Lessons from a Lifetime of
Leadership in the Pentagon*** (2019); see in particular his account of the
subtleties involved in blocking overruns on the multi-hundred-billion-dollar
F-35 fighter jet project.

The smiling, friendly—and astonishingly unscrupulous—Frank Lorenzo
is well described in the book by *Business Week*'s then labor editor, Aaron
Bernstein, *Grounded: Frank Lorenzo and the Destruction of Eastern Airlines* (1990).
I also interviewed a number of the participants on both sides; partly for

useful detail, partly from astonishment at what had taken place. To carry the story forward, I can't highly enough recommend Eileen Appelbaum and Rosemary Batt's ***Private Equity at Work: When Wall Street Manages Main Street*** (2014), ideal for showing how the gaps Lorenzo wormed his way into still remain, letting modern Lorenzos take what others have built.

In both the Eastern and Empire State Building stories, the dynamics of resentment vs. gratitude play a central role. We today live at the end of a long arms race here. Ordinary people hate being cheated, so manipulators become ingenious, so we become more ingenious against them, etc. Since in different settings even the noblest of us end up as fine manipulators—anyone who's had a parent, or a spouse, or a child, might have experienced this once or twice—a great deal of our life is spent handling the results.

Robert Sapolsky's lengthy yet consistently wry ***Behave: The Biology of Humans at Our Best and Worst*** (2017) goes through the biological literature on this and related matters: how we detect the briefest of inconsistent looks; how we compare promises with results; how we even, quite often, get surges of oxytocin in our bloodstream when we feel justice has been done. It clarifies why unscrupulous political actors of all eras will try to stir up resentment, even when it's not justified. They understand they'll get those forces of righteous indignation on their side.

In our world where such resentment and gratitude lurk, navigation is never easy. The insights from Aristotle mentioned earlier are one guide; the Hillel question discussed in my text—highlighting a wise intermediate path not just for survival, but for morally "good" survival—is another. Joseph Telushkin's brief *Hillel: If Not Now, When?* (2010) uses a comfortable, conversational tone to place that sage in the most profound of contexts.

All these problems arise because we're competing for limited resources. That's why blocking your competitors by any means available is such an understandable temptation. The bizarre extremes this can lead to are laid out in S. E. Finer's exceptionally well-written ***The History of Government from the Earliest Times*** (1997); see his "Note on Mamluk Egypt" on the slave dynasties that controlled—to say they "ran" it is overgenerous—that unlucky country for centuries. Even today, most political systems fail to make decent actions the logical choice for the average citizen. The effect is stark when you compare neighboring countries, as with the successes of Botswana vs. the failures of adjacent yet ill-governed Zimbabwe. *Why Nations Fail: The Origins of Power, Prosperity and Poverty*, by Daron Acemoglu and James A. Robinson (2012), is excellent on the background there and more generally.

America's founders understood that good intentions will always fail without the right institutions in place to carry them out. ***The Federalist Papers*** are a masterpiece on how they thought this problem could be avoided. Lin-Manuel Miranda's hip-hop musical *Hamilton* is the perfect form for showing how contesting personalities always get in the way.

For Ursula Graham Bower's exploits, if you read her *Naga Path* (1950) you'll encounter a happy young woman, undaunted and fulfilled. Watch her lengthy video reminiscences with Alan Macfarlane forty years later— also conveniently available online—and you'll see an elder grande dame of cut-glass enunciation living those years again. Vicky Thomas's *The Naga Queen: Ursula Graham Bower and Her Jungle Warriors, 1939–45* (2012) draws on a number of family papers and interviews to expand this. (The British Army officer who mockingly asked, "Ha ha—very funny. Who made this up?" makes his entrance on p. 64.) Bower's travails with her mother were neither the first nor the last time such family struggles would inspire great achievement, as Deborah Tanner's timeless *You're Wearing That?: Understanding Mothers and Daughters in Conversation* (2006) illuminates. For a voice on the Naga side, Tezenlo Thong's *Progress and Its Impact On the Nagas: A Clash of Worldviews* (2016) fights the image Bower had to overcome, of a people who lived in darkness until superior outsiders brought them the light.

The wider setting of Bower's reconnaissance operations is well set out in William Slim's justifiably classic ***Defeat Into Victory*** (original edition 1956), which delivers an account of exactly what its title promises. I'd supplement it with Ronald Lewin's *Slim: The Standardbearer* (1976) and *Burma: The Longest War* (1984) by Louis Allen. I had two deeply informative conversations with Slim's son John, the 2nd Viscount Slim, whose own military career began in India just as his father's campaigns were coming to a close.

To organize Bower's story, I used Arnold van Gennep's framework of transitions, where his original *Rites of Passage* (1909; many later printings) remains a first-rate source. Popularized by Joseph Campbell, van Gennep's ideas found a fertile home in Hollywood: first in *Star Wars* (Luke Skywalker needing to sojourn on a distant planet and learn from a wise, wide-eyed being before he could return strengthened), then *The Lion King* (Simba needing to sojourn in a distant jungle and learn from a wise, wide-eyed being before he too could return strengthened), and others. David Brooks's reflective *The Second Mountain: The Quest for a Moral Life* (2019) builds on many of those themes.

PART THREE: DEFENDING

When Leo Durocher was in his great battle with Hodges's Brooklyn team, I was twelve and spending a lot of time at Chicago's Wrigley Field after the games, for my friends and I could get free tickets for the next day in exchange for staying late to help clean the stands. Sometimes we'd stop to watch him do interviews at that late hour as he stood awkwardly in the natural grass, the so-recently-full stadium stretching empty beyond. He wouldn't always be irritated when he began, but somehow, some way, he almost always would be near bursting by the end.

Paul Dickson's biography *Leo Durocher: Baseball's Prodigal Son* (2017) gets across what it must feel like to experience the world that way, where, aside from a very small number of people on your side—and even they can't be trusted for long—everyone else is just waiting to take advantage of you, and so in simple defense you can never give in, but instead have to constantly be on the attack.

For a hint of what the opposite life might feel like, see the online video where Gil Hodges's widow Joan describes with no-nonsense affection what actually happened the evening when her husband strolled out to collect his recalcitrant player from the middle of a game—search "gil hodges pulls cleon jones." Those ideals lived on with the basketball coach Phil Jackson (whose unflappable manner leading his Chicago Bulls to victory against their tough arch-rivals in Detroit—proudly self-labeled "the Bad Boys"—is still a sensitive matter for humiliated Pistons fans). *Eleven Rings*, by Phil Jackson and Hugh Delehanty (2013) elaborates on the humane strengths required. In Hollywood, where hissy fits abound, the great director Sidney Lumet was another of the rare grown-ups in the room. His *Making Movies* (1995) is a neat parallel to Phil Jackson's book, showing what's needed to carry this firm but fair approach to even larger scales.

Perhaps the most suitable lens through which to view Microsoft's descent in the Ballmer years is the one primatologist Frans de Waal brings out in his *Our Inner Ape: The Best and Worst of Human Nature* (2005). Leaders like Ballmer act as if they believe in what might be called the "alpha male" theory. Dominant apes strut and grunt and terrorize others to run their communities, supporters of this view hold, and although we might not like that, it's just what real life requires. But what de Waal noticed matched what Sapolsky described about hunter gatherers: that chimpanzees rising this way tend to have short careers, ending in exile or murder. It's the most successful alphas who "protect the underdog, keep the peace and reassure those who are distressed." When fights occur, such an alpha will stand "impressively between screaming parties with his arms raised, until things calm down." This is why Ballmer got so frustrated at his underlings not doing what in his distinctive manner he asked them to do. As the American general Martin Dempsey, one-time chairman of the Joint Chiefs of Staff, put it succinctly: "Imposed solutions rarely last."

Microsoft's system of rating employees by "stack ranking" found its Virgil in Kurt Eichenwald, whose irresistible "Microsoft's Downfall: Inside the Executive E-mails and Cannibalistic Culture that Felled a Tech Giant" ran in the August 2012 issue of *Vanity Fair*. "Every current and former Microsoft employee I interviewed—*every one*—cited stack ranking as the most destructive process inside of Microsoft." The assessment of Steve Ballmer as the "worst CEO" was by columnist Adam Hartung in *Forbes* in May 2012; the use of office furniture as a weapon—and Mr. Lucovsky's deft footwork in avoidance—is referenced in Stephen Levy's *In the Plex: How Google Thinks, Works, and Shapes Our Lives* (2011). This builds on court documents Lucovsky's team filed, placing the incident in November 2004, a matter which Lucovsky confirmed in the delightfully titled November 2011 *Wired* article "Man Survives Steve Ballmer's

Flying Chair to Build '21st Century Linux.'" "Why does [Ballmer throwing a chair] surprise anyone?" Lucovsky asked there. "If you play golf with Steve and he loses a five-cent bet, he's pissy for the next week."

How a sensible leader can do better is the subject of Satya Nadella's well-received autobiography, *Hit Refresh: The Quest to Rediscover Microsoft's Soul and Imagine a Better Future for Everyone*, with Greg Shaw and Jill Tracie Nichols (2017). A long interview he and his wife Anu gave in *Good Housekeeping* (November 2017) provides more personal background. As with the vaccine story, I had a number of talks with venture capitalists, past employees, and several outside firms to learn more.

Ballmer and Nadella differed on a fundamental matter: Under what circumstances can cooperation in a harsh environment actually work? This is at the heart of whether we default toward an open or a closed view of external threats. If cooperation will be destructive, then it's not fair to your own side to even start. *Moral Sentiments and Material Interests: The Foundations of Cooperation in Economic Life*, ed. Herbert Gintis et al. (2005), is an excellent collection, bringing concepts from law, game theory and experimental economics to bear on how reciprocity actually works. Elinor Ostrom's famous *Governing the Commons: The Evolution of Institutions for Collective Action* (1990) is still good at showing how in a wide range of cases—irrigation, fishing rights, forest use—cooperation can be sustained. The participants just need to be allowed the self-policing oversight they all easily understand. This is exactly what would have been crushed in the Mamluk Egypt that Finer described, and which the rigidity of stack ranking brought down in Microsoft.

REFLECTION: WHO ARE WE?

The heart of the Bligh chapter—and what made it the pivot of this book—is the question of how we can sustain our identity, given that the trade-offs required are inevitably so much more than we at first imagine. The childlike Lewis Carroll tried to reject the whole problem, by creating his wonderful character Alice, who boldly scoffs at these problems when she takes her impromptu journey in Wonderland. David Hume however places it at the center of his *Treatise of Human Nature*: "For my part, when I enter most intimately into what I call myself, I always stumble on some particular perception or other . . . I never can catch *myself*." This is a further reason the decency we want is so hard to sustain. Any of the many collections of **Hume's Essays** are excellent at seeing this explored.

Rebecca Solnit's memoir *Recollections of My Nonexistence* (2020) and the earlier *A Field Guide to Getting Lost* (2005) show how disturbingly sexism and other forces can crash down on the still-forming personality . . . yet also the way that communities which understand can provide the strength to fight back. *Two Sisters* by Åsne Seierstad (2016), just as calmly written, describes two young sisters from Norway who also found what seemed the ideal way to live a good and fair life, but this was by giving themselves over to the murderous Islamic state—an act which satisfied them until, with horror, they realized where they were now stuck.

Even away from such extremes, the more successful we are, the more the opportunities to fail open up. The rock musician Paul Hewson (Bono) has spoken earnestly about how important it is that taxes in rich countries are spent helping the poorest on Earth; he even used his U2 Vertigo Tour to promote the ONE campaign to fight poverty and disease worldwide. But there are taxes and there are taxes. As Bloomberg Markets pointed out, to Hewson's great discomfort, profits from the $389 million-gross ticket receipts were "funneled through companies that are mostly registered in Ireland and structured to minimize taxes."

Hewson apologized for that oversight, but humans wobble. Shortly after, he began even more secretively—in an act only revealed years later by the leak of the Panama Papers—to shift other profits he made into a Maltese company which incorporated a Lithuanian company which transferred ownership to a Guernsey company . . . at the end of which he once again would be able to keep it all.

How to do better? The great UN head Dag Hammarskjöld shared Hewson's positive goals but prepositioned himself to resist the difficulties he knew would arise. His worldly yet still optimistic philosophy is in his posthumously published *Markings* (1964): "We are not permitted to choose the frame of our destiny. But what we put into it is ours." This was what

Dietrich Bonhoeffer, featured at the end of Chapter 7, also shared, as Charles Marsh's 2014 biography *Strange Glory: A Life of Dietrich Bonhoeffer* eloquently explains. Another account of a man pushing back against intense social pressure is *The Von Hassell Diaries 1938–1944* (originally published 1948), by Ulrich Von Hassel, a proud German conservative who kept his moral bearings. His account of how so many others did not was written on small scraps of paper—easier to hide during a Gestapo search—which he stuffed into tea cans and buried outside his home; they were dug up and printed after the war.

For greater depth on Bligh's own contrary pulls—the forced decency toward his men; the desperate desire for success in his mission—I'd start with Caroline Alexander's 2003 *The Bounty: The True Story of the Mutiny on the Bounty*. Her near 40-page evaluation of the sources is humbling. In *Captain Bligh's Portable Nightmare* by John Toohey (1999), the nightmare is not just being cast on to a small launch in the middle of the Pacific. It's also the overwhelming irritations Bligh felt rush up whenever the greatest immediate dangers abated. And a brilliant, fresh angle is taken in the 1992 work ***Mr Bligh's Bad Language: Passion, Power and Theatre on the* Bounty**, by Greg Dening, who asked the simple yet fertile question of why the key actors presented themselves to each other as they did.

THE TEST: PROPAGANDA MASTER; PRESIDENT; WAR

Here all the themes start coming together. The link is what George Orwell described so well in his *Nineteen Eighty-Four*, published shortly after the events this book leads up to occurred. How does what takes place inside the individual mind connect with what society allows? Here too, when young, we fantasize that the causality will run in one direction only: from our inner desires to an outer world that responds to us. It was Orwell's genius to look at how politicians can manage to keep doing that for long stretches of time, leaving reality behind.

This is why Henry Frankfurter's brief essay *On Bullshit* (original edition 1986, reprinted 2005) is so apt. What he describes there isn't just lying, but rather the sort of lying where both sides know what's being asserted isn't true, yet the teller has enough power that he or she doesn't care. Nor can the listeners object. At first they're too weak, and then, worst of all, in time they even stop wanting to object.

Many people in public life have spent years in that world. One who had the honesty to describe what it was like, after publicly repenting (admittedly, he was forced to), is the Briton Damian McBride. His well-named account *Power Trip: A Decade of Policy, Plots and Spin* (2013) achieves a tone which is, finally, honest throughout. "I wasn't always a nasty bastard," he begins, "but you could argue the signs were there." Others drawn to power usually manage to find repentance easier to resist. For just one of many modern examples, this time on the opposite side of the political spectrum, Alex Gibney and Alexis Bloom's documentary on long-time Fox News head Roger Ailes, *Divide and Conquer* (2018), can be recommended; his career is given longer background in Gabriel Sherman's 2017 *The Loudest Voice in the Room*. Both McBride and Ailes were still old-school, dealing with print and TV. Understanding what amorality can achieve with the next stage of communications technology—bots and the like—is well surveyed in McKay Coppins's article "The Billion-Dollar Disinformation Campaign to Reelect the President," *The Atlantic* (March 2020).

Moral collapse is rarely a sudden event, but rather the end of a long series of poor decisions and oversights—just like industrial accidents, and for similar reasons. For a modern example of how far this can go, Jim Frederick's *Black Hearts: One Platoon's Descent into Madness in Iraq's Triangle of Death* (2010) is gripping in its slow inevitability; deservedly taught at West Point and other military academies. He also shows how two adjacent platoons avoided that moral collapse. Good leadership made the difference, even in the same brutal setting.

The general literature for the Goebbels and FDR chapters is immense, so I'll stick to a handful of mostly recent works that are directly relevant. For Goebbels, Peter Longerich's *Goebbels: A Biography* (2015) is simply brilliant, not least in showing how insecure he was throughout his life—desperately needing to play himself up in public pronouncements and his private diaries alike. Longerich also shows how much of his ministry's resources Goebbels used not directly for propaganda—though that, of course, was substantial—but for spreading the *impression* that he was a genius at propaganda.

Combined with Toby Thacker's equally telling *Joseph Goebbels: Life and Death* (2009), one sees not just the external stages of his life but, because Goebbels kept that diary from the bitter early days back at home in Rheydt in 1923, all the way until his death in 1945, a great vividness of his inner life too. It's ironic that this master of untruth worked so hard, in private, to preserve what he knew actually was true: When cross-referenced against other sources, these diaries prove to be remarkably accurate.

All dictatorial societies build on past traditions, and Bismarck had done a good job identifying his own *Reichsfeinde*—"enemies of the empire"—a few decades earlier: Poles, Catholics, trade unionists and others. Fritz Stern illuminates the subtleties in his *Gold and Iron: Bismarck, Bleichröder, and the Building of the German Empire* (1977), recounting an unexpected almost-friendship that was central; Katja Hoyer's *Blood and Iron: The Rise and Fall of the German Empire, 1871-1918* (2021) is briefer, but goes wider in context on that formative time, which led to so many resentments after it failed.

The secretary who remembered Goebbels tripping up the stairs "like a little duke," Brunhilde Pomsel, lived on and on, until finally, in 2013— age 102—she agreed to a lengthy series of interviews for the documentary *Ein Deutsches Leben* (*A German Life*). What was he really like, the young interviewers wanted to know? Pomsel reflected. She remembered being at the *Sportpalast* in 1943 when he'd yelled out his question about wanting total war, bringing the crowds to their feet. Frau Goebbels had been in the row behind them, SS men alongside.

She and another secretary from his office had tried not to look at each other. "Until then we hadn't known that side of Goebbels . . . He was unrecognizable . . . A person you see almost every day in the office—nicely turned out, elegant, almost a noble elegance—and then that raging dwarf." The full edited transcripts are in *The Work I Did: A Memoir of the Secretary to Goebbels*, by Brunhilde Pomsel (adapted by Thore D. Hansen, 2018). The prescient Dostoevsky remark about the gentleman of jeering physiognomy appears in his somewhat frantic *Notes from Underground*.

The problem with biographies of Franklin Delano Roosevelt tends to be that of hagiography. Because what he achieved was so impressive, it's easy to overlook how dangerous his inconsistency and cowardice turned out to be: how much he failed at, and how much he didn't even try. Even so, enough biographers have overcome this problem that choice remains difficult. Two which I can heartily recommend to start with are Jean Edward Smith's *FDR* (2007), and, focusing on the middle part of his life, Geoffrey C. Ward's *A First-Class Temperament: The Emergence of Franklin D. Roosevelt* (1989). Ward's title comes from Oliver Wendell Holmes's remark after meeting the new president: "A second-class intellect. But a first-class temperament."

Of the many associated individuals, Roosevelt's most important adviser, Harry Hopkins, had the great fortune to have his life written by playwright and Algonquin wit Robert Sherwood (who also was Roosevelt's speechwriter). His **Roosevelt and Hopkins** (1948; reissued 2001) captures this fine, indispensable man. "It required a soaring imagination to conceive Lend-Lease, and it required the shrewdest kind of manipulation to get it passed by Congress."

All of them shared the luck of having Marguerite LeHand on their side. Kathryn Smith's *The Gatekeeper: Missy LeHand, FDR and the Untold Story of the Partnership that Defined a Presidency* (2016) tells her story, while the bit part played by one oddly named vessel comes out in *FDR on His Houseboat: The Larooco Log, 1924–1926*, ed. Karen Chase (2016); the facsimile drawings in Roosevelt's hand are touching, as he struggled to be the shallow, party-loving soul he realized he no longer actually was.

His labor secretary, Frances Perkins, accomplished the extraordinary feat of getting Social Security legislation not merely passed, but constructed in a manner to sustain bipartisan support nearly a century into the future. Kirstin Downey's *The Woman Behind the New Deal: The Life of Frances Perkins, FDR's Secretary of Labor and His Moral Conscience* (2009) shows how, even revealing some of the mysteries in the large red envelope of "Notes on the Male Mind" which Perkins turned to, only half-jokingly, with such effect. *The Five Giants: A Biography of the Welfare State*, by Nicholas Timmins (2001) shows how efforts for similar transformations succeeded at least partially in the UK, with a special highlight on Perkins's approximate equivalent, the ex-miner Nye Bevan, who also was, as contemporaries put it, "an artist in the use of power."

Largely for length reasons, I had to slight Eleanor Roosevelt, which was unfair to that woman who did so much to overcome her difficult early years. Her story is best understood in the context of her wider family, and for that, *The Roosevelts: An Intimate History* by Geoffrey C. Ward (2014) is ideal. It's based on the Ken Burns documentary of the same title, and the photo research by Susanna Steisel is tremendous; I've spent a lot of time with these characters over the years, and still discovered shots I hadn't known existed.

If Roosevelt had foundered, demagogues could easily have taken over, as many commentators at the time thought possible. William Manchester's *American Caesar: Douglas MacArthur, 1880–1964* (1978) describes one likely candidate. The novel *All the King's Men* by Robert Penn Warren (1946), although not directly based on the life of the crowd-rousing Huey Long—the man Roosevelt considered the most dangerous after MacArthur—is excellent on how charismatic leaders twist all the tools we've seen to corrupt those near them.

That was the reason this final half of the book had to be a dual biography, matching what Blake understood. Roosevelt and Goebbels—it could have been Hitler, but Goebbels's role in distorting communications made him especially relevant today—each reveal key operations of the human mind, and in particular how we configure those operations in different ways: that underlings can be respected or not, outsiders can be accepted or not, and all the rest. The clarity that comes from such contrasts is a fundamental property of how we think. (Linguistics scholars, for example, note that a sound only seems high in pitch when we can compare it to a sound we call low.) Ordinary gossip matches this too. Graham Bower's mother could be appalled at what her daughter was wearing, but only because she had a feeling about how very different it was from what she *should* be wearing.

The point isn't that it takes a comparison with Roosevelt to conclude that Goebbels was bad. It's that, as noted, without such comparisons, we'd get little of the crucial detail about what makes each side work, and what makes them fail. Goebbels's exaggerating of crowds and trying to close down newspapers that disagreed with him and vilifying opponents is now just a historical curio; the strengths of Roosevelt's reverse operations are clear. But had he been less skilled in carrying them out, one can only wonder at how differently history—facing challenges Roosevelt couldn't have envisaged—might have turned out.

ACKNOWLEDGMENTS

THE BOOK IS dedicated to the memory of Kathleen Griffin, with whom I shared most of my twenties, when we lived in a little village in the foothills of the Alps. She'd faced harsh experiences in her life, yet drawn the conclusion that she'd do what she could to help others facing their own difficulties. That's the reason I find positive choice so admirable in this book.

This is little use if it comes out as a naive blandness, but from Kathleen's Cornish, Irish and French ancestry, no one was ever going to accuse her of being bland. She had a remarkable ability to swear fluently in several languages; she succeeded in the competitive world of national broadcasting as well. But she also, for years, was the kindest of BBC trainers, helping novice journalists who were at times almost overcome by their awkwardness.

When practical action was called for, she was there too. At a lake near our village once, when a friend got into trouble in deep water, she shot toward him from shore even as the rest of us on land dithered and wondered what to do. Although he was a strong man, and flailing desperately, she had him steadied and safe by the time anyone else made it there; when we did get him back, she sat with him quietly, soothingly, so that along with his physical recovery, he'd not be embarrassed at so losing composure in the water.

Had I been a better person, I'd have appreciated her more. That I didn't is one of the great regrets of my life. The desire to do better—perhaps the central theme of this book—is one I far too well understand.

To make the histories that carry that theme come alive, I had to learn more about different fields than I could know from my own experience. Luckily, I've been blessed with friends who've had far more interesting lives than my own. They range from past heads of UK special forces, to those who've navigated the rougher terrains of Hollywood studios, or of grandmaster chess boards—and, for one especially brave soul, classrooms of hyper-eager youngsters. A few of my most-detailed sources couldn't be listed—the Tower of London still has space, apparently, for those violating their professions' codes of *omertà*—but for the others, big thanks go to:

- In animal behavior: Martin Franklin, Ben Tapley.
- In aviation: David Finnimore, Neil MacDougall, Neil Passmore, Matthew Whitfield; also the late Murray Alpert.
- In business, finance and the countering of Machiavellians: James Beresford, Edward Bonham-Carter, David Carr, Michael Cohrs, Leslie Dighton, Karin Forseke, Penny Freer, Ari Freisinger, Lachlan French, Stephen Huxter, Andrey Kruglykhin, Stacey Mullin, Jacqueline Novogratz, Peter Schmitz, Rohan Silva, Ashvin Sologar, Maarten van Wesemael, Rick Wheatley, Nadine and Richard Windsor.
- The worlds of chess and other strategic arts: Georgia Inés Falcon Melford, Jon Lawson, Malcolm Pein, Jonathan Rowson.
- Construction and other large projects: Paul Atherley, Niall Barr, Matt Cartwright, Cornelia Dibua, Lia Freisinger, Mungo Melvin, Alan Middleton, Colm Reilly, Sam Singh, Josephine Tan.
- Education, listening and communications: Sarah Blackwood, Louise Callaghan, Clarissa Farr, Simon Goldhill, Simon Harper, Stuart Lawson, Michelle Robson, Tex Royale, Anthony Smith, Rob Waran, Maxine Windsor.
- Film and TV: Anita Anand, Jon Bennet, Bernie Caulfield, Danny Cohen, Frank Cottrell-Boyce, George Lamb, Lawrence Levy, Karl Warner.
- In law: Barry Bennett, Tess Jones, Anthony Julius, Derval Walsh.
- In medicine: Virginia Brown, Professor Pier Lambiase, Sir David Sloman.
- For military matters: James Dutton, Matthew Jones, Graeme Lamb, Floyd Woodrow MBE DCM.

– Philosophy, politics, history: Jeremy Bentham, Philip Bobbit, Oliver
   Carr, David Charters, Rob Colvile, Robert A. Hefner III, Frank
   McLynn, Mounzer Nasr, Martin Rees, Ngaire Woods, Jonathan Wolff.
– Physical sciences, and especially biology: Bob Brooks, Amir
   Moghaddam, Ted Schenkelberg, Aron Troen.
– For private detectives, and what they recognize of human behavior:
   Jim Mintz.
– Social sciences, especially anthropology, economics and psychology:
   Jeremy Carne, Hazel Gale, Julia Hobsbawm, John Kay, Theo Kelly,
   Susannah Kennedy, Andrew Mayo, Elizabeth Mishkin, Charlotte
   Mühlmann, Michael Muthukrishna, Tom Simpson, Rory Sutherland,
   Mike Woodford.
– Sports and competitiveness: Danny Freisinger, Graham Lloyd, Leon
   Taylor, Mark Walker, Guy Windsor.
– The world of tech: Derek Jean-Baptiste, John Markoff, David Rowan,
   Ajit Singh, David Spreng, Susan Zimmerman.

Several of the above individuals ranged across multiple categories, as also,
very much, did Lia Abady, Anthony Capo-Bianco, Angelica Carr, Panio
Gianopoulos, Janet Lew, Mandy Luo, and Howard Passell.

Extensive editing help came from Andrew Hill, Mike Skapinker, Julia
Stuart, Anelia Varela, Becca Windsor, Andrew Wright, and from the start,
my agent Patrick Walsh.

At The Bridge Street Press in London, Tim Whiting has a great take
on the editor's arts; in a warm, compassionate, and caring way, he identifies
chapters which are well written, well researched, and—being quite irrelevant
to the book—need to be well discarded. The humbled author, recognizing
Whiting is, alas, right again, is wise to agree. Holly Harley provided extensive further improvement to what I once, in foolish optimism, thought was a
final manuscript (though she eased the pain with a multitude of entertaining
parenthetical (and sometimes subparenthetical) comments). It's common
to take for granted a copy editor's work, but there are dozens of places in
this book where any fluency of expression came from copy editor Elizabeth

Dobson, not me. Further help came from Tamsyn Berryman, Clara Diaz, and Nico Taylor.

At Abrams in New York, Andrew Gibeley, Annalea Manalili and Jamison Stoltz made everything work.

Staff at the London Library on London's elegant St. James's Square once again helped guide me through their institution's unique resources; so too did staff at the British Library, on London's not-quite-so-enticing Euston Road. I've tried out ideas for this book in talks at a range of companies, and particularly gained from—I believe vigorous is the word—feedback at Adobe, Anglo American, General Dynamics, Goldman Sachs, Google, Microsoft, Mischcon de Reya, Ogilvy, Pfizer, Simpson Thacher & Bartlett, Six to Start, and Verizon; similarly from groups at the World Economic Forum. Several of them, as well as other specialist contacts, let me spend time ranging from days up to weeks in their organizations, a rare learning experience. A great many informants in Beirut helped too, when I spent time in and around that magnificent, battered city, learning about daily decisions in a world far from Oxford's peaceable halls, far from my native Chicago as well.

A number of friends have heard me go on about this book's topic at what is definitely unfair length, yet still remained willing to continue the mix of handholding plus analytics that authors so need. Commendation for long-lasting service here goes to Rebecca Abrams, Shanda Bahles, Sunny Bates, Julia Bindman, Sophie Chisholm, James Chiswell, Richard Cohen, Betty Sue Flowers, Tim Harford, Mark Hurst, Olivia Judson, Dan Newman, William Pitt, Ramana Rao and Sheana Tambourgi. Their counsel came in various mixes of city walks, park walks, beach walks, circuitous hotel walks, phone calls, quick phone calls, curb-sitting coffees at Borough Market, and electronic communication of virtually every known sort.

At times the aid was continued over Bodanis stir-fries (cheap and cheerful), Karma bakery treats (cheerful, and in addition tasty), and, when we could convince ourselves we deserved it, over Popolo restaurant meals, which those who've been lucky enough to get to, this East London restaurant will recognize as the paragon of culinary arts.

New friends Robert McCrum, Natascha McElhone, Roz Morris, Nick Shaw and Lotus Qi found themselves unexpectedly roped in to the "He'll never stop with the questions, will he?" crowd, and I must say have acquitted themselves with aplomb. From the next generation, two thirds of Natascha's and one third of Nick's offspring were old enough to be roped in too; the others are, I believe, waiting in the wings. Through it all, as ever, Gabrielle Walker, the warmest of friends, would—as long as supplied with sufficient Earl Grey tea—listen at length to any remaining queries, before asking one of her trademark apparently simple questions which, once I traced out the implications, often led to the needed solutions.

I've also been blessed with something else many of us don't get in life, which is a second chance, in home and heart. Claire has shown me what marriage can be, in years of shared dinners, gentle understanding, and, always, melodies that touch the soul; Sam and Sophie survived years of their dad's—usually inadvertent—embarrassing actions, ending up as adults of whom I'm intensely proud; Julius is a fast-growing, inventive stepson, who can be identified as the eager youngster offering wide-ranging talks on virtually every topic (with a special enthusiasm for First World War battleships) as we sit at meals, then repair to a much-loved purple sofa.

There time and space bend, for that's where, a near-generation before, I shared hours on end with the equally eager Sam and Sophie. Those years of stretched-out reading and movie watching and commenting during movie watching, and assiduous ice-cream sharing—as well as "dive on to the cushions from as dangerously elevated heights as possible" competitions— have vanished from existence, the light photons that recorded them either lost in the room's walls, or—for the lucky number that escaped through the windows—now far-dispersed through the galaxy, the accompanying sounds even more quickly vanished into the thermodynamic confusion of our planet's atmosphere. All that remains are memories, and over the generations, those will dissipate in granular jumps down to zero too.

Which on a bad day I find depressing, but on a good day—clicking attention back to the present world—I'm reminded why I write. Words fade, and lives fade, but what's passed on need not. Waves can cross the Pacific, with no individual water molecule traveling more than a few yards; sections of DNA that were extant before the Himalayas rose up are still extant, and active, inside us now. Ethics matters; how we live our life matters: words from thousands of years ago speak to us as if today. Writers get to scoop up knowledge at our moment in history and pass on what they've glimpsed.

For those who helped let this happen, I'm immensely grateful; for those who might add to its dispersion in the future, my thanks must remain here, waiting.

INDEX